Rodale books may be purchased for business or promotional use or for special sales. For information, please write to:

Special Markets Department, Rodale, Inc., 733 Third Avenue, New York, NY 10017

Printed in the United States of America

Rodale Inc. makes every effort to use acid-free ♾, recycled paper ♻.

Front cover photographs: Grilled Chicken Citrus Salad, page 78;
Scampi with Fettucine, page 239; Fresh Mozzarella and Tomato Pizza, page 379;
Photography © Rodale Inc. Photographer: Mitch Mandel.

Lime- and Chile-Rubbed Chicken Breasts, page 72
Photography © General Mills

Interior photography © General Mills

Library of Congress Cataloging-in-Publication Data

Crocker, Betty.
  Betty Crocker supper in a snap : 360 quick and delicious family favorite recipes.
      p.   cm.
  Includes index.
  ISBN 978-1-60961-026-5 hardcover
  1. Cooking, American.   2. Suppers.   3. Quick and easy cooking.   4. Cookbooks.   I. Title.   II. Title: Supper in a snap.
  TX715.C921384 2011
  641.5'55—dc22                                                                         2011003195

2  4  6  8   10  9  7  5  3  1   hardcover

**RODALE.**

We inspire and enable people to improve their lives and the world around them.

For more of our products visit rodalestore.com or call 800–848–4735

# Betty Crocker
# SUPPER *in a* SNAP

**360** Quick and Delicious Family Favorite Recipes

# Dear Friends,

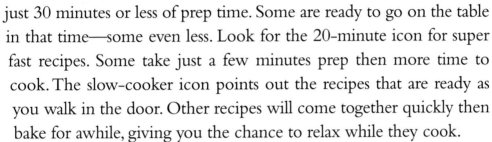

It's almost dinner time—how did the day go by so fast? It's tempting to just go with a bowl of cereal or order pizza, but doesn't a home-cooked dinner sound a lot better?

Consider this book your road map to dinner by the shortest route possible. Most recipes take just 30 minutes or less of prep time. Some are ready to go on the table in that time—some even less. Look for the 20-minute icon for super fast recipes. Some take just a few minutes prep then more time to cook. The slow-cooker icon points out the recipes that are ready as you walk in the door. Other recipes will come together quickly then bake for awhile, giving you the chance to relax while they cook.

There are fun meals like Quick Chicken Quesadillas and delectable treats like Rosemary Pork Roast with Carrots, plus pizza, sandwiches, breakfast for dinner—and even some super-streamlined soups. Who knew you could make chicken noodle soup with fresh veggies in only 30 minutes?

Time is something we could all use a second helping of, but most days we're lucky to steal a few free morsels at best. So on days when every minute counts, let *Betty Crocker Supper in a Snap* put you in the fast lane to dinner, so you can spend your precious free moments with the family, or anyone.

Warmly,

# contents

# "24/7": great tips for quick cooking

*What a busy week it's been! Priorities likely include simplifying life by making dinners more quickly. It's easy enough to phone in a pizza order, get fast food or open a can of soup; but let's face it, having a homemade meal is more satisfying! Once you know the easy tricks for quick cooking, you can make anything you want even faster! Browse all the fast-track tips below.*

**DO IT NOW, SAVE TIME LATER** Taking a few more moments to get ingredients ready ahead really saves you time in the long run. On one of those hectic nights when every extra minute counts, you will be glad you did. Here are some of the best ideas:

- **Burgers:** Make extra hamburger patties or meatballs and freeze in resealable food-storage plastic freezer bag up to 4 months.

- **Cooked Chicken:** Cook extra chicken and cut it up. Put desired amounts in resealable food-storage plastic freezer bags and freeze up to 4 months.

- **Ground Beef:** Brown extra ground beef and freeze desired amounts in resealable food-storage plastic freezer bags up to 3 months.

- **Meat and Poultry:** Cut raw meat and poultry into strips or cubes; arrange in single layer on foil-lined cookie sheet and freeze until firm. Put desired amounts into resealable food-storage plastic freezer bags and freeze up to 9 months.

- **Pasta and Rice:** Cook and drain extra pasta or rice. After draining, toss pasta or rice with a little olive oil or vegetable oil to keep it from sticking together. Put desired amounts in reseable food-storage plastic bags; refrigerate up to 5 days or freeze up to 6 months.

- **Veggies:** Chop, slice or dice fresh veggies like onions, bell peppers, carrots and celery. Arrange in single layer on foil-lined cookie sheet and freeze until firm. Put desired amounts in resealable food-storage plastic freezer bags and freeze up to 1 month.

**THINNER IS FASTER** To cook boneless skinless chicken breasts faster, pound them with a meat mallet or rolling pin between sheets of waxed paper or plastic wrap until they're about ¼ inch thick.

**NO CLEANUP** Line cookie sheets and baking pans with nonstick or regular foil before baking breaded chicken strips, fish sticks, French fries or anything similar. When it's baked, remove the food and toss the foil.

**A SPEEDIER MASH** To slash the cooking time for homemade mashed potatoes, cut the potatoes into 1- to 1½-inch pieces. This works great for other veggies, too!

**BOIL WATER FASTER** To jump-start boiling water, start with hot water and cover the saucepan with a lid.

**NO MORE STICKY SITUATIONS** When measuring syrup, honey or other sticky stuff, spray measuring spoons and cups with cooking spray first—it'll slide right out!

**QUICKER PASTA TOSS** If you frequently toss pasta with veggies, don't cook those veggies separately; just add frozen or fresh veggies to the pasta cooking water during the last few minutes of cooking, and drain the whole works together!

# gizmos, gadgets
## and other great stuff

*It's so true, having the right tool or gadget can shave off minutes when time really matters. We don't have room to list all the great little items available, but look for these handy kitchen helpers in department or discount stores, kitchenware stores, on the Internet or even in large supermarkets or hardware stores.*

**CHOPPER:** Manual choppers are great for handling small amounts of ingredients like onions, bell peppers, olives or other lightweight foods. The food goes into a glass or plastic hopper and a set of cutting blades does the work when you either press a plunger up and down or turn a handle. Or, by all means, use an electric mini-food processor.

**CUTTING WHEEL (ROLLING MINCER):** A cool little handheld tool with two cutting blades that you roll back and forth over fresh herbs, garlic or small green onions on a cutting board to finely chop or mince.

**FLEXIBLE CUTTING MAT:** Almost paper thin, these tough, flexible mats let you easily transfer ingredients from the mat to another container by folding the mat in half over the container and letting the ingredients fall in.

**KITCHEN SCISSORS:** Look for heavy-duty all-purpose kitchen scissors. Cut up fresh herbs, dried fruit, canned whole tomatoes and marshmallows; cut tortillas into strips or pita breads in half. A specific type of scissors called poultry scissors is designed to cut through chicken bones and thinner, lighter turkey bones (great to use if you economize by cutting up whole chickens into quarters or to cut the tips of chicken wings for zesty buffalo wings).

**NONSTICK ANYTHING:** Nonstick surfaces mean a lot less cleanup, especially when it comes to skillets! Just make sure always to use silicone or plastic utensils so the surface won't get scratched. Over time, all those scratches remove the coating and reduce the nonstick qualities.

**PASTA SERVER (PASTA FORK/ SPOON):** If your cooked pasta keeps slip-sliding away, get one of those dandy pasta servers! In one swoop, you can gather up pasta, and it works especially well for long pasta.

**POUR-OFF SIEVE:** A crescent-shaped straining device that fits over the rim of a variety of pot and pan sizes. All you do is tilt and pour off the liquid. If you usually toss your pasta with a sauce, this tool with its one-step process saves you from washing a colander!

**SPRING-LOADED SCOOP:** This multipurpose tool comes in various sizes for scooping ice cream, batters and doughs for baked goods, meatballs and melon balls. The nifty wire scraper inside these scoops neatly releases whatever is inside when the handle lever is pressed.

**WHISK:** Available in metal and silicone versions, this kitchen staple saves time as it blends and whips egg mixtures, sauces and lightweight batters. A good-quality wire whisk is made from a heavier-gauge metal, and has more wires and a solid metal handle, often about 1 inch in diameter. This type of whisk can hold up to denser, heavier mixtures better than inexpensive, lightweight or silicone models. In nonstick cookware, use only silicone whisks so they don't scratch. Stock multiple whisks in a variety of sizes so just the right one is always available and not in the dishwasher!

# the quick cook's pantry
## for the 5:30 challenge

*What's for dinner? Most of us start thinking about what's for dinner about an hour or two before we actually sit down to eat. Whether you're still at work or the kids are just getting off the bus, that's not very far ahead of time. A well-stocked pantry is a solution for this last-minute scramble and is a terrific meal-planning tool. Since we all like different foods and have different needs, no one pantry list works for everyone, but this list of quick picks provides the ingredients for a great start!*

### BREAD AND BAKING MIX

- Bisquick mix (for pancakes, biscuits, dumplings)
- Bread crumbs (plain or seasoned)
- Bread (your favorite type of loaf)
- Croutons
- English muffins
- French bread
- Frozen dinner rolls
- Pita breads
- Prebaked Italian pizza crusts
- Refrigerated dough products (biscuits, rolls, pizza dough, pie crust)
- Stuffing mix or cubes
- Taco shells
- Tortillas

### CONDIMENTS

- Balsamic vinegar
- Barbecue sauce
- Bouillon granules or cubes
- Dried herbs (basil, oregano, Italian seasoning, marjoram, thyme)
- Honey
- Jams, jellies, marmalades, preserves
- Jarred chopped garlic
- Ketchup
- Maple syrup
- Marinades
- Mayonnaise or salad dressing
- Mustard (yellow, Dijon, honey-mustard)
- Pickles/olives
- Refrigerated or jarred pesto
- Salad dressings
- Salsa
- Seasonings and seasoning mixes (garlic powder and salt, lemon-pepper, Cajun, barbecue)
- Spices (cinnamon, ginger, cloves, pumpkin pie spice, chili powder, cumin)
- Soy sauce, teriyaki sauce
- Worcestershire sauce

### DAIRY CASE

- Butter or margarine
- Cheese spreads, cheese loaves
- Cream cheese
- Eggs or fat-free egg product
- Grated Parmesan cheese
- Half-and-half, whipping cream
- Milk
- Shredded, sliced, crumbled and cubed cheeses
- Sour cream

## FRUITS

- Frozen fruit
- Jarred and canned fruit
- Prewashed and precut fresh fruit

## MEAT, POULTRY, FISH AND SEAFOOD

- Boneless skinless chicken breasts
- Canned and vacuum-packed pouch products
- Deli products
- Frozen breaded chicken and fish
- Frozen meatballs
- Frozen peeled deveined shrimp or breaded shrimp
- Ground beef and turkey
- Heat-and-eat seasoned roasts
- Precooked sausage links and rings
- Precut meats and chicken
- Refrigerated seasoned meat and poultry strips
- Refrigerated shredded barbecued meat and poultry
- Rotisserie chicken
- Steaks and chops instead of roasts
- Thinly cut meats and poultry

## NONPERISHABLE STAPLES

- Canned beans (plain, refried or baked beans)
- Canned chicken and beef broth
- Canned seasoned tomato products
- Cooking spray
- Dried fruits
- Gravy and sauce mixes
- Jarred gravy
- Nuts
- Olive oil
- Pasta and pizza sauces
- Soups and chili
- Vegetable oil

## PASTAS AND GRAINS

- Angel hair or vermicelli pasta
- Couscous (plain or flavored)
- Flavored pasta and noodle mixes
- Flavored rice mixes
- Fresh refrigerated pasta (plain or filled)
- Frozen egg noodles
- Frozen ravioli or gnocchi
- Instant white or brown rice

## ULTRA-CONVENIENCE

- Boxed meal kits
- Frozen meal starter kits
- Frozen pizza
- Frozen seasoned pasta blends
- Make reservations
- Order pizza
- Pick up your favorite takeout
- Stop by the deli

## VEGETABLES

- Boxed instant potato mixes
- Canned veggies (mushrooms, corn)
- Frozen and refrigerated ready-to-cook potatoes
- Frozen veggies (plain or blends)
- Prewashed and precut fresh vegetables
- Ready-to-heat-and-eat refrigerated potato side dishes
- Salad kits

# 1 light bites

## Instant Appetizers

*Have you ever had an appetizer emergency and thought the only thing you could come up with was a bag of chips with dip or salsa? Well, the ideas here are a little more exciting than that!*

1 **Warmed Olives and Roasted Almonds with Lemon–Olive Oil Drizzle:** Heat oven to 350°F. In a shallow baking dish, mix equal amounts of your favorite mixture of olives (drained) and lightly salted roasted whole almonds. Drizzle lightly with extra-virgin olive oil, sprinkle with grated lemon peel and toss. Heat briefly just to warm olives. Serve with sliced crusty bread or crackers.

2 **Basil-Mascarpone Spread:** Onto a shallow serving dish, spread about 8 ounces of mascarpone cheese or softened cream cheese; spoon basil pesto over the top and sprinkle with chopped red bell pepper. Serve with baguette slices or crackers.

3 **Parmesan and Dates:** Cut a piece of Parmesan or Asiago cheese into cube-size chunks (they won't be nice and even, but that's okay). Top with the same size piece of dried date or fig; secure with a toothpick. Serve with baguette slices or crackers.

**4** **Blue Cheese Waffle Fries:** Heat frozen waffle fries or cottage fries in oven as directed on the package. About 2 to 5 minutes before they're done, remove them from the oven and sprinkle with crumbled blue or Gorgonzola cheese. Continue baking just until the cheese begins to melt. Have a bottle of Buffalo wings hot sauce available for those who like things spicy!

**5** **Italian Snack Mix:** Drizzle popcorn, mini bagel chips, mini pretzels and Parmesan- or pizza-flavored fish-shaped crackers with melted butter. Sprinkle with garlic powder, onion powder, dried basil leaves and dried oregano leaves; toss gently.

**6** **So-Simple Salsa Dip:** Mix equal parts of salsa and softened cream cheese, adding milk if needed. Serve with tortilla chips.

**7** **Yogonanas:** Poke end of wooden stick into banana half; roll banana in your favorite flavor of yogurt, then roll in crushed cereal, granola or cookies.

**8** **That Marshmallow Creme Fruit Dip:** In a medium bowl, beat an 8-ounce package of softened cream cheese, a 7-ounce jar of marshmallow creme and 1 tablespoon of milk or cream with an electric mixer until smooth and creamy. Serve with fresh fruit, cookies or graham crackers as dippers.

**9** **Pepperoni Pizza Nachos:** Heat oven to 400°F. On a foil-lined cookie sheet, arrange tortilla chips. Top with sliced pepperoni, pizza sauce and shredded mozzarella or pizza cheese blend. Bake 4 to 6 minutes or until hot and cheese is melted.

**10** **Graham Cracker Nachos:** On a serving plate, arrange graham crackers. Drizzle melted peanut butter or almond butter over crackers; top as desired with ingredients like mini marshmallows, mini candies, sliced fresh fruit, dried fruit, cereal or trail mix.

**This icon means:** 20 minutes or less

# Quick Chicken Quesadillas

1 package (6 oz) refrigerated cooked Southwest-flavor chicken breast strips*

½ cup chunky-style salsa

8 flour tortillas (6 to 8 inch)

Cooking spray

2 cups finely shredded Colby–Monterey Jack cheese blend (8 oz)

¼ cup sour cream

1 Cut chicken into bite-size pieces. In small bowl, mix chicken and salsa.

2 Spray 1 side of 1 tortilla with cooking spray; place sprayed side down in 10-inch skillet. Layer with ¼ of the chicken mixture and ½ cup of the cheese. Top with another tortilla; spray top of tortilla with cooking spray.

3 Cook uncovered over medium heat 4 to 6 minutes, carefully turning after 2 minutes, until golden brown and cheese is melted. Repeat with remaining tortillas, chicken mixture and cheese. To serve, cut quesadillas into wedges. Serve with sour cream and, if desired, additional salsa.

**4 servings (1 quesadilla each)**

* *Can't find the refrigerated seasoned chicken? Substitute 1½ cups chopped rotisserie or other cooked chicken.*

## Instant
**Success!**

*If you like veggies, try Quick Chicken-Vegetable Quesadillas. Just sprinkle 2 tablespoons chopped tomato, 1 tablespoon sliced ripe olives and 1 tablespoon sliced green onions over the cheese for each quesadilla.*

**1 Serving:** Calories 480; Total Fat 28g (Saturated Fat 15g; Trans Fat 1g); Cholesterol 95mg; Sodium 920mg; Total Carbohydrate 30g (Dietary Fiber 2g) • **Exchanges:** 2 Starch, 3 Lean Meat, 3½ Fat • **Carbohydrate Choices:** 2

# Buffalo-Style Chicken Nuggets

1 ½ cups Corn Chex® cereal

½ cup Original Bisquick® mix

2 teaspoons paprika

¼ teaspoon seasoned salt

¼ teaspoon ground red pepper (cayenne)

1 tablespoon vegetable oil

1 teaspoon red pepper sauce

1 lb boneless skinless chicken breasts, cut into 2-inch pieces

¼ cup ranch dressing

1 Heat oven to 425°F. In 1-gallon resealable food-storage plastic bag, crush cereal with rolling pin. Add Bisquick mix, paprika, seasoned salt and ground red pepper to cereal; mix well.

2 In small bowl, mix oil and red pepper sauce. Coat chicken pieces with oil mixture.

3 Shake about 6 chicken pieces at a time in bag of cereal mixture until coated. Shake off any extra mixture. On ungreased cookie sheet, place chicken pieces in single layer.

4 Bake about 10 minutes or until chicken is no longer pink in center. Serve chicken with dressing.

**4 servings**

## Easy
### Add-On

*Add a side of crunchy dippers such as celery and carrot sticks to serve with these spicy nuggets. Any of your favorite sauces or salad dressings can be used for dipping.*

**1 Serving:** Calories 340; Total Fat 17g (Saturated Fat 3g; Trans Fat 0g); Cholesterol 75mg; Sodium 590mg; Total Carbohydrate 20g (Dietary Fiber 1g) • **Exchanges:** 1 ½ Starch, 3 Very Lean Meat, 3 Fat • **Carbohydrate Choices:** 1

# Grilled Veggies and Steak

1 package (6 oz) small fresh portabella
   mushrooms

½ lb beef sirloin steak (about ¾ inch
   thick), cut into ¾-inch cubes

1 cup frozen pearl onions (from 1-lb
   bag), thawed

½ cup plus 2 tablespoons balsamic
   vinaigrette

½ cup halved grape or cherry
   tomatoes

1  Heat gas or charcoal grill. In large bowl, place mushrooms, beef, onions
and ½ cup of the vinaigrette; toss to coat. Let stand 10 minutes; drain. Place
mixture in grill basket (grill "wok"). Place basket on cookie sheet to carry
to grill to catch drips.

2  Place basket on grill. Cover grill; cook over medium-high heat 7 to
9 minutes, shaking basket or stirring beef mixture twice, until vegetables are
tender and beef is desired doneness. Stir in tomatoes.

3  Spoon beef mixture into serving dish. Stir in remaining 2 tablespoons
vinaigrette.

**4 servings**

## Make it a Meal

*Throw in a ciabatta loaf
or some petits pains,
and maybe a jar of
store-bought tapenade
spread for a light
summertime dinner.*

**1 Serving:** Calories 150; Total Fat 5g (Saturated Fat 1g; Trans Fat 0g); Cholesterol 30mg; Sodium 350mg; Total Carbohydrate 10g
(Dietary Fiber 1g) • **Exchanges:** 1 Vegetable, 2 Very Lean Meat, 1 Fa • **Carbohydrate Choices:** ½

# Tiny Meat and Cheese Bites

1 cup Giardiniera vegetable mix (from 16-oz jar), drained

40 cubes (½ inch) hard salami (about ½ lb)

40 cubes (½ inch) Swiss cheese (about 4 oz)

1 Cut larger vegetables into ½-inch pieces.

2 On each of 40 toothpicks, alternate pieces of salami, vegetables and cheese.

**8 servings (5 skewers each)**

## Instant
## **Success!**

*Giardiniera is a mixture of pickled vegetables, such as carrots, cauliflower, red pepper and celery. You can usually find it in the supermarket with the pickles and olives.*

**1 Serving:** Calories 170; Total Fat 14g (Saturated Fat 6g; Trans Fat 0g); Cholesterol 35mg; Sodium 800mg; Total Carbohydrate 2g (Dietary Fiber 0g) • **Exchanges:** 1½ High-Fat Meat • **Carbohydrate Choices:** 0

Betty Crocker Supper in a Snap

# Roast Beef Bruschetta

Prep Time **20 Minutes**
Start to Finish **30 Minutes**

1 loaf (1 lb) baguette French bread, cut into 30 (¼-inch) slices

2 tablespoons olive or vegetable oil

5 small plum (Roma) tomatoes

½ cup chive-and-onion cream cheese spread (from 8-oz container)

½ lb thinly sliced cooked roast beef

¼ teaspoon coarsely ground pepper

8 medium green onions, sliced (½ cup)

1  Heat oven to 375°F. Brush both sides of bread slices with oil. Place on ungreased cookie sheet. Bake about 5 minutes or until crisp. Cool 5 minutes.

2  Meanwhile, cut each tomato into 6 slices; set aside. Spread cream cheese over each bread slice. Top with beef; sprinkle with pepper. Top with tomato slices and onions.

**6 servings (5 bruschetta each)**

## Speed it Up

*It's great to be able to make some foods before you need them. Toast the bread slices a day ahead of time, and store loosely covered at room temperature. Top them up to 1 hour ahead, then cover and place in the fridge until serving.*

**1 Serving:** Calories 400; Total Fat 19g (Saturated Fat 7g; Trans Fat 1g); Cholesterol 45mg; Sodium 600mg; Total Carbohydrate 41g (Dietary Fiber 3g) • **Exchanges:** 2 ½ Starch, 1 Vegetable, 1 Lean Meat, 3 Fat • **Carbohydrate Choices:** 3

light bites

19

# Mini Salmon Wraps

Prep Time **20 Minutes**
Start to Finish **30 Minutes**

2 packages (3 oz each) cream cheese, softened

2 tablespoons horseradish sauce

6 spinach, tomato or plain flour tortillas (8 to 10 inch)

1 medium cucumber, peeled, finely chopped (1 cup)

¼ cup sour cream

¼ cup chopped fresh dill weed

¼ cup finely chopped red or yellow onion

8 oz salmon lox, cut into thin strips

1   In small bowl, mix cream cheese and horseradish sauce. Spread cream cheese mixture evenly over tortillas.

2   In small bowl, mix cucumber, sour cream, dill weed and onion; spread over cream cheese mixture. Arrange salmon strips over cucumber mixture. Roll up tortillas tightly.

3   Cover and refrigerate wraps 10 minutes or until ready to serve. If desired, cut each wrap into 8 pieces.

**6 servings (8 pieces each)**

## Speed it Up

*Beat the clock! Make these sophisticated wraps up to 24 hours ahead; cover with plastic wrap and refrigerate.*

**1 Serving:** Calories 310; Total Fat 17g (Saturated Fat 8g; Trans Fat 1g); Cholesterol 45mg; Sodium 610mg; Total Carbohydrate 27g (Dietary Fiber 1g) • **Exchanges:** 2 Starch, 1 Very Lean Meat, 3 Fat • **Carbohydrate Choices:** 2

Prep Time **15 Minutes**
Start to Finish **20 Minutes**

# Spicy Lemon Shrimp with Basil Mayonnaise

1 tablespoon grated lemon peel

3 tablespoons lemon juice

¾ teaspoon crushed red pepper flakes

½ teaspoon salt

2 cloves garlic, finely chopped

2 tablespoons olive or vegetable oil

1 lb uncooked deveined peeled large shrimp (22 to 25 shrimp), thawed if frozen, tail shells removed

½ cup loosely packed fresh basil leaves

½ cup low-fat mayonnaise or salad dressing

1 Set oven control to broil. In medium glass or plastic bowl, mix lemon peel, lemon juice, red pepper flakes, salt, garlic and 1 tablespoon of the oil. Add shrimp; toss to coat. In ungreased 15 × 10 × 1-inch pan, spread shrimp.

2 Broil shrimp with tops 2 to 3 inches from heat 3 to 5 minutes or until shrimp are pink.

3 In food processor, place basil and remaining 1 tablespoon oil. Cover; process until chopped. Add mayonnaise. Cover; process until smooth. Serve shrimp with mayonnaise.

**4 servings (6 shrimp and 2 tablespoons sauce each)**

## Instant **Success!**

*Using frozen shrimp is super convenient, but pat the thawed shrimp dry before adding to the oil mixture. Reach dinnertime even faster by making and refrigerating the basil mayonnaise up to a day before.*

**1 Serving:** Calories 250; Total Fat 18g (Saturated Fat 2.5g; Trans Fat 0g); Cholesterol 170mg; Sodium 690mg; Total Carbohydrate 4g (Dietary Fiber 0g) • **Exchanges:** 2½ Very Lean Meat, 3½ Fat • **Carbohydrate Choices:** 0

# Chewy Pizza Bread

1½ cups all-purpose flour

1½ teaspoons baking powder

½ teaspoon salt

¾ cup regular or nonalcoholic beer

½ cup tomato pasta sauce

⅓ cup shredded mozzarella cheese (1.5 oz)

Chopped fresh basil leaves, if desired

1 Heat oven to 425°F. Spray 8-inch square pan with cooking spray.

2 In medium bowl, mix flour, baking powder and salt. Stir in beer just until flour is moistened. Spread dough in pan. Spread pasta sauce over dough. Sprinkle with cheese.

3 Bake 15 to 20 minutes or until toothpick inserted in center comes out clean. Sprinkle with basil. Cut into 2-inch squares. Serve warm.

**4 servings (4 squares each)**

## Easy
### Add-On

*Pepperoni? Yes, go ahead and add slices of pepperoni on the sauce before topping with cheese.*

**1 Serving:** Calories 230; Total Fat 3.5g (Saturated Fat 1.5g; Trans Fat 0g); Cholesterol 5mg; Sodium 680mg; Total Carbohydrate 43g (Dietary Fiber 2g) • **Exchanges:** 3 Starch • **Carbohydrate Choices:** 3

# Veggie Quesadillas

1 cup shredded zucchini

1 small tomato, seeded, chopped
   (½ cup)

1 tablespoon chopped fresh or
   1 teaspoon dried oregano leaves

½ teaspoon garlic-pepper blend

8 whole wheat flour tortillas (8 inch)

2 cups shredded Italian cheese blend
   (8 oz)

Tomato pasta sauce or marinara sauce,
   heated, if desired

1 Heat oven to 350°F. In medium bowl, mix zucchini, tomato, oregano
and garlic-pepper blend.

2 On ungreased large cookie sheet, place 4 tortillas. Sprinkle ½ cup of the
cheese evenly over each of the 4 tortillas. Spoon ¼ of the vegetable mixture
over cheese. Top with remaining tortillas.

3 Bake about 6 minutes or until hot and cheese is melted. Cut each
quesadilla into wedges. Serve with pasta sauce.

**4 servings (1 quesadilla each)**

**Make** it
a **Meal**

*Ramp up supper by
adding a bagged salad
mix and dressing.*

**1 Serving:** Calories 300; Total Fat 16g (Saturated Fat 10g; Trans Fat 0.5g); Cholesterol 40mg; Sodium 680mg; Total
Carbohydrate 20g (Dietary Fiber 4g) • **Exchanges:** 1½ Starch, 2 Medium-Fat Meat, ½ Fat • **Carbohydrate Choices:** 1

# 2 chicken &turkey

## Fast Veggie Sides

*Serving plain cooked frozen or fresh vegetables is always an option, but in a few extra minutes, you can "doctor" veggies to make some really decent sides!*

**1** Green Beans with Shaved Asiago: Drizzle hot cooked green beans with extra-virgin olive oil, then, holding your vegetable peeler over the beans, shave slices of Asiago or Parmesan cheese on top.

**2** Asparagus with Toasted Nuts and Citrus Zest: Top hot cooked asparagus spears with slivered almonds or pine nuts that have been toasted in melted butter on top of the stove. Sprinkle with grated lemon or orange peel.

**3** Broccoli with Garlic-and-Herb Cream Sauce: Heat garlic-and-herb spreadable cheese in a small saucepan over low heat, stirring frequently, until smooth and creamy, adding milk or cream if needed. Spoon over hot cooked broccoli.

**4** Grape Tomato Sauté: Sauté whole grape tomatoes, jarred chopped garlic and Italian seasoning in extra-virgin olive oil just until tomatoes are hot. Season with salt and pepper to taste.

**5** Maple-Glazed Carrots: Mix together equal amounts of maple syrup and melted butter; toss with hot, cooked, well-drained baby carrots.

**6** Cheesy Corn: Mix together hot cooked corn and any flavor of process cheese sauce or salsa con queso dip; heat until hot.

**7** Ranch Veggies: Drizzle hot cooked veggies with ranch dressing.

**8** Broccoli Italiano: Toss hot, cooked broccoli florets with warmed zesty Italian dressing; sprinkle with grated Parmesan cheese or shredded Cheddar cheese.

**9** Cheesy Taco Broccoli: Toss hot, cooked broccoli florets with shredded taco-flavored cheese; sprinkle with crushed nacho-flavored tortilla chips.

**10** Sugar Snap Peas with Honey Butter: Mix together equal amounts of honey and melted butter; toss with hot cooked, well-drained sugar snap peas. Sprinkle with honey-roasted peanuts.

**This icon means:** 20 minutes or less

**This icon means:**  slow-cooker recipe

# Oven-Fried Chicken

¼ cup butter or margarine

½ cup all-purpose flour

1 teaspoon paprika

½ teaspoon salt

¼ teaspoon pepper

1 cut-up whole chicken (3 to 3 ½ lb)

1   Heat oven to 425°F. Melt butter in 13 × 9-inch pan in the oven.

2   In large food-storage plastic bag, mix flour, paprika, salt and pepper. Place a few pieces of chicken at a time in bag, seal bag and shake to coat with flour mixture. Place chicken, skin sides down, in a single layer in butter in pan.

3   Bake uncovered 30 minutes. Remove pan from oven; turn chicken pieces over, using tongs. Bake uncovered about 30 minutes longer or until juice of chicken is clear when thickest pieces are cut to bone (170°F for breasts; 180°F for thighs and legs on an instant-read thermometer). If chicken sticks to pan, loosen it gently with turner or fork.

**6 servings**

**Lighten Up Oven-Fried Chicken:** *Remove skin from chicken before cooking. Do not melt butter in pan; instead, spray pan with cooking spray. Decrease butter to 2 tablespoons; melt butter and drizzle over chicken after turning in step 3 for 11 grams of fat and 240 calories per serving.*

## Budget
Smart

*To save a little more money on this recipe, substitute 3½ lb of chicken thighs and drumsticks for the cut-up whole chicken. Just be sure to cook the pieces to 180°F.*

**1 Serving:** Calories 330; Total Fat 21g (Saturated Fat 9g, Trans Fat 1g); Cholesterol 105mg; Sodium 330mg; Total Carbohydrate 8g (Dietary Fiber 0g) • **Exchanges:** ½ Starch, 3½ Lean Meat, 2 Fat • **Carbohydrate Choices:** ½

# Oven-Baked Chicken

1 tablespoon butter or margarine

⅔ cup Original Bisquick mix

1½ teaspoons paprika

1 teaspoon salt or garlic salt

1 teaspoon Italian seasoning, if desired

¼ teaspoon pepper

1 cut-up whole chicken (3 to 3½ lb)

1  Heat oven to 425°F. In 13 × 9-inch (3-quart) glass baking dish, melt butter in oven.

2  In medium bowl, stir together Bisquick mix, paprika, salt, Italian seasoning and pepper. Coat chicken with Bisquick mixture. Place skin side down in heated dish.

3  Bake 35 minutes. Turn chicken; bake about 15 minutes longer or until juice of chicken is clear when thickest piece is cut to bone (170°F for breasts; 180°F for thighs and drumsticks).

**5 servings**

## Instant
## Success!

*Just like fried chicken but lighter and less messy, this is sure to become a household favorite. If you love dark meat and see chicken drumsticks or thighs on sale, snap them up and use them instead of a whole cut-up chicken. The baked chicken can be served hot, room temperature or cold, and it's a very welcome leftover!*

**1 Serving:** Calories 360; Total Fat 20g (Saturated Fat 7g, Trans Fat 1g); Cholesterol 110mg; Sodium 780mg; Total Carbohydrate 11g (Dietary Fiber 0g) • **Exchanges:** ½ Starch, 4½ Lean Meat, 1½ Fat • **Carbohydrate Choices:** 1

# Home-Style Chicken Dinner

Prep Time **30 Minutes**

Start to Finish **1 Hour 20 Minutes**

2 teaspoons dried basil leaves

1 teaspoon seasoned salt

1 teaspoon garlic pepper blend

2 tablespoons olive or vegetable oil

1 cut-up whole chicken (3- to 3½-lb), skin removed if desired

6 small unpeeled red potatoes, cut into quarters (2 cups)

2 medium dark-orange sweet potatoes, peeled, cut into 1-inch pieces (3 cups)

1 medium green bell pepper, cut into 1-inch pieces (1 cup)

3 plum (Roma) tomatoes, cut into quarters

## Instant Success!

*Sweet potatoes bring this homey classic right up to date and help make it a one-dish meal.*

1 Heat oven to 400°F. Spray 13 × 9-inch (3-quart) glass baking dish with cooking spray. In large bowl, mix basil, seasoned salt, garlic pepper and oil. Brush about half of the mixture on chicken. Add remaining ingredients to bowl; toss to coat.

2 Place vegetables in baking dish. Place chicken on vegetables. Brush with any remaining oil mixture.

3 Bake uncovered 45 to 50 minutes or until vegetables are tender and juice of chicken is clear when centers of thickest pieces are cut to bone (170°F for breasts; 180°F for thighs and drumsticks). Serve with pan juices.

**4 servings**

**1 Serving:** Calories 610; Total Fat 27g (Saturated Fat 7g, Trans Fat 0.5g); Cholesterol 130mg; Sodium 480mg; Total Carbohydrate 51g (Dietary Fiber 7g) • **Exchanges:** 2 Starch, 1 Other Carbohydrate, 1 Vegetable, 5 Medium-Fat Meat • **Carbohydrate Choices:** 3½

# Taco Chicken with Corn Salsa

1 package (1.25 oz) taco seasoning mix

4 boneless skinless chicken breasts (about 1¼ lb)

2 tablespoons vegetable oil

1 can (11 oz) whole kernel corn with red and green peppers, drained

1 medium avocado, pitted, peeled and chopped

2 tablespoons finely chopped red onion

2 tablespoons chopped fresh cilantro

1 tablespoon lime juice

1 teaspoon honey

1 In medium bowl, reserve 2 teaspoons of the taco seasoning mix. Coat chicken with remaining taco seasoning mix.

2 In 12-inch skillet, heat oil over medium heat. Cook chicken in oil 3 to 5 minutes, turning once, until brown. Reduce heat to medium-low. Cook about 8 minutes, turning once, until juice of chicken is clear when center of thickest part is cut (170°F).

3 Meanwhile, add remaining ingredients to reserved taco seasoning mix; toss gently. Serve salsa with chicken.

**4 servings**

## Instant **Success!**

*This lively little salsa can be made ahead of time, but be sure to add the avocado just before serving to preserve its color and texture.*

**1 Serving:** Calories 410; Total Fat 18g (Saturated Fat 3.5g; Trans Fat 0g); Cholesterol 85mg; Sodium 690mg; Total Carbohydrate 26g (Dietary Fiber 5g) • **Exchanges:** 1 Starch, ½ Other Carbohydrate, 4½ Very Lean Meat, 3 Fat • **Carbohydrate Choices:** 2

# Tuscan Rosemary Chicken and White Beans

Prep Time **30 Minutes**
Start to Finish **30 Minutes**

⅛ cup Italian dressing

4 boneless skinless chicken breasts (about 1 ¼ lb)

¼ cup water

2 medium carrots, sliced (1 cup)

2 medium stalks celery, sliced (1 cup)

¼ cup coarsely chopped drained sun-dried tomatoes in oil

1 teaspoon dried rosemary leaves, crushed

1 can (19 oz) cannellini beans, drained, rinsed

1 In 12-inch skillet, heat dressing over medium–high heat. Cook chicken in dressing 2 to 3 minutes on each side or until lightly browned.

2 Reduce heat to medium-low. Add water, carrots, celery, tomatoes and rosemary to skillet. Cover; simmer about 10 minutes or until carrots are crisp-tender and juice of chicken is clear when center of thickest part is cut (170°F).

3 Stir in beans. Cover; cook 5 to 6 minutes or until beans are thoroughly heated.

**4 servings**

## Easy
### Add-On

*The flavorful pan juices are just begging to be soaked up with a hunk of crusty bread!*

**1 Serving:** Calories 440; Total Fat 14g (Saturated Fat 2g; Trans Fat 0g); Cholesterol 90mg; Sodium 320mg; Total Carbohydrate 34g (Dietary Fiber 9g) • **Exchanges:** 2 Starch, 1 Vegetable, 5 Very Lean Meat, 2 Fat • **Carbohydrate Choices:** 2

# Two-Pepper Chicken with Honey Butter

4 boneless skinless chicken breasts (about 1 ¼ lb)

1 tablespoon black peppercorns, crushed

1 tablespoon white peppercorns, crushed

1 tablespoon vegetable oil

¼ cup butter or margarine, softened

2 tablespoons honey

1 Coat both sides of chicken with peppercorns. In 10-inch skillet, heat oil over medium-high heat. Cook chicken in oil 15 to 20 minutes, turning once, until juice of chicken is clear when center of thickest part is cut (170°F).

2 In small bowl, mix butter and honey. Top chicken with honey butter.

**4 servings**

## Instant
## Success!

*How do you crush peppercorns? If you don't have a pepper mill, it's easy using a mortar and pestle, mini-food processor, or spice or coffee grinder. The low-tech method is to place them in a resealable plastic bag and pound with a meat mallet or rolling pin.*

**1 Serving:** Calories 340; Total Fat 20g (Saturated Fat 9g; Trans Fat 1g); Cholesterol 115mg; Sodium 160mg; Total Carbohydrate 10g (Dietary Fiber 0g) • **Exchanges:** ½ Other Carbohydrate, 4½ Very Lean Meat, 3½ Fat • **Carbohydrate Choices:** ½

# Moroccan Spiced Chicken

Prep Time **30 Minutes**
Start to Finish **30 Minutes**

1 tablespoon paprika

½ teaspoon salt

½ teaspoon ground cumin

¼ teaspoon ground allspice

¼ teaspoon ground cinnamon

4 boneless skinless chicken breasts
(about 1¼ lb)

1 tablespoon vegetable oil

2 cups water

1 teaspoon vegetable oil

1½ cups uncooked couscous

¼ cup raisins, if desired

1 small papaya, peeled, seeded and
sliced

1 In small bowl, mix paprika, salt, cumin, allspice and cinnamon. Coat
both sides of chicken with spice mixture.

2 In 10-inch skillet, heat 1 tablespoon oil over medium heat. Cook
chicken in oil 15 to 20 minutes, turning once, until juice of chicken is clear
when center of thickest part is cut (170°F).

3 Meanwhile, in 2-quart saucepan, heat water and 1 teaspoon oil just
to boiling. Stir in couscous; remove from heat. Cover; let stand 5 minutes.
Fluff couscous before serving; stir in raisins. Serve chicken with couscous
and papaya.

**4 servings**

## Make it a Meal

*Looking for something
quick but fancy to serve
guests? Dress up this
dish with warmed pita
folds drizzled with
olive oil or melted
butter or with Middle
Eastern flatbread.*

**1 Serving:** Calories 470; Total Fat 10g (Saturated Fat 2g; Trans Fat 0g); Cholesterol 85mg; Sodium 380mg; Total Carbohydrate
55g (Dietary Fiber 5g) • **Exchanges:** 3½ Starch, 4½ Very Lean Meat, 1 Fat • **Carbohydrate Choices:** 3½

# Chicken in Fresh Herbs

4 boneless skinless chicken breasts
(about 1¼ lb)

1 medium shallot, chopped

¼ cup chopped fresh chervil leaves

¼ cup chopped fresh tarragon leaves

½ cup dry white wine or chicken broth

1 tablespoon lemon juice

½ teaspoon salt

Cracked pepper, if desired

1 Heat 10-inch skillet over medium-high heat until hot.

2 Cook all ingredients except pepper in skillet 15 to 20 minutes, turning chicken once, until juice of chicken is clear when center of thickest part is cut (170°F). Sprinkle with pepper.

**4 servings**

## Instant
## Success!

*This fresh farmers'
market dish uses chervil,
an herb with a sweet
flavor reminiscent of
onion and parsley.
It looks very similar
to Italian flat-leaf
parsley, which can be
used as a substitute.
The tarragon has a
delicate licorice flavor.*

**1 Serving:** Calories 170; Total Fat 4.5g (Saturated Fat 1.5g; Trans Fat 0g); Cholesterol 85mg; Sodium 380mg; Total Carbohydrate 0g (Dietary Fiber 0g) • **Exchanges:** 4½ Very Lean Meat, ½ Fat • **Carbohydrate Choices:** 0

# Feta-Topped Chicken

Prep Time **10 Minutes**
Start to Finish **25 Minutes**

4 boneless skinless chicken breasts
   (about 1 ¼ lb)

2 tablespoons balsamic vinaigrette
   dressing

1 teaspoon Italian seasoning

¼ teaspoon seasoned pepper

1 large plum (Roma) tomato, cut into
   8 slices

¼ cup crumbled feta cheese (1 oz)

1 Set oven control to broil. Brush both sides of chicken breasts with
dressing. Sprinkle both sides with Italian seasoning and seasoned pepper.
Place on rack in broiler pan.

2 Broil with tops 4 inches from heat about 10 minutes, turning once,
until juice of chicken is clear when center of thickest part is cut (170°F).
Top with tomato and cheese. Broil 2 to 3 minutes longer or until cheese is
lightly browned.

**4 servings**

## Make it a Meal

*Boil some orzo pasta
while the chicken is
cooking. Toss the hot
pasta with a little of
the dressing, or drizzle
with olive oil and
sprinkle with garlic
salt before tossing.*

**1 Serving:** Calories 230; Total Fat 9g (Saturated Fat 2.5g; Trans Fat 0g); Cholesterol 95mg; Sodium 230mg; Total Carbohydrate
3g (Dietary Fiber 0g) • **Exchanges:** 4½ Very Lean Meat, 1½ Fat • **Carbohydrate Choices:** 0

chicken & turkey

# Barbecue Chicken and Vegetable Supper

1 tablespoon vegetable oil

4 boneless skinless chicken breasts
    (about 1¼ lb)

½ teaspoon salt

2 cups frozen whole green beans
    (from 14-oz bag)

2 cups refrigerated red potato wedges
    (from 20-oz bag)

1 jar (12 oz) chicken gravy

⅓ cup barbecue sauce

1 In 12-inch nonstick skillet, heat oil over medium–high heat. Add chicken; sprinkle with salt. Cook 4 minutes, turning once, until browned.

2 Add beans, potatoes, gravy and barbecue sauce; stir to coat and mix. Cover; cook 5 to 8 minutes, stirring occasionally, until beans and potatoes are tender and juice of chicken is clear when center of thickest part is cut (170°F).

**4 servings**

## Instant Success!

*Gravy lovers, this saucy skillet supper is your meal ticket! Try substituting frozen potato wedges or steak fries (no need to thaw first!) if you can't find the refrigerated potato wedges.*

**1 Serving:** Calories 400; Total Fat 13g (Saturated Fat 3g; Trans Fat 0g); Cholesterol 85mg; Sodium 1220mg; Total Carbohydrate 33g (Dietary Fiber 6g) • **Exchanges:** 1 Starch, 1 Other Carbohydrate, 1 Vegetable, 4½ Very Lean Meat, 2 Fat • **Carbohydrate Choices:** 2

# Zesty Roasted Chicken and Potatoes

6 boneless skinless chicken breasts (about 1¾ lb)

8 small (unpeeled) red potatoes, cut into quarters (about 1 lb)

⅓ cup mayonnaise or salad dressing

3 tablespoons Dijon mustard

½ teaspoon pepper

2 cloves garlic, finely chopped, or ¼ teaspoon garlic powder

Chopped fresh chives, if desired

1 Heat oven to 350°F. Spray 15 × 10 × 1-inch pan with cooking spray.

2 Place chicken and potatoes in pan. In small bowl, mix remaining ingredients except chives; brush over chicken and potatoes.

3 Roast uncovered 30 to 35 minutes or until potatoes are tender when pierced with a fork and juice of chicken is clear when center of thickest part is cut (170°F). Sprinkle with chives.

**6 servings**

**Lighten Up Zesty Roasted Chicken and Potatoes:** *Use low-fat mayonnaise for 9 grams of fat and 270 calories per serving.*

**1 Serving:** Calories 310; Total Fat 14g (Saturated Fat 2.5g, Trans Fat 0g); Cholesterol 85mg; Sodium 330mg; Total Carbohydrate 15g (Dietary Fiber 2g) • **Exchanges:** 1 Starch, 4 Very Lean Meat, 2 Fat • **Carbohydrate Choices:** 1

# Chicken Marsala

Prep Time **45 Minutes**

Start to Finish **45 Minutes**

¼ cup all-purpose flour

¼ teaspoon salt

¼ teaspoon pepper

4 boneless skinless chicken breasts
   (about 1 ¼ lb)

2 tablespoons olive or vegetable oil

2 cloves garlic, finely chopped

1 cup sliced mushrooms (3 oz)

¼ cup chopped fresh parsley or
   1 tablespoon parsley flakes

½ cup dry Marsala wine or chicken
   broth

1 In shallow dish, mix flour, salt and pepper. Coat chicken with flour mixture; shake off excess flour.

2 In 10-inch skillet, heat oil over medium-high heat. Cook garlic, mushrooms and parsley in oil 5 minutes, stirring frequently.

3 Add chicken to skillet. Cook uncovered about 8 minutes, turning once, or until chicken is brown. Add wine. Cook uncovered 8 to 10 minutes longer, turning once, or until juice of chicken is clear when center of thickest part is cut (170°F).

**4 servings**

## Budget Smart

*This twist on veal marsala is both easy and impressive—especially the second time you make it. That's because marsala wine has a much longer shelf life than most wines and if you buy it once, you can hold on to it for the next time you make this recipe!*

**1 Serving:** Calories 290; Total Fat 11g (Saturated Fat 2g, Trans Fat 0g); Cholesterol 85mg; Sodium 230mg; Total Carbohydrate 9g (Dietary Fiber 0g) • **Exchanges:** ½ Starch, 4½ Very Lean Meat, 2 Fat • **Carbohydrate Choices:** ½

# Chicken with Mushrooms and Carrots

4 slices bacon, chopped

4 boneless skinless chicken breasts (about 1¼ lb)

¼ teaspoon pepper

2 cups ready-to-eat baby-cut carrots

1 cup chicken broth

¼ cup dry white wine or chicken broth

1 tablespoon cornstarch

½ teaspoon dried thyme leaves

¼ teaspoon salt

4 oz small fresh mushrooms, cut in half (about 1⅓ cups)

1 In 12-inch nonstick skillet, cook bacon over medium heat 6 to 8 minutes, stirring occasionally, until crisp. Remove bacon to paper towel to drain.

2 Add chicken to bacon drippings in skillet; sprinkle with pepper. Cook over medium heat 4 to 5 minutes, turning once, until well browned. Add carrots and ¼ cup of the broth. Cover; cook 7 to 9 minutes or until carrots are crisp-tender and juice of chicken is clear when center of thickest part is cut (170°F).

3 Meanwhile, to remaining chicken broth, add wine, cornstarch, thyme and salt; mix well. Add broth mixture and mushrooms to skillet. Cook 3 to 5 minutes, stirring once or twice, until bubbly. Cover; cook about 3 minutes longer, or until mushrooms are tender. Sprinkle with bacon.

**4 servings**

## Speed it Up

*To make this luscious chicken recipe even faster, buy presliced mushrooms and toss them straight into the skillet.*

**1 Serving:** Calories 260; Total Fat 8g (Saturated Fat 2.5g; Trans Fat 0g); Cholesterol 95mg; Sodium 710mg; Total Carbohydrate 9g (Dietary Fiber 2g) • **Exchanges:** ½ Other Carbohydrate, 1 Vegetable, 5 Very Lean Meat, 1 Fat • **Carbohydrate Choices:** ½

# Lemon Chicken with Olives

4 boneless skinless chicken breasts (about 1 ¼ lb)

2 teaspoons olive or canola oil

1 tablespoon lemon juice

1 teaspoon salt-free lemon-pepper seasoning

¼ cup sliced ripe olives

4 thin slices lemon

**1** Set oven control to broil. Spray broiler pan rack with cooking spray. Starting at thickest edge of each chicken breast, cut horizontally almost to opposite side. Open cut chicken breast so it is an even thickness.

**2** In small bowl, mix oil and lemon juice. Drizzle over both sides of chicken breasts. Sprinkle both sides with lemon–pepper seasoning. Place on rack in broiler pan.

**3** Broil with tops 4 inches from heat about 10 minutes, turning once, until juice of chicken is clear when center of thickest part is cut (170°F). During last 2 minutes of broiling, top with olives and lemon slices.

**4 servings**

## Instant
## Success!

*Lemon, olives and chicken go together so beautifully that many recipes combine them (try the Mediterranean Chicken Packets, page 60). This recipe uses both lemon juice and whole lemon slices from the same lemon: Cut off the 4 lemon slices, then squeeze the remainder for the tablespoon of juice.*

**1 Serving:** Calories 170; Total Fat 7g (Saturated Fat 1.5g, Trans Fat 0g); Cholesterol 75mg; Sodium 140mg; Total Carbohydrate 0g (Dietary Fiber 0g); • **Exchanges:** 4 Very Lean Meat, ½ Fat • **Carbohydrate Choices:** 0

# Grilled Taco-Barbecue Chicken

Prep Time **25 Minutes**
Start to Finish **25 Minutes**

2 tablespoons taco seasoning mix (from 1-oz package)

1 teaspoon dried oregano leaves

4 boneless skinless chicken breasts (about 1¼ lb)

1 tablespoon olive or vegetable oil

¼ cup barbecue sauce

2 tablespoons chili sauce

½ teaspoon ground cumin

1 Heat gas or charcoal grill. In shallow bowl, mix taco seasoning mix and oregano. Brush chicken with oil; sprinkle with taco seasoning mixture.

2 Place chicken on grill. Cover grill; cook 10 to 15 minutes or until juice of chicken is clear when center of thickest part is cut (170°F).

3 Meanwhile, in small microwavable bowl, mix barbecue sauce, chili sauce and cumin. Cover; microwave on High 30 to 60 seconds or until hot. Serve sauce over chicken.

**4 servings**

**Oven Directions:** *Heat oven to 375°F. Line shallow baking pan with foil, or spray with cooking spray. Place coated chicken in pan. Bake 25 to 30 minutes or until juice of chicken is clear when center of thickest part is cut (170°F).*

## Instant Success!

*Taking chicken breasts south of the border is a great way to spice up a weeknight summer dinner. This recipe puts your spice cabinet to work with taco seasoning, dried oregano and cumin.*

**1 Serving:** Calories 240; Total Fat 8g (Saturated Fat 2g, Trans Fat 0g); Cholesterol 85mg; Sodium 780mg; Total Carbohydrate 11g (Dietary Fiber 0g) • **Exchanges:** ½ Other Carbohydrate, 4½ Very Lean Meat, 1 Fat • **Carbohydrate Choices:** 1

# Parmesan-Dijon Chicken

¾ cup dry bread crumbs

¼ cup grated Parmesan cheese

2 tablespoons Dijon mustard

¼ cup butter or margarine, melted

6 boneless skinless chicken breasts
(about 1¾ lb)

1 Heat the oven to 375°F.

2 In large food-storage plastic bag, mix bread crumbs and cheese. In shallow dish, stir mustard into melted butter until well mixed.

3 Pat chicken dry with paper towels. Dip 1 piece of chicken at a time into butter mixture, coating all sides. Then place in bag of crumbs, seal bag and shake to coat with crumb mixture. In ungreased 13×9-inch pan, place chicken in a single layer.

4 Bake uncovered 20 to 30 minutes, turning chicken over once with tongs, until juice of chicken is clear when center of thickest pieces are cut (170°F). If chicken sticks to pan during baking, loosen it gently with turner or fork.

**6 servings**

## Make it a Meal

*The bread crumb–Parmesan-mustard crust keeps the chicken moist and juicy. Use any leftover chicken to make Parmesan-Dijon sandwiches for the next day's lunch—top with lettuce, tomato and some additional Dijon mustard.*

**1 Serving:** Calories 330; Total Fat 17g (Saturated Fat 8g, Trans Fat 0g); Cholesterol 110mg; Sodium 540mg; Total Carbohydrate 11g (Dietary Fiber 0g) • **Exchanges:** ½ Starch, 5 Very Lean Meat, 3 Fat • **Carbohydrate Choices:** 1

# Chicken Milano

### SALAD

1 cup tightly packed arugula leaves

½ cup diced tomatoes

2 tablespoons diced red onion

### DRESSING

1 tablespoon olive or vegetable oil

2 teaspoons red wine vinegar

⅛ teaspoon salt

### CHICKEN

2 tablespoons all-purpose flour

1 cup Italian-style crispy bread crumbs

1 egg

4 boneless skinless chicken breasts
   (about 1 ¼ lb)

2 tablespoons olive or vegetable oil

¼ cup crumbled tomato-basil or regular
   feta cheese (1 oz)

1 In medium bowl, place salad ingredients. In small bowl, beat dressing ingredients with wire whisk. Pour over salad; toss to coat.

2 On separate plates, place flour and bread crumbs. In medium bowl, beat egg with fork. Coat both sides of chicken with flour. Dip chicken into beaten egg, then coat well with bread crumbs.

3 In 12-inch nonstick skillet, heat 2 tablespoons oil over medium heat. Add chicken; cook 8 to 10 minutes, turning once, until juice of chicken is clear when center of thickest part is cut (170°F) and coating is golden brown. Serve chicken topped with salad and sprinkled with cheese.

**4 servings**

## Easy Add-On

*This is a poultry spin on a classic veal dish from Milan, Italy. The arugula and tomato salad is the traditional accompaniment, but baby spinach leaves would work, too. Chicken can be cut into strips and tossed with additional arugula or other green for an easy crispy chicken salad.*

**1 Serving:** Calories 440; Total Fat 24g (Saturated Fat 4g, Trans Fat 0g); Cholesterol 145mg; Sodium 650mg; Total Carbohydrate 21g (Dietary Fiber 0g) • **Exchanges:** 1 Starch, ½ Other Carbohydrate, 4½ Very Lean Meat, 4 Fat • **Carbohydrate Choices:** 1½

# Mediterranean Chicken Packets

1 package (4 oz) crumbled tomato-basil feta cheese (1 cup)

2 tablespoons grated lemon peel

1 teaspoon dried oregano leaves

4 boneless skinless chicken breasts (about 1¼ lb)

4 plum (Roma) tomatoes, each cut into 3 slices

1 small red onion, finely chopped (1 cup)

20 pitted kalamata olives or pitted jumbo ripe olives

1 Heat gas or charcoal grill. Cut 4 (18 × 12-inch) sheets of heavy-duty foil. In small bowl, mix cheese, lemon peel and oregano. On center of each foil sheet, place 1 chicken breast, 3 tomato slices, ¼ cup onion and 5 olives. Spoon ¼ of the cheese mixture over chicken and vegetables on each sheet.

2 For each packet, bring up 2 sides of foil over chicken and vegetables so edges meet. Seal edges, making a tight ½-inch fold; fold again, allowing space for heat circulation and expansion. Fold other sides to seal.

3 Place packets on grill over medium heat. Cover grill; cook 20 to 25 minutes, rotating packets ½ turn after 10 minutes, until juice of chicken is clear when center of thickest part is cut (170°F). Place packets on plates. To serve, cut large X across top of each packet; carefully fold back foil to allow steam to escape.

**4 servings**

## Speed it Up

*Grilling chicken breasts with vegetables and seasoning in foil packets is a wonderful way to lock in all those flavors, and cleanup is a breeze! The crumbled tomato-basil feta is really convenient, but you can also crumble your own plain or flavored feta— or try using goat cheese for an interesting twist.*

**1 Serving:** Calories 290; Total Fat 13g (Saturated Fat 6g, Trans Fat 0g); Cholesterol 110mg; Sodium 570mg; Total Carbohydrate 7g (Dietary Fiber 2g) • **Exchanges:** 1 Vegetable, 5 Very Lean Meat, 2 Fat • **Carbohydrate Choices:** ½

# Grilled Chicken Breasts with Tomato-Basil Butter

6 boneless skinless chicken breasts
   (about 1¾ lb)

2 teaspoons garlic-pepper blend

½ cup butter or margarine, softened

1 tablespoon chopped fresh or
   1 teaspoon dried basil leaves

3 tablespoons tomato paste

1   Brush grill rack with vegetable oil. Heat gas or charcoal grill. Sprinkle chicken with garlic–pepper blend.

2   Place chicken on grill. Cover grill; cook over medium heat 15 to 20 minutes, turning once, until juice of chicken is clear when center of thickest part is cut (170°F).

3   In small bowl, mix remaining ingredients. Serve chicken topped with butter mixture.

**6 servings**

## Instant
## Success!

*Don't want to waste tomato paste when a recipe calls for a small amount? Use the squeeze tube version that can be refrigerated after being opened. Or spoon extra canned tomato paste in 1-tablespoon-size dollops on a foil-lined cookie sheet and freeze until solid, then store in a resealable plastic bag in the freezer.*

**1 Serving:** Calories 300; Total Fat 20g (Saturated Fat 11g; Trans Fat 1g); Cholesterol 120mg; Sodium 250mg; Total Carbohydrate 2g (Dietary Fiber 0g) • **Exchanges:** 4 Very Lean Meat, 3½ Fat • **Carbohydrate Choices:** 0

# Grilled Sesame-Ginger Chicken

2 tablespoons teriyaki sauce

1 tablespoon sesame seed, toasted

1 teaspoon ground ginger

4 boneless skinless chicken breasts (about 1¼ lb)

1 Brush grill rack with vegetable oil. Heat gas or charcoal grill. In small bowl, mix teriyaki sauce, sesame seed and ginger.

2 Place chicken on grill. Cover grill; cook over medium heat 15 to 20 minutes, brushing frequently with sauce mixture and turning after 10 minutes, until juice of chicken is clear when center of thickest part is cut (170°F). Discard any remaining sauce mixture.

**4 servings**

## Instant Success!

*To toast sesame seed, cook in an ungreased heavy skillet over medium-low heat 5 to 7 minutes, stirring frequently until browning begins, then stirring constantly until golden brown.*

**1 Serving:** Calories 190; Total Fat 6g (Saturated Fat 1.5g; Trans Fat 0g); Cholesterol 85mg; Sodium 420mg; Total Carbohydrate 2g (Dietary Fiber 0g) • **Exchanges:** 4 ½ Very Lean Meat, 1 Fat • **Carbohydrate Choices:** 0

# Grilled Raspberry-Glazed Chicken

½ cup raspberry jam

1 tablespoon Dijon mustard

6 boneless skinless chicken breasts
(about 1¾ lb)

1½ cups fresh or frozen (thawed and
drained) raspberries

1 Brush grill rack with vegetable oil. Heat gas or charcoal grill. In small bowl, mix jam and mustard.

2 Place chicken on grill. Cover grill; cook over medium heat 15 to 20 minutes, brushing occasionally with jam mixture and turning once, until juice of chicken is clear when center of thickest part is cut (170°F). Discard any remaining jam mixture.

3 Serve chicken topped with raspberries.

**6 servings**

## Make it a Meal

*It's patio perfect! This fruity grilled chicken goes nicely with coleslaw and garlic bread. Watermelon wedges and frozen pops cool things off for dessert.*

**1 Serving:** Calories 250; Total Fat 4.5g (Saturated Fat 1g; Trans Fat 0g); Cholesterol 80mg; Sodium 140mg; Total Carbohydrate 22g (Dietary Fiber 2g) • **Exchanges:** ½ Fruit, 1 Other Carbohydrate, 4 Very Lean Meat, ½ Fat • **Carbohydrate Choices:** 1 ½

# Grilled Maple- and Cranberry-Glazed Chicken

Prep Time **25 Minutes**
Start to Finish **25 Minutes**

1 can (16 oz) whole berry cranberry sauce

½ cup maple-flavored syrup

½ teaspoon salt

6 boneless skinless chicken breasts (about 1¾ lb)

1 Brush grill rack with vegetable oil. Heat gas or charcoal grill. In small bowl, mix half of the cranberry sauce and the syrup; reserve remaining sauce. Sprinkle salt over chicken.

2 Place chicken on grill. Cover grill; cook over medium heat 10 minutes; turn chicken. Cover grill; cook 5 to 10 minutes longer, brushing occasionally with cranberry-syrup mixture, until juice of chicken is clear when center of thickest part is cut (170°F). Serve with remaining cranberry sauce.

**6 servings**

## Make it a Meal

*Team this sweetly glazed chicken with your favorite stuffing mix and a convenient form of mashed potatoes like the refrigerated version or one of the flavored instant varieties.*

**1 Serving:** Calories 360; Total Fat 4.5g (Saturated Fat 1g; Trans Fat 0g); Cholesterol 80mg; Sodium 320mg; Total Carbohydrate 50g (Dietary Fiber 0g • **Exchanges:** 3 ½ Other Carbohydrate, 4 Very Lean Meat, ½ Fat • **Carbohydrate Choices:** 3

# Grilled Cheddar-Stuffed Chicken Breasts

4 boneless skinless chicken breasts
(about 1¼ lb)

¼ teaspoon salt

¼ teaspoon pepper

1 piece (3 oz) Cheddar cheese

1 tablespoon butter or margarine,
melted

¼ cup chunky-style salsa

1 Heat gas or charcoal grill. Between pieces of plastic wrap or waxed paper, place each chicken breast smooth side down; gently pound with flat side of meat mallet or rolling pin until about ¼ inch thick. Sprinkle with salt and pepper.

2 Cut cheese into 4 slices, about 3 × 1 × ¼ inch. Place 1 slice cheese on center of each chicken piece. Roll chicken around cheese, folding in sides. Secure with toothpicks. Brush rolls with butter.

3 Place chicken rolls, seam sides down, on grill. Cover grill; cook over medium heat about 15 minutes, turning after 10 minutes, until chicken is no longer pink in center. Remove toothpicks before serving. Serve with salsa.

**4 servings**

## Make it a Meal

*Enjoy these chicken rolls with deli coleslaw and hot cooked instant rice tossed with black beans. The rice can cook at the same time as the chicken!*

**1 Serving:** Calories 280; Total Fat 15g (Saturated Fat 8g; Trans Fat 0g); Cholesterol 115mg; Sodium 450mg; Total Carbohydrate 1g (Dietary Fiber 0g) • **Exchanges:** 5 Very Lean Meat, 2½ Fat • **Carbohydrate Choices:** 0

# Lime- and Chili-Rubbed Chicken Breasts

2 teaspoons chili powder

2 teaspoons packed brown sugar

2 teaspoons grated lime peel

½ teaspoon salt

¼ teaspoon garlic powder

⅛ teaspoon ground red pepper (cayenne)

4 boneless skinless chicken breasts (about 1¼ lb)

2 teaspoons olive or canola oil

1 Heat gas or charcoal grill. In small bowl, mix chili powder, brown sugar, lime peel, salt, garlic powder and ground red pepper. Rub both sides of chicken with oil, then with spice mixture.

2 Place chicken on grill over medium heat. Cover grill; cook 10 to 15 minutes, turning once or twice, until juice of chicken is clear when center of thickest part is cut (170°F).

**4 servings**

## Instant Success!

*Refrigerating the "rubbed" chicken 20 to 30 minutes before grilling really enhances the flavor. You can also bake the chicken. Place the rubbed chicken in a foil-lined shallow baking pan and bake in a 375°F oven for 25 to 30 minutes.*

**1 Serving:** Calories 200; Total Fat 7g (Saturated Fat 1.5g; Trans Fat 0g); Cholesterol 85mg; Sodium 390mg; Total Carbohydrate 3g (Dietary Fiber 0g) • **Exchanges:** 4½ Very Lean Meat, 1 Fat • **Carbohydrate Choices:** 0

# Chicken Sesame Stir-Fry

1 cup water

Dash salt

½ cup uncooked instant brown rice

2 tablespoons reduced sodium soy sauce

1 teaspoon lemon juice

2 teaspoons cornstarch

½ teaspoon toasted sesame oil

1 teaspoon canola oil

½ lb uncooked chicken breast tenders (not breaded), pieces cut in half lengthwise

1½ cups frozen bell pepper and onion stir-fry (from 1-lb bag), thawed, drained

½ teaspoon sesame seed

## Instant Success!

*Want to cook with Chinese flavors but not sure which flavorings you really need? Start with soy sauce and toasted sesame oil—they're the most frequently called for ingredients in a range of Chinese-style dishes, like this simple stir-fry. Toasted sesame oil lends a delightful, unmistakable Chinese flavor but must be used sparingly. Store it in the refrigerator to preserve freshness.*

**1** In 1-quart saucepan, heat ⅔ cup of the water and the salt to boiling over high heat. Stir in rice. Reduce heat to low. Cover; simmer about 10 minutes or until water is absorbed. Fluff with fork.

**2** Meanwhile, in small bowl, stir remaining ⅓ cup water, the soy sauce, lemon juice, cornstarch and sesame oil; set aside.

**3** Heat nonstick wok or 10-inch skillet over medium-high heat. Add canola oil; rotate wok to coat side. Add chicken; cook and stir 2 to 3 minutes. Add stir-fry vegetables; cook and stir 3 to 5 minutes or until chicken is no longer pink in center and vegetables are crisp-tender.

**4** Stir soy sauce mixture into chicken mixture; heat to boiling. Cook and stir until sauce is thickened. Sprinkle with sesame seed. Serve with rice.

**2 servings**

**1 Serving:** Calories 300; Total Fat 5g (Saturated Fat 0g, Trans Fat 0g); Cholesterol 50mg; Sodium 750mg; Total Carbohydrate 35g (Dietary Fiber 2g) • **Exchanges:** 1½ Starch, ½ Other Carbohydrate, 1 Vegetable, 3 Very Lean Meat, ½ Fat • **Carbohydrate Choices:** 2

# Extra-Easy Pad Thai–Style Chicken

1 tablespoon vegetable oil

1 lb uncooked chicken breast tenders (not breaded), cut in half crosswise

2 eggs, beaten

2 cups water

2 packages (3 oz each) chili-flavor ramen noodles

¼ cup lime juice

4 medium green onions, sliced (¼ cup)

½ cup chopped salted peanuts

4 teaspoons chopped fresh cilantro

1 In 12-inch nonstick skillet, heat oil over medium-high heat. Cook chicken in oil 4 to 5 minutes, stirring frequently, until browned. Stir in eggs. Cook 2 to 3 minutes, stirring occasionally, until eggs are firm.

2 Stir in water, noodles with contents of seasoning packets and lime juice. Cover; cook 5 minutes, stirring once or twice to separate noodles.

3 Stir to mix all ingredients; spoon onto serving plates. Sprinkle with onions, peanuts and cilantro.

**4 servings**

## Instant
## Success!

*If you can't find the chili-flavor ramen noodles in your neck of the woods, try chicken-, shrimp- or vegetable-flavor. Fish sauce is often used in traditional pad thai; if you'd like to try it, replace 2 tablespoons of the water with fish sauce.*

**1 Serving:** Calories 490; Total Fat 25g (Saturated Fat 5g; Trans Fat 2.5g); Cholesterol 155mg; Sodium 930mg; Total Carbohydrate 30g (Dietary Fiber 4g) • **Exchanges:** 2 Starch, 4½ Lean Meat, 2 Fat • **Carbohydrate Choices:** 2

# Grilled Chicken Citrus Salad

⅔ cup citrus vinaigrette dressing

4 boneless skinless chicken breasts
(about 1¼ lb)

1 bag (10 oz) ready-to-eat romaine
lettuce

2 unpeeled apples, cubed (about 2 cups)

½ cup coarsely chopped dried apricots

2 medium green onions, sliced
(2 tablespoons)

½ cup chopped honey-roasted
peanuts

1 Heat gas or charcoal grill. Place 2 tablespoons of the dressing in small bowl. Brush all sides of chicken with the 2 tablespoons dressing.

2 In large bowl, toss lettuce, apples, apricots and onions; set aside.

3 Place chicken on grill. Cover grill; cook over medium heat 8 to 10 minutes, turning once, until juice of chicken is clear when center of thickest part is cut (170°F).

4 Add remaining dressing to lettuce mixture; toss. On 4 plates, divide lettuce mixture. Cut chicken crosswise to slices; place on lettuce. Sprinkle with peanuts.

**4 servings**

## Instant
## Success!

*With so many
wonderful prewashed
salad greens available,
feel free to use your
favorite for this recipe.*

**1 Serving:** Calories 550; Total Fat 31g (Saturated Fat 4g; Trans Fat 0g); Cholesterol 90mg; Sodium 510mg; Total Carbohydrate 30g (Dietary Fiber 6g) • **Exchanges:** 1 Fruit, ½ Other Carbohydrate, 1 Vegetable, 5½ Very Lean Meat, 5½ Fat • **Carbohydrate Choices:** 2

Betty Crocker Supper in a Snap

# Summer Harvest Chicken-Potato Salad

4 medium red potatoes (1 lb), cut into ¾-inch cubes

½ lb fresh green beans, trimmed, cut into 1-inch pieces (about 2 cups)

½ cup plain fat-free yogurt

⅓ cup fat-free ranch dressing

1 tablespoon prepared horseradish

¼ teaspoon salt

Dash pepper

2 cups cut-up cooked chicken breast

⅔ cup thinly sliced celery

Torn salad greens, if desired

**1** In 2-quart saucepan, heat 6 cups lightly salted water to boiling. Add potatoes; return to boiling. Reduce heat; simmer uncovered 5 minutes. Add green beans; cook uncovered 8 to 12 minutes longer or until potatoes and beans are crisp-tender.

**2** Meanwhile, in small bowl, mix yogurt, dressing, horseradish, salt and pepper; set aside.

**3** Drain potatoes and green beans; rinse with cold water to cool. In large serving bowl, mix potatoes, green beans, chicken and celery. Pour yogurt mixture over salad; toss gently to coat. Line plates with greens; spoon salad onto greens.

**4 servings**

## Easy Add-On

*Can't decide between chicken or potato salad? Here you get the best of both! This summery salad keeps the calories down by using fat-free yogurt and ranch dressing, but you can use regular if that's what you have on hand. You could also substitute 2 cups of chopped cooked ham for the chicken.*

**1 Serving:** Calories 270; Total Fat 3.5g (Saturated Fat 1g, Trans Fat 0g); Cholesterol 60mg; Sodium 410mg; Total Carbohydrate 32g (Dietary Fiber 5g) • **Exchanges:** 1½ Starch, ½ Other Carbohydrate, 1 Vegetable, 2½ Very Lean Meat • **Carbohydrate Choices:** 2

# Italian Chopped Salad

6 cups chopped (1 large bunch or
  2 small bunches) romaine lettuce

2 large tomatoes, chopped (2 cups)

2 medium cucumbers, chopped
  (1½ cups)

1 cup cut-up cooked chicken or turkey

1 package (3 oz) Italian salami,
  chopped

1 can (15 oz) cannellini beans

1 cup fresh small basil leaves

⅔ cup red wine vinaigrette or Italian
  dressing or homemade dressing

In large bowl, place lettuce, tomatoes, cucumbers, chicken, salami, beans and basil leaves. Pour vinaigrette over salad, and toss until ingredients are coated.

**4 servings**

**Homemade Italian Dressing:** *In a container with a tight-fitting lid, combine 1 cup olive or vegetable oil, ¼ cup white or cider vinegar, 2 tablespoons finely chopped onion, 1 teaspoon dried basil, 1 teaspoon sugar, 1 teaspoon ground mustard, ½ teaspoon salt, ½ teaspoon dried oregano leaves, ¼ teaspoon pepper, and 2 finely chopped cloves garlic. Cover and shake all ingredients. Shake before using. Store tightly covered in refrigerator.*

## Easy
Add-On

*This main-dish salad benefits from cannellini beans, which cost little and are high in fiber. Try adding canned beans to other salads to make them more substantial.*

**1 Serving:** Calories 500; Total Fat 29g (Saturated Fat 6g, Trans Fat 0g); Cholesterol 55mg; Sodium 1050mg; Total Carbohydrate 33g (Dietary Fiber 9g) • **Exchanges:** 1 Starch, ½ Other Carbohydrate, 2 Vegetable, 3 Medium-Fat Meat, 2½ Fat • **Carbohydrate Choices:** 2

# Sausalito Chicken and Seafood Salad

Prep Time **20 Minutes**
Start to Finish **20 Minutes**

6 cups bite-size pieces assorted salad greens

1 cup diced rotisserie or other cooked chicken

1 large avocado, pitted, peeled and sliced

1 package (8 oz) refrigerated imitation crabmeat chunks

1 can (4 oz) whole green chiles, drained, sliced lengthwise

¾ cup frozen (thawed) guacamole (from 12-oz container)

½ cup sour cream

1 large tomato, chopped (1 cup)

Lime or lemon wedges

1 Among 4 plates, divide salad greens. Top with chicken, avocado, crabmeat and chiles.

2 In small bowl, mix guacamole and sour cream; spoon over salad. Top with tomato. Garnish with lime wedges.

**4 servings**

## Make it a Meal

*Sausalito is a quaint town across the bay from San Francisco that's known for its outdoor cafes and wonderful seafood. This refreshing (and refreshingly simple) salad will transport you there!*

**1 Serving:** Calories 360; Total Fat 21g (Saturated Fat 6g; Trans Fat 0g); Cholesterol 65mg; Sodium 1400mg; Total Carbohydrate 20g (Dietary Fiber 9g) • **Exchanges:** 1 Other Carbohydrate, 1 Vegetable, 3 Lean Meat, 2 ½ Fat • **Carbohydrate Choices:** 1

# Turkey Salad with Fruit

1 container (6 oz) peach, orange or lemon yogurt (⅔ cup)

¼ teaspoon ground ginger

10 oz cooked turkey or chicken, cut into ½-inch pieces (2 cups)

2 medium stalks celery, thinly sliced (1 cup)

1 medium green onion with top, cut into ⅛-inch slices

1 can (11 oz) mandarin orange segments, drained

1 can (8 oz) sliced water chestnuts, drained

1 cup seedless green grapes

4 cups mixed salad greens

1 In large bowl, mix yogurt and ginger. Stir in remaining ingredients except salad greens. Cover with plastic wrap; refrigerate at least 2 hours.

2 On 4 plates, arrange salad greens. Top greens with turkey salad.

**4 servings**

**Simple Swap:** *Substitute 2 cups cut-up cooked ham for the turkey.*

## Speed it Up

*Containers of fruit yogurt make great snacks, and here you use one to make a simple dressing for this turkey and fruit salad. Use whichever flavor you like best!*

**1 Serving:** Calories 270; Total Fat 6g (Saturated Fat 2g, Trans Fat 0g); Cholesterol 65mg; Sodium 135mg; Total Carbohydrate 29g (Dietary Fiber 4g) • **Exchanges:** ½ Starch, ½ Fruit, ½ Other Carbohydrate, 1 Vegetable, 3 Very Lean Meat, 1 Fat • **Carbohydrate Choices:** 2

Prep Time **20 Minutes**
Start to Finish **20 Minutes**

# Chicken Alfredo over Biscuits

1 tablespoon vegetable oil

½ teaspoon dried thyme leaves

¼ teaspoon salt

¼ teaspoon pepper

1 lb boneless skinless chicken breasts, cut into 1-inch pieces

1 bag (1 lb) frozen mixed vegetables

1 container (10 oz) refrigerated Alfredo pasta sauce

½ teaspoon Dijon mustard

8 baking powder biscuits

1 In 10-inch nonstick skillet, heat oil, thyme, salt and pepper over medium-high heat. Cook chicken in oil mixture, stirring occasionally, until no longer pink in center.

2 Stir in remaining ingredients except biscuits; reduce heat to medium. Cover; cook 5 to 6 minutes, stirring occasionally, until hot.

3 Split open biscuits. Serve chicken mixture over biscuits.

**4 servings**

## Make it a Meal

*Ah, comfort food—with a quick twist! If you do have a few extra minutes, add a cup of sliced celery in step 1 for crunch. A side dish can be as simple as sliced apples and pears sprinkled with nuts and a dash of cinnamon.*

**1 Serving:** Calories 720; Total Fat 38g (Saturated Fat 18g; Trans Fat 2.5g); Cholesterol 140mg; Sodium 1340mg; Total Carbohydrate 55g (Dietary Fiber 6g) • **Exchanges:** 2 Starch, 1½ Other Carbohydrate, 4½ Very Lean Meat, 7 Fat • **Carbohydrate Choices:** 3½

# Mustardy Chicken and Dumplings

**Easy**
Add-On

*To make this zesty one-dish meal zestier, add another teaspoon of mustard.*

1 tablespoon vegetable oil

4 boneless skinless chicken breasts (about 1¼ lb), cut into bite-size pieces

1 medium onion, chopped (½ cup)

2 cups milk

2 cups frozen mixed vegetables

1 can (10¾ oz) condensed cream of chicken soup

1 tablespoon yellow mustard

1½ cups Original Bisquick® mix

**1** In 4-quart Dutch oven, heat oil over medium-high heat. Cook chicken and onion in oil 6 to 8 minutes, stirring occasionally, until chicken is no longer pink in center and onion is tender.

**2** Stir in 1½ cups of the milk, the mixed vegetables, soup and mustard. Heat to boiling.

**3** In small bowl, stir Bisquick mix and remaining ½ cup milk until soft dough forms. Drop dough by 6 spoonfuls onto chicken mixture; reduce heat to low. Cover; cook 20 minutes.

**6 servings**

**1 Serving:** Calories 390; Total Fat 15g (Saturated Fat 4g, Trans Fat 1g); Cholesterol 65mg; Sodium 930mg; Total Carbohydrate 36g (Dietary Fiber 3g) • **Exchanges:** 2 Starch, ½ Other Carbohydrate, 3 Very Lean Meat, 2½ Fat • **Carbohydrate Choices:** 2½

# Chicken and Noodles Skillet

1 tablespoon vegetable oil

1 lb boneless skinless chicken breasts, cut into bite-size pieces

1 medium onion, chopped (½ cup)

1 cup ready-to-eat baby-cut carrots, cut lengthwise in half

1 cup frozen cut broccoli

1 cup uncooked egg noodles (2 oz)

1 can (14 oz) chicken broth

1 can (10¾ oz) condensed cream of chicken soup

Chopped fresh parsley, if desired

1 In 12-inch nonstick skillet, heat oil over medium–high heat. Cook chicken and onion in oil 6 to 8 minutes, stirring frequently, until browned and onion is just tender.

2 Stir in remaining ingredients except parsley. Heat to boiling; reduce heat. Cover and simmer 10 minutes. Uncover and simmer 5 to 8 minutes longer, stirring occasionally, until chicken is no longer pink in center and noodles are tender. Sprinkle with parsley.

**4 servings**
**(1 ¼ cups each)**

**1 Serving:** Calories 340; Total Fat 13g (Saturated Fat 3.5g, Trans Fat 0g); Cholesterol 85mg; Sodium 1080mg; Total Carbohydrate 24g (Dietary Fiber 3g) • **Exchanges:** 1 Starch, 2 Vegetable, 3½ Lean Meat, ½ Fat • **Carbohydrate Choices:** 1½

# Mediterranean Chicken Stew

2 teaspoons olive or vegetable oil

2 lb boneless skinless chicken thighs

1 teaspoon garlic salt

¼ teaspoon pepper

2 teaspoons dried oregano leaves

2 cans (14.5 oz each) diced tomatoes with garlic and onion, undrained

1 can (14 oz) quartered artichoke hearts, drained

1 package (10 oz) couscous (1½ cups)

1 can (6 oz) pitted medium ripe olives, drained

1 In 12-inch skillet, heat oil over medium-high heat. Sprinkle chicken with garlic salt, pepper and oregano. Cook chicken in oil 8 minutes, turning once, until brown on both sides; drain. In 4- to 4½-quart slow cooker, place chicken, tomatoes and artichokes.

2 Cover and cook on Low heat setting 5 to 6 hours.

3 Cook couscous as directed on package. Stir olives into stew. To serve, spoon stew over couscous.

**5 servings (1½ cups each)**

**Simple Swap:** *Not an onion lover? Diced tomatoes with roasted garlic can be substituted for the diced tomatoes with garlic and onion.*

## Speed it Up

*This savory stew is underway in just 10 minutes and all ready by the time you're home for dinner. The addition of couscous makes this stew a meal in itself.*

**1 Serving:** Calories 620; Total Fat 21g (Saturated Fat 5g, Trans Fat 0); Cholesterol 110mg; Sodium 980mg; Total Carbohydrate 60g (Dietary Fiber 10g) • **Exchanges:** 3 Starch, ½ Other Carbohydrate, 1 Vegetable, 5 Lean Meat, 1 Fat • **Carbohydrate Choices:** 4

# Chicken and Garlic Ravioli with Peppers and Sun-Dried Tomatoes

Prep Time **30 Minutes**
Start to Finish **30 Minutes**

2 packages (9 oz each) refrigerated chicken and roasted garlic-filled ravioli

½ cup julienne sun-dried tomatoes in oil and herbs (from 8-oz jar), drained, 2 tablespoons oil reserved

1 bag (1 lb) frozen bell pepper and onion stir-fry, thawed, drained

2 cups shredded provolone cheese (8 oz)

1 Cook and drain ravioli as directed on package.

2 In 12-inch skillet, heat reserved oil from tomatoes over medium heat. Cook bell pepper mixture in oil 2 minutes, stirring occasionally. Stir in tomatoes and ravioli. Cook, stirring occasionally, until hot.

3 Sprinkle with cheese; remove from heat. Cover; let stand 1 to 2 minutes or until cheese is melted.

**6 servings**

## Instant Success!

*Our best friends are always there for us, as it is with shredded mozzarella cheese— it's a great "pinch hitter" if you don't have provolone.*

**1 Serving:** Calories 390; Total Fat 19g (Saturated Fat 8g; Trans Fat 0g); Cholesterol 35mg; Sodium 540mg; Total Carbohydrate 35g (Dietary Fiber 3g) • **Exchanges:** 1½ Starch, ½ Other Carbohydrate, 1 Vegetable, 2 High-Fat Meat, ½ Fat • **Carbohydrate Choices:** 2

# Chicken and Ravioli Carbonara

2 tablespoons Italian dressing

1 lb boneless skinless chicken breasts, cut into ½-inch strips

¾ cup chicken broth

1 package (9 oz) refrigerated cheese-filled ravioli

½ cup half-and-half

4 slices bacon, crisply cooked, crumbled

Shredded Parmesan cheese, if desired

Chopped fresh parsley, if desired

1 In 10-inch skillet, heat dressing over high heat. Cook chicken in dressing 2 to 4 minutes, turning occasionally, until brown.

2 Add broth and ravioli to skillet. Heat to boiling; reduce heat to medium. Cook uncovered about 4 minutes or until ravioli are tender and almost all broth has evaporated.

3 Stir in half-and-half; reduce heat. Simmer uncovered 3 to 5 minutes or until sauce is hot and desired consistency (cook longer for a thicker sauce). Sprinkle with bacon, cheese and parsley.

**4 servings**

## Instant Success!

*Betty Crocker Kitchens testing often shows interesting results. The less time this sauce is cooked, the thinner it will be; if cooked longer, the sauce will become thick and coat the ravioli. The choice is yours—some people like to have more sauce to dip their bread into!*

**1 Serving:** Calories 460; Total Fat 21g (Saturated Fat 9g; Trans Fat 0g); Cholesterol 125mg; Sodium 750mg; Total Carbohydrate 30g (Dietary Fiber 1g) • **Exchanges:** 1 Starch, 1 Other Carbohydrate, 5 Very Lean Meat, 3½ Fat • **Carbohydrate Choices:** 2

# Cacciatore-Style Chicken

Prep Time **55 Minutes**

Start to Finish **55 Minutes**

3 boneless skinless chicken breasts
   (¾ to 1 lb)

1 tablespoon olive or vegetable oil

1 medium onion, chopped (½ cup)

2 cloves garlic, finely chopped

½ cup chopped green bell pepper

¾ cup sliced zucchini or yellow summer
   squash

¾ cup sliced mushrooms

1 can (14.5 oz) diced tomatoes,
   undrained

½ teaspoon Italian seasoning

⅛ teaspoon pepper

2 cups uncooked bow-tie (farfalle),
   radiatore (nuggets) or rotini pasta

1 Cut each chicken breast half crosswise into 3 pieces. In 10-inch skillet, heat oil over medium-high heat. Cook chicken in oil about 5 minutes, stirring frequently, until brown; move chicken to one side of skillet.

2 Add onion, garlic, bell pepper, zucchini and mushrooms to other side of skillet. Cook vegetables about 3 minutes, stirring occasionally, until crisp-tender.

3 Stir tomatoes, Italian seasoning and pepper into vegetables and chicken. Heat to boiling; reduce heat. Cover and simmer 25 minutes or until chicken is no longer pink in center. Meanwhile, cook and drain pasta as directed on package.

4 Uncover chicken mixture and simmer 5 minutes longer. Serve over pasta.

**4 servings**

## Speed it Up

*This simple spin on the Italian classic is made easy by using boneless chicken breasts, which you can buy in bulk for extra savings. The canned diced tomatoes are another great budget staple.*

**1 Serving:** Calories 280; Total Fat 8g (Saturated Fat 1.5g, Trans Fat 0g); Cholesterol 80mg; Sodium 310mg; Total Carbohydrate 29g (Dietary Fiber 3g) • **Exchanges:** 1½ Starch, 1 Vegetable, 2½ Very Lean Meat, 1 Fat • **Carbohydrate Choices:** 2

Prep Time **20 Minutes**
Start to Finish **20 Minutes**

# Crispy Chicken and Fettuccine

1 package (12 oz) frozen southern-style chicken nuggets

1 package (9 oz) refrigerated fettuccine

1 can (14.5 oz) Italian-seasoned diced tomatoes, undrained

1 can (15 oz) tomato sauce

2 tablespoons chopped fresh parsley

2 tablespoons shredded Parmesan cheese

1 Heat oven to 400°F. Bake chicken nuggets as directed on package. If desired, cut chicken nuggets in half.

2 Meanwhile, cook and drain fettuccine as directed on package. Leave fettuccine in colander after draining. In same saucepan, heat tomatoes and tomato sauce over medium heat, stirring occasionally, until thoroughly heated.

3 Add fettuccine, chicken and parsley to tomato sauce; toss to coat. Sprinkle with cheese.

**4 servings**

## Instant
## Success!

*"Gotta" love that refrigerated pasta! It cooks much more quickly than dried, so follow the directions on the package carefully.*

**1 Serving:** Calories 530; Total Fat 20g (Saturated Fat 5g; Trans Fat 2.5g); Cholesterol 55mg; Sodium 1490mg; Total Carbohydrate 58g (Dietary Fiber 5g) • **Exchanges:** 2½ Starch, ½ Other Carbohydrate, 2 Vegetable, 2½ High-Fat Meat • **Carbohydrate Choices:** 4

Betty Crocker Supper in a Snap

# Bow Ties with Chicken and Asparagus

4 cups uncooked bow-tie (farfalle) pasta (8 oz)

1 lb fresh asparagus spears

1 tablespoon canola oil

1 lb boneless skinless chicken breasts, cut into 1-inch pieces

1 package (8 oz) sliced fresh mushrooms (3 cups)

2 cloves garlic, finely chopped

1 cup fat-free chicken broth with 33% less sodium

1 tablespoon cornstarch

4 medium green onions, sliced (¼ cup)

2 tablespoons chopped fresh basil leaves

Salt, if desired

¼ cup finely shredded Parmesan cheese (1 oz)

1 Cook and drain pasta as directed on package, omitting salt.

2 Meanwhile, break off tough ends of asparagus as far down as stalks snap easily. Wash asparagus; cut into 1-inch pieces.

3 In 12-inch nonstick skillet, heat oil over medium-high heat. Add chicken; cook 2 minutes, stirring occasionally. Stir in asparagus, mushrooms and garlic. Cook 6 to 8 minutes, stirring occasionally, until chicken is no longer pink in center and vegetables are tender.

4 In small bowl, gradually stir broth into cornstarch. Stir in onions and basil. Stir cornstarch mixture into chicken mixture. Cook and stir 1 to 2 minutes or until thickened and bubbly. Season with salt. Toss with pasta. Sprinkle with cheese.

**6 servings (1½ cups each)**

## Instant
## Success!

*If you don't want to buy fresh basil just for this recipe, you could use parsley instead, or use up the remaining basil by making pesto (see page 276).*

**1 Serving:** Calories 320; Total Fat 7g (Saturated Fat 2g, Trans Fat 0g); Cholesterol 50mg; Sodium 210mg; Total Carbohydrate 37g (Dietary Fiber 3g) • **Exchanges:** 2 Starch, 1 Vegetable, 2½ Very Lean Meat, 1 Fat • **Carbohydrate Choices:** 2½

# Chicken Alfredo

8 oz uncooked linguine

2 teaspoons butter or margarine

2 tablespoons finely chopped shallot

1 clove garlic, finely chopped

1 pint (2 cups) fat-free half-and-half

3 tablespoons all-purpose flour

½ cup reduced-fat sour cream

¼ cup shredded fresh Parmesan cheese

½ teaspoon salt

⅛ teaspoon white pepper

1¼ lb chicken breast strips for stir-fry

1 jar (7 oz) roasted red bell peppers, drained, thinly sliced

⅓ cup shredded fresh Parmesan cheese

2 tablespoons chopped fresh parsley

1 In 4-quart Dutch oven, cook linguine as directed on package. Drain; rinse with hot water. Return to Dutch oven to keep warm.

2 Meanwhile, in 2-quart saucepan, melt butter over medium heat. Add shallot and garlic; cook and stir 1 minute. In medium bowl, beat half-and-half and flour with wire whisk; add to saucepan. Heat to boiling, stirring frequently. Beat in sour cream with wire whisk. Reduce heat to low; cook 1 to 2 minutes or until heated. Remove from heat; stir in ¼ cup cheese, the salt and pepper.

3 Heat 12-inch nonstick skillet over medium-high heat. Add chicken; cook about 5 minutes, stirring frequently, until no longer pink in center.

4 Add chicken, bell peppers and sauce to linguine; stir to mix. Cook over low heat until hot. Garnish each serving with cheese and parsley.

**6 servings**

## Speed it Up

*Don't be intimidated by the long list of ingredients—many are kitchen staples with plenty of uses, so you'll get a lot of mileage from any extras. To streamline this list, substitute foods you already have—slice your own strips from 1¼ lb chicken breasts, use black pepper instead of white or cut up a red bell pepper instead of using the jarred roasted peppers.*

**1 Serving:** Calories 430; Total Fat 12g (Saturated Fat 6g, Trans Fat 0g); Cholesterol 80mg; Sodium 710mg; Total Carbohydrate 47g (Dietary Fiber 2g) • **Exchanges:** 2 Starch, 1 Other Carbohydrate, 4 Very Lean Meat, 1½ Fat • **Carbohydrate Choices:** 3

# Chicken- and Spinach-Stuffed Shells

Prep Time **30 Minutes**

Start to Finish **1 Hour 10 Minutes**

18 uncooked jumbo pasta shells (from 12- or 16-oz package)

2 cups frozen cut leaf spinach, thawed

1 egg, slightly beaten

5 oz cooked chicken or turkey, chopped (1 cup)

1 container (15 oz) whole-milk ricotta cheese or 2 cups cottage cheese

¼ cup grated Parmesan cheese

1 jar (26 oz) tomato pasta sauce

2 cups shredded Italian cheese blend (8 oz)

1 Heat oven to 350°F. Cook pasta shells as directed on package.

2 Meanwhile, place thawed spinach in strainer and squeeze with fingers to remove liquid. Place spinach on paper towels or clean kitchen towel and squeeze out any remaining liquid until spinach is dry.

3 In medium bowl, mix spinach, egg, chicken, ricotta cheese and Parmesan cheese. In strainer, drain pasta shells. Rinse with cool water; drain.

4 In 13 × 9-inch (3-quart) glass baking dish, spread 1 cup of the pasta sauce. Spoon about 2 tablespoons ricotta mixture into each pasta shell. Arrange shells, filled sides up, on sauce in baking dish. Spoon remaining sauce over stuffed shells.

5 Cover dish with foil. Bake 30 minutes. Carefully remove foil; sprinkle with Italian cheese blend. Bake uncovered 5 to 10 minutes longer or until cheese is melted.

**6 servings (3 shells each)**

## Easy Add-On

*If you don't have cooked chicken or turkey in your fridge, you could substitute chopped ham—or leave out meat altogether for a vegetarian version. It's important to get the spinach as dry as possible, so don't skip the towel-squeezing step. If the kids are around, they'd probably love to help you fill the cooked shells with the cheese mixture.*

**1 Serving:** Calories 580; Total Fat 27g (Saturated Fat 14g, Trans Fat 0.5g); Cholesterol 130mg; Sodium 1060mg; Total Carbohydrate 49g (Dietary Fiber 4g) • **Exchanges:** 2 Starch, 1 Other Carbohydrate, 4 Medium-Fat Meat, 1 Fat • **Carbohydrate Choices:** 3

# Super-Easy Chicken Manicotti

1 jar (26 to 30 oz) tomato pasta sauce (any variety)

¾ cup water

1 teaspoon garlic salt

1½ lb uncooked chicken breast tenders (not breaded) (14 tenders)

14 uncooked manicotti pasta shells (8 oz)

2 cups shredded mozzarella cheese (8 oz)

Chopped fresh basil leaves, if desired

1 Heat oven to 350°F. In medium bowl, mix pasta sauce and water. In ungreased 13 × 9-inch (3-quart) glass baking dish, spread about one-third of the pasta sauce.

2 Sprinkle garlic salt on chicken. Insert chicken into uncooked manicotti shells, stuffing from each end of shell to fill if necessary. Place shells on pasta sauce in baking dish. Pour remaining pasta sauce evenly over shells, covering completely. Cover tightly with foil.

3 Bake about 1 hour or until shells are tender. Sprinkle with cheese. Bake uncovered about 5 minutes longer or until cheese is melted. Sprinkle with basil.

**7 servings**

## Budget Smart

*This is probably the easiest manicotti recipe you'll ever see. It's only slightly more work (and a bit cheaper) to start with uncooked boneless skinless chicken breasts instead of tenders; slice them into 1¼-inch strips before using. Be sure to wash your hands thoroughly after handling the raw chicken.*

**1 Serving:** Calories 450; Total Fat 13g (Saturated Fat 5g, Trans Fat 0g); Cholesterol 75mg; Sodium 1130mg; Total Carbohydrate 48g (Dietary Fiber 3g) • **Exchanges:** 3 Starch, 4 Lean Meat • **Carbohydrate Choices:** 3

# Pesto Turkey and Pasta

3 cups uncooked bow-tie (farfalle) pasta (6 oz)

2 cups cubed cooked turkey breast

½ cup basil pesto

½ cup coarsely chopped roasted red bell peppers (from 7-oz jar)

¼ cup sliced ripe olives

1 In 3-quart saucepan, cook and drain pasta as directed on package.

2 In same saucepan, mix drained pasta, turkey, pesto and bell peppers. Heat over low heat, stirring constantly, until hot. Garnish with olives.

**4 servings**

## Speed it Up

*Can't boil water any faster, right? Actually you can! Fill the saucepan with hot tap water; cover it and turn the burner on high. Dinner's that much closer!*

**1 Serving:** Calories 430; Total Fat 19g (Saturated Fat 3.5g; Trans Fat 0g); Cholesterol 65mg; Sodium 530mg; Total Carbohydrate 37g (Dietary Fiber 4g) • **Exchanges:** 2½ Starch, 3 Lean Meat, 1½ Fat • **Carbohydrate Choices:** 2½

Betty Crocker Supper in a Snap

# Turkey Pasta Primavera

1 package (9 oz) refrigerated fettuccine
   or linguine

2 tablespoons Italian dressing

1 bag (1 lb) frozen broccoli, carrots and
   cauliflower, thawed, drained

2 cups cut-up cooked turkey
   or chicken

1 teaspoon salt

2 large tomatoes, seeded, chopped
   (2 cups)

¼ cup freshly grated Parmesan cheese

2 tablespoons chopped fresh parsley

1   Cook and drain fettuccine as directed on package.

2   Meanwhile, in 10-inch skillet, heat dressing over medium–high heat.
Cook vegetable mixture in dressing, stirring occasionally, until crisp-tender.

3   Stir turkey, salt and tomatoes into vegetables. Cook about 3 minutes or
just until turkey is hot. Spoon turkey mixture over fettuccine. Sprinkle with
cheese and parsley.

**4 servings**

## Instant
## Success!

*Here's a quick, easy
and healthy pasta for
a busy weeknight.
Primavera is Italian
for "spring-style,"
and any dish labeled
primavera includes
plenty of vegetables. For
an even less expensive
version, substitute 9 oz
of dried pasta for the
fresh; it'll take just a
little longer to cook.*

**1 Serving:** Calories 400; Total Fat 12g (Saturated Fat 3g, Trans Fat 0g); Cholesterol 65mg; Sodium 980mg; Total Carbohydrate
44g (Dietary Fiber 6g) • **Exchanges:** 2 Starch, 2 Vegetable, 3½ Lean Meat • **Carbohydrate Choices:** 3

# Caribbean Turkey Stew

2 teaspoons olive oil

1 turkey breast tenderloin (½ lb), cut into 1-inch pieces

1 small onion, coarsely chopped (¼ cup)

1 clove garlic, finely chopped

2 small red potatoes, cut into eighths (¾ cup)

½ dark-orange sweet potato, peeled, cut into 1-inch pieces (¾ cup)

1 can (14 oz) chicken broth

¼ teaspoon ground nutmeg

⅛ teaspoon pepper

1 dried bay leaf

½ cup frozen sweet peas, thawed

1 In 3-quart saucepan, heat oil over medium-high heat. Add turkey, onion and garlic; cook 4 to 5 minutes, stirring frequently, until onion is softened.

2 Stir in remaining ingredients except peas. Heat to boiling. Reduce heat to medium-low; cover and cook 15 minutes or until potatoes are tender and turkey is no longer pink in center.

3 Stir in peas. Cover; cook 2 to 3 minutes, stirring occasionally, until peas are hot. Remove bay leaf.

**2 servings (1 ¾ cups each)**

## Instant
## Success!

*Sweet potatoes are from the morning glory family and originated in the tropical areas of South America. They're available year-round and inexpensive, and they add a sweet touch to this tasty weeknight dinner for two.*

**1 Serving:** Calories 390; Total Fat 7g (Saturated Fat 1.5g, Trans Fat 0g); Cholesterol 75mg; Sodium 940mg; Total Carbohydrate 47g (Dietary Fiber 7g) • **Exchanges:** 2½ Starch, ½ Other Carbohydrate, 4 Very Lean Meat, ½ Fat • **Carbohydrate Choices:** 3

# Turkey–Wild Rice Casserole

Prep Time 25 Minutes

Start to Finish 5 Hours
25 Minutes

4 slices bacon, cut into ½-inch pieces

1 lb turkey breast tenderloins, cut into ½- to 1-inch pieces

2 medium carrots, coarsely chopped (1 cup)

1 medium onion, coarsely chopped (½ cup)

1 medium stalk celery, sliced (½ cup)

1 cup uncooked wild rice

1 can (10¾ oz) condensed cream of chicken soup

2½ cups water

2 tablespoons reduced-sodium soy sauce

¼ to ½ teaspoon dried marjoram leaves

⅛ teaspoon pepper

**1** In 12-inch skillet, cook bacon over medium heat, stirring occasionally, until almost crisp. Stir in turkey, carrots, onion and celery. Cook about 2 minutes, stirring frequently, until turkey is brown.

**2** Spoon turkey mixture into 3- to 4-quart slow cooker. Stir in remaining ingredients.

**3** Cover; cook on Low heat setting 5 to 6 hours.

**5 servings**

## Budget Smart

*Turkey makes such wonderful soups, stews and casseroles—and it's so inexpensive—that it's a shame not to have it more often through the year instead of just at Thanksgiving. This lightly creamy casserole gets a lot of flavor from the bacon that gets sautéed at the start.*

**1 Serving:** Calories 340; Total Fat 8g (Saturated Fat 2.5g, Trans Fat 0g); Cholesterol 70mg; Sodium 870mg; Total Carbohydrate 38g (Dietary Fiber 4g) • **Exchanges:** 2½ Starch, 3 Very Lean Meat, 1 Fat • **Carbohydrate Choices:** 2½

# Onion-Topped Turkey Divan

1 bag (14 oz) frozen broccoli florets, thawed

2 cups diced cooked turkey

1 can (10¾ oz) condensed cream of chicken soup

½ cup mayonnaise or salad dressing

½ cup milk

1 cup shredded Cheddar cheese (4 oz)

1 cup French-fried onions (from 2.8-oz can), coarsely crushed

1  Heat oven to 350°F. Spray 8-inch square (2-quart) glass baking dish with cooking spray.

2  Layer broccoli and turkey in baking dish. In medium bowl, mix soup, mayonnaise and milk; stir in cheese. Spread over turkey and broccoli. Cover baking dish with foil.

3  Bake 30 minutes. Sprinkle with onions. Bake uncovered 20 to 25 minutes longer or until bubbly and broccoli is tender.

**4 servings (1 cup each)**

## Easy
### Add-On

*Everyone loves those canned French-fried onions that go on top of the famous potluck vegetable dish of green beans with cream of mushroom gravy. Try them on other casseroles to add crunch, like this easy turkey and broccoli divan.*

**1 Serving:** Calories 560; Total Fat 37g (Saturated Fat 12g, Trans Fat 2.5g); Cholesterol 110mg; Sodium 1130mg; Total Carbohydrate 22g (Dietary Fiber 3g) • **Exchanges:** 1½ Starch, 4 Lean Meat, 5 Fat • **Carbohydrate Choices:** 1½

# Honey-Mustard Turkey with Snap Peas

Prep Time **10 Minutes**
Start to Finish **25 Minutes**

1 lb uncooked turkey breast slices, about ¼ inch thick

½ cup Dijon and honey marinade

1 cup ready-to-eat baby-cut carrots, cut lengthwise in half

2 cups frozen sugar snap peas

1 In shallow glass or plastic dish, place turkey. Pour marinade over turkey; turn slices to coat evenly. Cover dish and let stand 10 minutes at room temperature.

2 Spray 10-inch skillet with cooking spray; heat over medium heat. Drain most of marinade from turkey. Cook turkey in skillet about 5 minutes, turning once, until brown.

3 Add carrots, lifting turkey to place carrots on bottom of skillet. Top turkey with peas. Cover and simmer about 7 minutes or until carrots are tender and turkey is no longer pink in center.

**4 servings**

## Instant Success!

*Using pre-cut ingredients can shave precious minutes from a meal, as in this 25-minute dinner. If you'd prefer to shave pennies, use regular carrots, peeled and cut into ¼-inch slices instead of the baby-cut carrots. Slicing your own turkey breast saves even more.*

**1 Serving:** Calories 260; Total Fat 11g (Saturated Fat 2g, Trans Fat 0g); Cholesterol 75mg; Sodium 260mg; Total Carbohydrate 10g (Dietary Fiber 3g) • **Exchanges:** ½ Other Carbohydrate, 1 Vegetable, 4 Very Lean Meat, 1½ Fat • **Carbohydrate Choices:** ½

# Turkey and Green Chile Stuffing Casserole

2 tablespoons butter or margarine

1 medium onion, chopped (½ cup)

1 small red bell pepper, chopped (½ cup)

4 cups seasoned cornbread stuffing mix

1 cup frozen whole kernel corn

1 can (4.5 oz) chopped green chiles, undrained

1½ cups water

2 turkey breast tenderloins (about ¾ lb each)

½ teaspoon chili powder

½ teaspoon peppered seasoned salt

1 Heat oven to 350°F. Spray 11 × 7-inch (2-quart) glass baking dish with cooking spray. In 12-inch nonstick skillet, melt butter over medium-high heat. Cook onion and bell pepper in butter 2 to 3 minutes, stirring frequently, until tender. Stir in stuffing mix, corn, chiles and water. Spread stuffing mixture in baking dish.

2 Sprinkle both sides of turkey tenderloins with chili powder and peppered seasoned salt. Place on stuffing, pressing into stuffing mixture slightly. Spray sheet of foil with cooking spray. Cover baking dish with foil, sprayed side down.

3 Bake 1 hour. Uncover and bake 10 to 15 minutes longer or until juice of turkey is no longer pink when centers of thickest pieces are cut.

**6 servings**

## Instant
## Success!

*Turkey and chile stuffing combine to make this easy one-dish meal with a Tex-Mex twist. The chopped canned chiles are mildly spicy, but not hot. If you do want more heat, just add a little more chili powder.*

**1 Serving:** Calories 360; Total Fat 7g (Saturated Fat 3g, Trans Fat 0.5g); Cholesterol 85mg; Sodium 990mg; Total Carbohydrate 43g (Dietary Fiber 3g) • **Exchanges:** 3 Starch, 3½ Very Lean Meat, ½ Fat • **Carbohydrate Choices:** 3

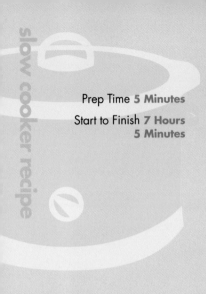

Prep Time **5 Minutes**

Start to Finish **7 Hours 5 Minutes**

# Herbed Turkey Breast

4- to 5-lb bone-in turkey breast, thawed if frozen

2 tablespoons honey mustard

½ teaspoon dried rosemary leaves, crumbled

½ teaspoon dried thyme leaves

½ teaspoon dried basil leaves

½ teaspoon garlic pepper

¼ teaspoon salt

½ cup chicken broth

**1** Spray 5- to 6-quart slow cooker with cooking spray. Place turkey in cooker. Brush with honey mustard. Sprinkle with rosemary, thyme, basil, garlic pepper and salt. Pour broth around turkey.

**2** Cover and cook on Low heat setting 7 to 8 hours.

**8 servings**

**Simple Swap:** *If you don't have honey mustard, stir 2 teaspoons of honey into 1½ tablespoons of plain mustard.*

## Budget
### Smart

*As we learn every year at Thanksgiving, turkey is the bird that keeps right on giving. It yields plenty and costs less per pound than most meats. Use leftover herbed turkey in casseroles, soups and salads. Or slice it for turkey sandwiches. Wrap the breast tightly and store in the fridge for up to 3 days.*

**1 Serving:** Calories 280; Total Fat 12g (Saturated Fat 3.5g, Trans Fat 0g); Cholesterol 115mg; Sodium 270mg; Total Carbohydrate 0g (Dietary Fiber 0g) • **Exchanges:** 6 Very Lean Meat, 1½ Fat • **Carbohydrate Choices:** 0

# Turkey–Butternut Squash Ragout

Prep Time **15 Minutes**

Start to Finish **7 Hours**
**15 Minutes**

1½ lb turkey thighs (about 2 medium), skin removed

1 small butternut squash (about 2 lb), peeled, seeded and cut into 1½-inch pieces (3 cups)

1 medium onion, cut in half and sliced

1 can (16 oz) baked beans, undrained

1 can (14.5 oz) diced tomatoes with Italian seasonings, undrained

2 tablespoons chopped fresh parsley, if desired

1 Spray 3- to 4-quart slow cooker with cooking spray. In cooker, mix all ingredients except parsley.

2 Cover and cook on Low heat setting 7 to 8 hours.

3 Place turkey on cutting board. Remove meat from bones; discard bones. Return turkey to cooker. Just before serving, sprinkle with parsley.

**4 servings**

## Budget
Smart

*Turkey thighs—and most other turkey parts—are often on sale right after Thanksgiving, but turkey is a fairly economical meat year-round. After 7 to 8 hours in a slow cooker, the meat will practically fall right off the bone.*

**1 Serving:** Calories 380; Total Fat 6g (Saturated Fat 2g, Trans Fat 0g); Cholesterol 115mg; Sodium 730mg; Total Carbohydrate 46g (Dietary Fiber 10g) • **Exchanges:** 3 Starch, 1 Vegetable, 3 Very Lean Meat • **Carbohydrate Choices:** 3

# 3 beef & pork

## Speedy Potato, Pasta & Rice Sides

*Instant potatoes and packaged rice and noodle mixes are wonderful to keep on hand; but if you want a little bit more adventure, try one of these fast and easy ideas.*

1 **Chipotle-Cheddar Mashed Potatoes:** Stir chopped canned chipotle chiles in adobo sauce and shredded Cheddar cheese into your mashed potatoes.

2 **Rich and Creamy Roasted Garlic Mashed Potatoes:** Make a package of mashed potatoes seasoned with roasted garlic as directed on the package, except substitute whipping cream or half-and-half for the milk.

3 **Barbecued Steak Fries:** Heat oven as directed on package of frozen steak fries. On foil-lined cookie sheet, arrange fries; spray lightly with cooking spray and sprinkle with barbecue seasoning. Turn fries over and repeat with other side if desired. Bake as directed on package.

**4** **Easy Bacon-Cheese Fries:** Heat your favorite type of frozen French fries as directed on the package. Place in shallow serving platter; spoon any flavor warm process cheese sauce or salsa con queso dip over potatoes. Sprinkle with purchased precooked bacon bits and sliced green onion.

**5** **Cheesy Pasta:** Toss hot cooked pasta with extra-virgin olive oil and shredded or grated Asiago, Parmesan or Romano cheese. Heat gently if necessary. Sprinkle with dried basil leaves or parsley flakes.

**6** **Artichoke Pasta Toss:** Toss hot cooked pasta with a jar (or as many jars as needed) of undrained marinated artichokes (cut into quarters if needed). Heat gently if necessary.

**7** **Basil Pasta Toss:** Toss hot cooked pasta with basil pesto; sprinkle with shredded or grated Parmesan cheese. Heat gently if necessary.

**8** **Dill and Lemon-Pepper Pasta:** Toss hot cooked pasta with purchased dill dip and a bit of lemon-pepper seasoning. Heat gently if necessary.

**9** **Salsa Rice:** Stir salsa and sliced ripe olives into hot cooked rice. Heat gently if necessary; sprinkle with shredded taco-flavored cheese or Cheddar cheese.

**10** **Rice Alfredo with Bacon:** Stir purchased Alfredo sauce into hot cooked rice. Heat gently if necessary; sprinkle with precooked bacon bits.

**This icon means:**   20 minutes or less

**This icon means:**   slow-cooker recipe

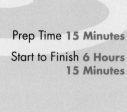
**Prep Time 15 Minutes**

**Start to Finish 6 Hours 15 Minutes**

# Herbed Beef Roast

3-lb beef boneless tip roast

1 teaspoon mixed dried herb leaves (such as marjoram, basil and oregano)

1 teaspoon salt

½ teaspoon pepper

2 cloves garlic, finely chopped

1 cup balsamic or red wine vinegar

1 If beef roast comes in netting or is tied, do not remove. Spray 12-inch skillet with cooking spray; heat over medium-high heat. Cook beef in skillet about 5 minutes, turning occasionally, until brown on all sides. Sprinkle with herbs, salt and pepper.

2 In 4- to 5-quart slow cooker, place garlic. Place beef on garlic. Pour vinegar over beef.

3 Cover and cook on Low heat setting 6 to 8 hours. Remove netting or strings from beef.

**12 servings**

## Budget
### Smart

*Tip roast is an inexpensive cut of beef, and it works perfectly in this slow-cooked roast. If it's not tied, see if the butcher at the market will tie it for you, for more even browning and cooking. A cup of vinegar may seem like a lot, but you'll find the beef comes out perfectly tender and delicious.*

**1 Serving:** Calories 170; Total Fat 8g (Saturated Fat 3g, Trans Fat 0g); Cholesterol 60mg; Sodium 250mg; Total Carbohydrate 1g (Dietary Fiber 0g) • **Exchanges:** 3 Lean Meat • **Carbohydrate Choices:** 0

# Flank Steak with Smoky Honey Mustard Sauce

Prep Time **30 Minutes**
Start to Finish **30 Minutes**

### SAUCE

¼ cup honey mustard dressing

1 tablespoon frozen (thawed) orange juice concentrate

1 tablespoon water

1 small clove garlic, finely chopped

1 chipotle chile in adobo sauce (from 7-oz can), finely chopped

### STEAK

1 beef flank steak (about 1½ lb)

6 flour tortillas (8 inch; from 11.5-oz package)

1 Heat gas or charcoal grill. In small bowl, mix sauce ingredients; reserve 2 tablespoons in separate bowl. Make cuts about ½ inch apart and ⅛ inch deep in diamond pattern in both sides of beef. Brush reserved sauce on both sides of beef.

2 Place beef on grill over medium heat. Cover grill; cook 17 to 20 minutes, turning once, until desired doneness. Cut beef across grain into thin slices. Serve with remaining sauce and tortillas.

**6 servings**

## Instant Success!

*For grilling steaks on the cheap, flank steak is one of your best bets. It's full of beefy flavor and less expensive than tenderloin or strip steak. To ensure the flank steak comes out tender and not chewy, score the meat before grilling as described in step 1. After grilling, slice it thinly across the grain or across the natural fibers in the meat. Leftover steak would be fantastic in sandwiches.*

**1 Serving:** Calories 360; Total Fat 16g (Saturated Fat 4.5g, Trans Fat 1.5g); Cholesterol 55mg; Sodium 460mg; Total Carbohydrate 22g (Dietary Fiber 0g) • **Exchanges:** 1½ Starch, 4 Lean Meat, ½ Fat • **Carbohydrate Choices:** 1½

Prep Time **10 Minutes**
Start to Finish **20 Minutes**

# Strip Steaks with Mango-Peach Salsa

¼ cup finely chopped red bell pepper

2 teaspoons finely chopped seeded jalapeño chiles

1 teaspoon finely chopped or grated gingerroot or ¼ teaspoon ground ginger

¼ cup peach preserves

1 tablespoon lime juice

1 small mango, cut lengthwise in half, pitted and chopped (1 cup)

4 boneless beef New York strip steaks (about 1½ lb)

1 to 2 teaspoons Caribbean jerk seasoning

1 In medium bowl, mix bell pepper, chiles and gingerroot. Stir in preserves, lime juice and mango.

2 Set oven control to broil. Sprinkle both sides of beef with jerk seasoning. Place on rack in broiler pan. Broil with tops 4 to 6 inches from heat 6 to 10 minutes, turning once, until desired doneness. Serve with salsa.

**4 servings**

## Instant Success!

*Fresh mango will be slightly soft to the touch. Cut lengthwise into two pieces, cutting as close to the seed as possible. Make crisscross cuts ½ inch apart into mango flesh. Turn each mango half inside out and scrape off the pieces. Canned or jarred mangoes also can be used for this recipe; be sure to drain well before using.*

**1 Serving:** Calories 360; Total Fat 12g (Saturated Fat 4.5g; Trans Fat 0.5g); Cholesterol 75mg; Sodium 130mg; Total Carbohydrate 24g (Dietary Fiber 1g) • **Exchanges:** 1½ Other Carbohydrate, 5½ Very Lean Meat, 2 Fat • **Carbohydrate Choices:** 1½

# Balsamic-Garlic Marinated Steak

4 cloves garlic, finely chopped, or
½ teaspoon garlic powder

½ cup balsamic vinegar

¼ cup chili sauce or ketchup

2 tablespoons packed brown sugar

2 tablespoons olive or vegetable oil

½ teaspoon Italian seasoning

¼ teaspoon salt

¼ teaspoon coarse ground pepper

1 boneless beef top round steak, 1 to
1½ inches thick (1½ lb)

**1** In shallow glass dish or resealable food-storage plastic bag, mix garlic and remaining ingredients except beef. Add beef; turn to coat with marinade. Cover dish with plastic wrap or seal bag. Refrigerate at least 8 hours but no longer than 12 hours, turning beef occasionally.

**2** Heat gas or charcoal grill. Remove beef from marinade, reserving the marinade.

**3** Place beef on grill over medium heat. Cover grill; cook 12 to 18 minutes for medium-rare or 17 to 21 minutes for medium doneness, turning and brushing with marinade once or twice. Discard any remaining marinade. To serve, cut beef across grain into slices.

**6 servings**

**Easy**
Add-On

*Bewildered by all the vinegars available? Along with white and red wine vinegar, balsamic vinegar is one of the most useful choices. Created in the area of Modena, Italy, from grapes, it is rich with a dark molasses color and sweet taste. It's versatile enough to use in salad dressings, marinades, soups and stews, and sauces.*

**1 Serving:** Calories 190; Total Fat 7g (Saturated Fat 1.5g, Trans Fat 0g); Cholesterol 65mg; Sodium 220mg; Total Carbohydrate 6g (Dietary Fiber 0g); • **Exchanges:** ½ Other Carbohydrate, 3½ Very Lean Meat, 1 Fat • **Carbohydrate Choices:** ½

# Grilled Steak and Potato Salad

Prep Time **30 Minutes**
Start to Finish **30 Minutes**

¾ lb small red potatoes, cut in half

⅔ cup honey Dijon dressing and marinade

1 boneless beef top sirloin steak, ¾ inch thick (¾ lb)

¼ teaspoon salt

¼ teaspoon coarsely ground pepper

4 cups bite-size pieces romaine lettuce

2 medium tomatoes, cut into thin wedges

½ cup thinly sliced red onion

1  Heat gas or charcoal grill. In 2- or 2½-quart saucepan, place potatoes; add enough water to cover potatoes. Heat to boiling; reduce heat to medium. Cook uncovered 5 to 8 minutes or just until potatoes are tender.

2  Drain potatoes; place in medium bowl. Add 2 tablespoons of the dressing; toss to coat. Place potatoes in grill basket (grill "wok") if desired. Brush beef steak with 1 tablespoon of the dressing; sprinkle with salt and pepper.

3  Place beef and potatoes on grill. Cover grill; cook over medium heat 8 to 15 minutes, turning once, until beef is desired doneness and potatoes are golden brown. Cut beef into thin slices.

4  Among 4 plates, divide lettuce, tomatoes and onion. Top with beef and potatoes; drizzle with remaining dressing. Sprinkle with additional pepper if desired.

**4 servings**

## Easy
### Add-On

*You won't have to twist the arm of blue cheese lovers to agree to a generous sprinkle of crumbled blue or Gorgonzola cheese on top of their salads.*

**1 Serving:** Calories 470; Total Fat 31g (Saturated Fat 16g; Trans Fat 1.5g); Cholesterol 130mg; Sodium 480mg; Total Carbohydrate 1g (Dietary Fiber 0g) • **Exchanges:** 7 Lean Meat, 2 Fat • **Carbohydrate Choices:** 0

# Grilled Rosemary-Dijon Steaks

¼ cup Dijon mustard

2 teaspoons chopped fresh or
  ½ teaspoon dried rosemary leaves,
  crushed

1 teaspoon coarsely ground pepper

2 cloves garlic, finely chopped

4 boneless beef top loin steaks, about
  1 inch thick (about 1½ lb)

**1** Heat gas or charcoal grill. In small bowl, mix mustard, rosemary, pepper and garlic; spread on both sides of beef.

**2** Place beef on grill. Cook uncovered over medium heat 1 minute on each side to seal in juices. Cover grill; cook 8 to 9 minutes longer for medium doneness, turning once.

**4 servings**

## Make it a Meal

*Celebrate life's simple pleasures! Serve the steak with grilled corn on the cob and microwaved "baked" potatoes with sour cream and butter.*

**1 Serving:** Calories 190; Total Fat 9g (Saturated Fat 3g; Trans Fat 0g); Cholesterol 50mg; Sodium 410mg; Total Carbohydrate 2g (Dietary Fiber 0g) • **Exchanges:** 4 Lean Meat • **Carbohydrate Choices:** 0

# Grilled Lemon-Pepper Steaks

4 beef sirloin or rib eye steaks, 1 inch thick (about 2 lb)

½ teaspoon garlic salt

¼ cup butter or margarine, melted

2 tablespoons chopped fresh or 1 tablespoon dried basil leaves

2 teaspoons lemon-pepper seasoning

2 medium bell peppers (any color), cut lengthwise in half, seeded

1 Spray grill rack with cooking spray. Heat gas or charcoal grill.

2 Trim fat on beef steaks to ½-inch thickness if necessary. Sprinkle garlic salt over beef. In small bowl, mix butter, basil and lemon-pepper seasoning; brush over beef and bell pepper halves.

3 Place beef and bell peppers on grill. Cover grill; cook over medium heat 10 to 15 minutes for medium beef doneness, turning once. Brush tops of steaks with butter mixture. Cut bell peppers into strips. Serve over beef.

**4 servings**

## Instant
## **Success!**

*Keep your steaks nice and juicy! Make sure the grill is hot before adding the steaks. A hot grill quickly sears the outside of the meat, sealing in the juices.*

**1 Serving:** Calories 360; Total Fat 18g (Saturated Fat 9g; Trans Fat 1g); Cholesterol 145mg; Sodium 430mg; Total Carbohydrate 4g (Dietary Fiber 1g) • **Exchanges:** 1 Vegetable, 6½ Lean Meat • **Carbohydrate Choices:** 0

# Beef and Potato Stew

Prep Time **20 Minutes**
Start to Finish **8 Hours 35 Minutes**

1 cup sun-dried tomatoes (not in oil)

1½ lb beef stew meat

12 small new potatoes (1½ lb), cut in half

1 medium onion, cut into 8 wedges

1½ cups ready-to-eat baby-cut carrots

1 can (14 oz) beef broth

1½ teaspoons seasoned salt

1 dried bay leaf

½ cup water

¼ cup all-purpose flour

1 Cover dried tomatoes with boiling water. Let stand 10 minutes; drain. Coarsely chop tomatoes.

2 In 3½- to 4-quart slow cooker, mix tomatoes and remaining ingredients except water and flour.

3 Cover and cook on Low heat setting 8 to 9 hours.

4 Mix water and flour; gradually stir into stew. Increase heat setting to High. Cover and cook 10 to 15 minutes or until slightly thickened. Remove bay leaf.

**6 servings**

## Budget Smart

*When picking out stew meat, do some comparison shopping. Chuck is often the cut of meat used in beef stew, so if the beef chuck costs less per pound than the precut stew meat, buy that instead. To use, just cut it into ¾-inch pieces.*

**1 Serving:** Calories 350; Total Fat 14g (Saturated Fat 5g, Trans Fat 0.5g); Cholesterol 70mg; Sodium 900mg; Total Carbohydrate 34g (Dietary Fiber 4g) • **Exchanges:** 2 Starch, 1 Vegetable, 3 Lean Meat • **Carbohydrate Choices:** 2

# Beef Stew

1 tablespoon vegetable oil

1 lb boneless beef chuck, tip or round roast, trimmed of fat, cut into 1-inch cubes

3 cups water

½ teaspoon salt

⅛ teaspoon pepper

2 medium carrots, cut into 1-inch pieces

1 large unpeeled baking potato (russet or Idaho), cut into 1½-inch pieces

1 medium green bell pepper, cut into 1-inch pieces

1 medium stalk celery, cut into 1-inch pieces

1 small onion, chopped (¼ cup)

1 teaspoon salt

1 dried bay leaf

½ cup cold water

2 tablespoons all-purpose flour

1 In 12-inch skillet or 4-quart Dutch oven, heat oil over medium heat 1 to 2 minutes. Add beef; cook 10 to 15 minutes, stirring occasionally, until brown on all sides.

2 Remove skillet from heat, then add water, ½ teaspoon salt and the pepper. Heat to boiling over high heat. Once mixture is boiling, reduce heat just enough so mixture bubbles gently. Cover; cook 2 hours to 2 hours 30 minutes or until beef is almost tender.

3 Stir in remaining ingredients except cold water and flour. Cover; cook about 30 minutes longer or until vegetables are tender when pierced with a fork. Remove and discard bay leaf.

4 In tightly covered jar or container, shake cold water and flour; gradually stir into beef mixture. Heat to boiling, stirring constantly. Boil and stir 1 minute, until thickened.

**4 servings**

## Budget
### Smart

*Stews are great choices for budget-smart cooking because the best meat cuts for stew are often the least expensive, too. Beef chuck, tip and round roast are all fairly cheap cuts of beef and will cook into a tender and flavorful beef stew.*

**1 Serving:** Calories 350; Total Fat 17g (Saturated Fat 6g, Trans Fat 0.5g); Cholesterol 65mg; Sodium 980mg; Total Carbohydrate 25g (Dietary Fiber 4g) • **Exchanges:** 1½ Starch, 1 Vegetable, 2½ Lean Meat, 1½ Fat • **Carbohydrate Choices:** 1½

# Old-Time Beef and Vegetable Stew

1 lb boneless beef sirloin steak, cut into ½-inch cubes

1 bag (1 lb) frozen stew vegetables, thawed, drained

1 can (15 oz) thick-and-zesty seasoned or plain tomato sauce

1 can (14 oz) beef broth

2 cans (5.5 oz each) spicy hot vegetable juice

**1** Spray 10-inch skillet with cooking spray; heat over medium-high heat. Cook beef in skillet about 10 minutes, stirring occasionally, until brown.

**2** Stir in remaining ingredients. Heat to boiling; reduce heat. Cover; simmer 5 minutes, stirring occasionally.

**6 servings**

## Instant **Success!**

*A bag of frozen stew vegetables—potatoes, carrots, onions and peas—is really handy for this recipe. The size of the veggie pieces varies from brand to brand, but all will be done by the end of the cooking time.*

**1 Serving:** Calories 170; Total Fat 3g (Saturated Fat 1g, Trans Fat 0g); Cholesterol 45mg; Sodium 850mg; Total Carbohydrate 16g (Dietary Fiber 3g) • **Exchanges:** 1 Starch, 2½ Very Lean Meat • **Carbohydrate Choices:** 1

# Italian-Style Shepherd's Pie

Prep Time **20 Minutes**
Start to Finish **50 Minutes**

1 lb boneless beef sirloin steak, trimmed of fat, cut into 1-inch cubes

1 cup sliced onion (about 1 medium)

2 medium carrots, sliced (1 cup)

½ teaspoon seasoned salt

¼ teaspoon pepper

1½ cups sliced fresh mushrooms

1 jar (14 oz) tomato pasta sauce (any variety)

½ package (7.2-oz size) roasted garlic mashed potatoes (1 pouch)

1 cup hot water

⅔ cup milk

2 tablespoons butter or margarine

2 tablespoons shredded fresh Parmesan cheese

1 Heat oven to 375°F. Spray 2-quart casserole or 11 × 7-inch (2-quart) glass baking dish with cooking spray. Heat 12-inch nonstick skillet over medium-high heat. Add beef, onion and carrots to skillet; sprinkle with seasoned salt and pepper. Cook 3 to 5 minutes, stirring frequently, until beef is brown.

2 Stir in mushrooms and pasta sauce. Heat to boiling. Cook over medium heat 5 minutes, stirring occasionally. Spread in casserole.

3 Make potatoes as directed on package for 4 servings, using 1 pouch potatoes and seasoning, water, milk and butter. Spoon into 8 mounds around edge of hot beef mixture. Sprinkle cheese over all.

4 Bake uncovered 25 to 30 minutes or until bubbly and potatoes are light golden brown.

**4 servings (1½ cups each)**

## Instant Success!

*Thanks to instant potatoes, this extra-easy shepherd's pie is quick to prep and ready in under an hour! Sirloin steak is often on sale, but you can also use ground beef in this recipe for added savings.*

**1 Serving:** Calories 430; Total Fat 15g (Saturated Fat 6g, Trans Fat 0.5g); Cholesterol 80mg; Sodium 860mg; Total Carbohydrate 48g (Dietary Fiber 5g) • **Exchanges:** 2 Starch, 1 Other Carbohydrate, 1 Vegetable, 3 Lean Meat, 1 Fat • **Carbohydrate Choices:** 3

# Beef Fajita Bowls

1 cup uncooked regular long-grain white rice

1 lb boneless beef sirloin steak

2 tablespoons vegetable oil

1 flour tortilla (8 inch), cut into 4 × ½-inch strips

1 bag (1 lb) frozen bell pepper and onion stir-fry

½ cup frozen whole kernel corn (from 1-lb bag)

1 cup chunky-style salsa

2 tablespoons lime juice

2 tablespoons chili sauce

½ teaspoon ground cumin

2 tablespoons chopped fresh cilantro

1 Cook rice as directed on package. Meanwhile, cut beef with grain into 2-inch strips; cut strips across grain into ⅛-inch slices. (Beef is easier to cut if partially frozen, 30 to 60 minutes.)

2 Heat 12-inch nonstick skillet over medium-high heat. Add oil; rotate skillet to coat bottom. Cook tortilla strips in oil 1 to 2 minutes on each side, adding additional oil if necessary, until golden brown and crisp. Drain on paper towel.

3 Add beef to skillet; stir-fry over medium-high heat 4 to 5 minutes or until beef is brown; remove beef from skillet. Add frozen bell pepper mixture and corn to skillet; stir-fry 1 minute. Cover; cook 2 to 3 minutes, stirring twice, until crisp-tender. Stir in beef, salsa, lime juice, chili sauce and cumin. Cook 2 to 3 minutes, stirring occasionally, until hot. Stir in cilantro. Among 4 bowls, divide rice. Top with beef mixture and tortilla strips.

**4 servings**

## Speed it Up

*You'll be "bowl-ed" over by this super-easy twist on fajitas. To make this even quicker, top with packaged tortilla chips instead. Then reduce the amount of oil for sautéing the beef to 1 tablespoon.*

**1 Serving:** Calories 510; Total Fat 12g (Saturated Fat 2.5g; Trans Fat 0g); Cholesterol 65mg; Sodium 1030mg; Total Carbohydrate 66g (Dietary Fiber 4g) • **Exchanges:** 3½ Starch, ½ Other Carbohydrate, 1 Vegetable, 3 Lean Meat • **Carbohydrate Choices:** 4½

# Szechuan Beef and Bean Sprouts

Prep Time **20 Minutes**
Start to Finish **30 Minutes**

1 lb boneless beef eye of round steak, trimmed of fat

¼ cup reduced-sodium chicken broth

1 tablespoon reduced-sodium soy sauce

1 tablespoon Szechuan sauce

⅛ teaspoon crushed red pepper flakes

4 plum (Roma) tomatoes, cut into 8 pieces

2 cups fresh bean sprouts (4 oz)

1 tablespoon chopped fresh cilantro

1 Cut beef with grain into 2-inch strips; cut strips across grain into ⅛-inch slices. (Beef is easier to cut if partially frozen, 30 to 60 minutes.) In medium bowl, stir together broth, soy sauce, Szechuan sauce and pepper flakes. Stir in beef. Let stand 10 minutes.

2 Drain beef; reserve marinade. Heat 12-inch nonstick skillet over medium-high heat. Add half of the beef to skillet; cook and stir 2 to 3 minutes or until brown. Remove beef from skillet. Repeat with remaining beef. Return all beef to skillet.

3 Add reserved marinade, the tomatoes and bean sprouts to beef in skillet; stir-fry about 1 minute or until vegetables are warm. Sprinkle with cilantro.

**4 servings (1¼ cups each)**

## Budget Smart

*Stir-fries are a great way to prepare inexpensive but tougher cuts of beef, such as eye and round, because the meat stays tender from being sliced thinly and cooked quickly.*

**1 Serving:** Calories 200; Total Fat 6g (Saturated Fat 1.5g, Trans Fat 0g); Cholesterol 65mg; Sodium 430mg; Total Carbohydrate 6g (Dietary Fiber 1g) • **Exchanges:** 1 Vegetable, 4 Very Lean Meat, 1 Fat • **Carbohydrate Choices:** ½

# Ramen-Beef Stir-Fry

1 lb boneless beef sirloin

2 cups water

1 package (3 oz) Oriental-flavor ramen
noodle soup mix

1 bag (14 to 16 oz) fresh stir-fry
vegetables

¼ cup stir-fry sauce

1 Cut beef into thin strips. Spray 12-inch skillet with cooking spray;
heat over medium-high heat. Cook beef in skillet 3 to 5 minutes, stirring
occasionally, until brown. Remove beef from skillet.

2 In same skillet, heat water to boiling. Break block of noodles from soup
mix into water; stir until slightly softened. Stir in vegetables. Heat to boiling.
Boil 4 to 5 minutes, stirring occasionally, until vegetables are crisp-tender.

3 Stir in contents of seasoning packet from soup mix, stir-fry sauce and
beef. Cook 2 to 3 minutes, stirring frequently, until hot.

**4 servings**

**1 Serving:** Calories 290; Total Fat 8g (Saturated Fat 2.5g; Trans Fat 1.5g); Cholesterol 65mg; Sodium 1150mg; Total
Carbohydrate 23g (Dietary Fiber 3g) • **Exchanges:** 1 Starch, 1 Vegetable, 3½ Lean Meat • **Carbohydrate Choices:** 1½

# Orange Teriyaki Beef with Noodles

Prep Time **25 Minutes**
Start to Finish **25 Minutes**

1 lb boneless beef sirloin, cut into thin strips

1 can (14 oz) beef broth

¼ cup teriyaki stir-fry sauce

2 tablespoons orange marmalade

Dash ground red pepper (cayenne)

1 ½ cups fresh snap pea pods

1 ½ cups uncooked fine egg noodles (3 oz)

1 Spray 12-inch skillet with cooking spray; heat over medium–high heat. Cook beef in skillet 2 to 4 minutes, stirring occasionally, until brown. Remove beef from skillet; keep warm.

2 Add broth, stir-fry sauce, marmalade and red pepper to skillet. Heat to boiling. Stir in pea pods and noodles; reduce heat to medium. Cover and cook about 5 minutes or until noodles are tender.

3 Stir in beef. Cook uncovered 2 to 3 minutes or until sauce is slightly thickened.

**4 servings**

## Instant Success!

*Okay, you're not wild about orange marmalade, so use peach or apricot jam or preserves instead. For a side salad, pick up a bag of washed spinach and toss with mandarin orange segments. Drizzle with a favorite dressing and sprinkle with chopped green onions.*

**1 Serving:** Calories 270; Total Fat 4.5g (Saturated Fat 1.5g; Trans Fat 0g); Cholesterol 85mg; Sodium 1160mg; Total Carbohydrate 25g (Dietary Fiber 1g) • **Exchanges:** 1 Starch, ½ Other Carbohydrate, 4 Very Lean Meat, ½ Fat • **Carbohydrate Choices:** 1 ½

# Bow-Tie Pasta with Beef and Tomatoes

2 cups uncooked bow-tie (farfalle) pasta (4 oz)

1 tablespoon olive or vegetable oil

1 cup frozen bell pepper and onion stir-fry (from 1-lb bag)

1 lb beef strips for stir-fry or thinly sliced flank steak

1 can (14.5 oz) Italian-style stewed tomatoes, undrained

1 teaspoon garlic salt

¼ teaspoon pepper

Fresh basil leaves, if desired

Freshly shredded Parmesan cheese, if desired

1 Cook and drain pasta as directed on package.

2 Meanwhile, in 12-inch skillet, heat oil over medium–high heat. Cook bell pepper mixture in oil 3 minutes, stirring frequently. Stir in beef. Cook 5 to 6 minutes, stirring frequently, until beef is no longer pink.

3 Stir in tomatoes, garlic salt and pepper. Cook 2 to 3 minutes, stirring frequently and breaking up tomatoes slightly with spoon, until mixture is hot. Stir in pasta. Cook 1 to 2 minutes, stirring constantly, until pasta is well coated and hot. Garnish with basil. Serve with cheese.

**4 servings**

## Speed it Up

*This handy one-dish pasta recipe is already fast, but it's even faster (and handier) if you substitute leftover cold pasta you might have in the fridge for the uncooked pasta. No need to warm it up first; just heat it an extra minute or two after stirring into the sauce.*

**1 Serving:** Calories 350; Total Fat 12g (Saturated Fat 3.5g; Trans Fat 0g); Cholesterol 50mg; Sodium 520mg; Total Carbohydrate 29g (Dietary Fiber 3g) • **Exchanges:** 1½ Starch, 1 Vegetable, 3½ Very Lean Meat, 2 Fat • **Carbohydrate Choices:** 2

# Parmesan Orzo and Meatballs

1½ cups frozen bell pepper and onion stir-fry (from 1-lb bag)

2 tablespoons Italian dressing

1 can (14 oz) beef broth

1 cup uncooked orzo or rosamarina pasta (6 oz)

16 frozen cooked meatballs (from 16-oz bag)

1 large tomato, chopped (1 cup)

2 tablespoons chopped fresh parsley

¼ cup shredded Parmesan cheese (1 oz)

1 In 12-inch nonstick skillet, cook bell pepper mixture and dressing over medium–high heat 2 minutes, stirring frequently.

2 Stir in broth; heat to boiling. Stir in pasta and meatballs. Heat to boiling; reduce heat to low. Cover; cook 10 minutes, stirring occasionally.

3 Stir in tomato. Cover; cook 3 to 5 minutes or until most of liquid has been absorbed and pasta is tender. Stir in parsley. Sprinkle with cheese.

**4 servings**

## Instant Success!

*Orzo is a rice-shaped pasta that cooks fairly quickly. It's also kid-friendly because it is easier to eat than long spaghetti.*

**1 Serving:** Calories 360; Total Fat 14g (Saturated Fat 4.5g; Trans Fat 0.5g); Cholesterol 65mg; Sodium 700mg; Total Carbohydrate 39g (Dietary Fiber 4g) • **Exchanges:** 1½ Starch, ½ Other Carbohydrate, 1 Vegetable, 2 Medium-Fat Meat, ½ Fat • **Carbohydrate Choices:** 2½

# Impossibly Easy Cheeseburger Pie

1 lb lean (at least 80%) ground beef

1 large onion, chopped (1 cup)

½ teaspoon salt

1 cup shredded Cheddar cheese (4 oz)

½ cup Original Bisquick® mix

1 cup milk

2 eggs

1 Heat oven to 400°F. Spray 9-inch glass pie plate with cooking spray.

2 In 10-inch skillet, cook beef and onion over medium-high heat 5 to 7 minutes, stirring occasionally, until beef is thoroughly cooked; drain. Stir in salt. Spread in pie plate. Sprinkle with cheese.

3 In medium bowl, stir remaining ingredients with wire whisk or fork until blended. Pour into pie plate.

4 Bake about 25 minutes or until knife inserted in center comes out clean.

**6 servings**

## Make it a Meal

*This is one of the most-requested Bisquick recipes of all time! It's a big hit with kids and a very tasty way to stretch a pound of ground beef to serve six. Serve with a salad or oven fries—and don't forget the ketchup!*

**1 Serving:** Calories 300; Total Fat 19g (Saturated Fat 9g, Trans Fat 1g); Cholesterol 140mg; Sodium 510mg; Total Carbohydrate 11g (Dietary Fiber 0g) • **Exchanges:** ½ Starch, 3 Medium-Fat Meat, 1 Fat • **Carbohydrate Choices:** 1

# Meat Loaf

Prep Time **20 Minutes**

Start to Finish **1 Hour
25 Minutes**

1 lb lean (at least 80%) ground beef

¼ cup milk

2 teaspoons Worcestershire sauce

1 teaspoon chopped fresh or
 ¼ teaspoon dried sage leaves

¼ teaspoon salt

¼ teaspoon ground mustard

⅛ teaspoon pepper

1 clove garlic, finely chopped, or
 ⅛ teaspoon garlic powder

1 egg

2 slices bread, torn into small pieces

3 tablespoons chopped onion

⅓ cup ketchup, chili sauce or barbecue
 sauce

1 Heat oven to 350°F. In large bowl, mix all ingredients except ketchup.

2 In ungreased baking pan, spread beef mixture. Shape mixture into
8 × 4-inch loaf in pan. Spread ketchup over top.

3 Bake uncovered 50 to 60 minutes until meat and juices are no longer
pink or until meat thermometer inserted in center of loaf reads 160°F and
center of loaf is no longer pink.★ Let stand 5 minutes; remove from pan.

★*If you like bell pepper, onions and celery in your meat loaf, you may find that it may remain pink
even though the beef is cooked to 160°F in the center. It's due to the natural nitrate content of these
ingredients. So it is best to always check meat loaf with a thermometer to make sure it is thoroughly
cooked.*

**4 servings**

Simple Swap: *Substitute ground turkey for the ground beef. Bake about
60 minutes or until meat thermometer inserted in center of loaf reads 165°F.*

## Easy
### Add-On

*Check your
supermarket for ground
meat labeled "meat
loaf combination"
(usually a blend of
ground pork, veal and
beef) especially if it's on
sale. Use it instead of
the ground beef for an
Italian-style meat loaf.*

**1 Serving:** Calories 290; Total Fat 15g (Saturated Fat 6g, Trans Fat 1g); Cholesterol 125mg; Sodium 560mg; Total Carbohydrate
15g (Dietary Fiber 0g) • **Exchanges:** ½ Starch, ½ Other Carbohydrate, 3 Medium-Fat Meat • **Carbohydrate Choices:** 1

# Mini Meat Loaves

½ cup ketchup

2 tablespoons packed brown sugar

1 lb lean (at least 80%) ground beef

½ lb ground pork

½ cup Original Bisquick® mix

¼ teaspoon pepper

1 small onion, finely chopped (¼ cup)

1 egg

1 Heat oven to 450°F. In small bowl, stir ketchup and brown sugar until mixed; reserve ¼ cup for topping. In large bowl, stir remaining ingredients and remaining ketchup mixture until well mixed.

2 Spray 13 × 9-inch pan with cooking spray. Place meat mixture in pan; pat into 12 × 4-inch rectangle. Cut lengthwise down center and then crosswise into sixths to form 12 loaves. Separate loaves, using spatula, so no edges are touching. Brush loaves with reserved ¼ cup ketchup mixture.

3 Bake 18 to 20 minutes or until loaves are no longer pink in center and meat thermometer inserted in center of loaves reads 160°F.

**6 servings (2 loaves each)**

## Speed it Up

*These cute little loaves bake much faster than a traditional whole loaf, plus you get more of that tangy crust. Stick with the "mini" theme by serving small boiled potatoes and cooked baby-cut carrots (both of which also cook up extra-fast!).*

**1 Serving:** Calories 300; Total Fat 16g (Saturated Fat 6g; Trans Fat 1g); Cholesterol 105mg; Sodium 430mg; Total Carbohydrate 16g (Dietary Fiber 0g) • **Exchanges:** ½ Starch, ½ Other Carbohydrate, 3 Medium-Fat Meat • **Carbohydrate Choices:** 1

# Grilled Hamburgers with Roasted Sweet Onions

Prep Time **25 Minutes**
Start to Finish **25 Minutes**

Cooking spray

4 lean ground beef patties (4 to 6 oz each)

2 tablespoons steak sauce

1 package (1 oz) onion soup mix (from 2-oz box)

2 large Bermuda or other sweet onions, cut in half, then thinly sliced and separated (6 cups)

2 tablespoons packed brown sugar

1 tablespoon balsamic vinegar

1 Heat gas or charcoal grill. Cut 2 (12 × 8-inch) sheets of heavy-duty foil; spray with cooking spray. Brush beef patties with steak sauce; sprinkle with half of the soup mix (dry).

2 Place half of the onions on center of each foil sheet. Sprinkle with remaining soup mix, brown sugar and vinegar. Bring up 2 sides of foil so edges meet. Seal edges, making tight ½-inch fold; fold again, allowing space for circulation and expansion. Fold other sides to seal.

3 Place packets and beef patties on grill. Cover grill; cook over medium heat 10 to 15 minutes, turning patties and rotating packets ½ turn once or twice, until meat thermometer inserted in center of patties reads 160°F. To serve onions, cut large X across top of each packet; carefully fold back foil to allow steam to escape. Serve onions with patties.

**4 servings**

## Make it a Meal

*Everything tastes better grilled! Lightly grill some hamburger buns for added crunchiness. Throw some frozen fries in the oven before starting the recipe. You'll be chowing down in no time!*

**1 Serving:** Calories 320; Total Fat 13g (Saturated Fat 5g; Trans Fat 1g); Cholesterol 70mg; Sodium 790mg; Total Carbohydrate 30g (Dietary Fiber 4g) • **Exchanges:** 1½ Starch, 1½ Vegetable, 2 Medium-Fat Meat, ½ Fat • **Carbohydrate Choices:** 2

# Monterey Skillet Hamburgers

1 lb lean (at least 80%) ground beef

1 can (4.5 oz) chopped green chiles, drained

2 tablespoons chopped fresh cilantro

1 teaspoon chili powder

½ teaspoon salt

⅛ teaspoon ground red pepper (cayenne)

1 medium red onion, thinly sliced

1 medium avocado, pitted, peeled and sliced

4 slices (1 oz each) Monterey Jack cheese

**1** In large bowl, mix beef, chiles, cilantro, chili powder, salt and red pepper. Shape mixture into 4 patties, about ½ inch thick.

**2** Spray 10-inch skillet with cooking spray; heat over medium-high heat. Cook onion in skillet 1 to 2 minutes, stirring occasionally, just until tender. Remove from skillet.

**3** Add beef patties to skillet. Cook 10 to 12 minutes, turning once, until meat thermometer inserted in center of patties reads 160°F. Top patties with onion, avocado and cheese. Cover; heat until cheese is melted.

**4 servings**

## Instant
## Success!

*To get to that luscious avocado quickly, first cut it lengthwise in half around the pit. On a solid surface and with your other hand out of the way, hit the pit with the blade of a sharp knife so it sticks, then twist the knife to easily remove the pit from the avocado. Carefully remove the pit from the knife with a paper towel because it's very slippery. Peel off the leathery skin with your fingers.*

**1 Serving:** Calories 400; Total Fat 28g (Saturated Fat 11g; Trans Fat 1g); Cholesterol 95mg; Sodium 980mg; Total Carbohydrate 8g (Dietary Fiber 4g) • **Exchanges:** ½ Other Carbohydrate, 4 Medium-Fat Meat, 1½ Fat • **Carbohydrate Choices:** ½

# Cincinnati Chili

10 oz uncooked spaghetti

1 lb lean (at least 80%) ground beef

1 medium onion, chopped (½ cup)

1 clove garlic, finely chopped

1 jar (26 to 28 oz) chunky vegetable-style tomato pasta sauce

1 can (15 to 16 oz) kidney beans, drained, rinsed

2 tablespoons chili powder

½ cup shredded Cheddar cheese (2 oz), if desired

3 medium green onions, sliced, if desired

1 Cook and drain spaghetti as directed on package. Meanwhile, in 10-inch skillet, cook beef, onion and garlic over medium heat 8 to 10 minutes, stirring occasionally, until beef is brown; drain.

2 Stir pasta sauce, beans and chili powder into beef; reduce heat. Simmer uncovered 10 minutes, stirring occasionally. Serve sauce over spaghetti. Sprinkle with cheese and green onions.

**6 servings**

## Speed it Up

*Thin spaghetti and vermicelli both cook more quickly than regular spaghetti, so if you like pasta but need to shave minutes, try one of these options.*

**1 Serving:** Calories 550; Total Fat 14g (Saturated Fat 4g; Trans Fat 0.5g); Cholesterol 45mg; Sodium 860mg; Total Carbohydrate 78g (Dietary Fiber 10g) • **Exchanges:** 4 Starch, 1 Other Carbohydrate, 1 Vegetable, 2 Medium-Fat Meat • **Carbohydrate Choices:** 5

# Taco Supper Skillet

½ lb lean (at least 80%) ground beef

1 package (1.25 oz) taco seasoning
  mix

2¼ cups water

1½ cups uncooked wagon wheel pasta
  (5½ oz)

1½ cups frozen whole kernel corn
  (from 1-lb bag)

1 can (15 oz) pinto or kidney beans,
  drained, rinsed

1 medium tomato, chopped (¾ cup)

½ cup sour cream

1 cup shredded Cheddar cheese (4 oz)

1 tablespoon chopped fresh chives,
  if desired

1  In 12-inch skillet, cook beef over medium–high heat 5 to 7 minutes, stirring frequently, until brown; drain.

2  Stir seasoning mix, water, uncooked pasta, corn, beans and tomato into beef. Heat to boiling; stir. Reduce heat to medium–low. Cover; cook 10 to 15 minutes, stirring occasionally, until pasta is desired doneness and most of the liquid has been absorbed.

3  Stir in sour cream. Remove from heat. Sprinkle with cheese and chives. Cover; let stand 2 to 3 minutes or until cheese is melted.

**4 servings**

## Make it a Meal

*Pair this family-style supper with baked tortilla chips and fresh fruit salad served in lettuce cups. For speed, look for cut-up fresh fruit or jarred fruit in the produce section of the supermarket.*

**1 Serving:** Calories 640; Total Fat 23g (Saturated Fat 12g; Trans Fat 1g); Cholesterol 85mg; Sodium 590mg; Total Carbohydrate 73g (Dietary Fiber 12g) • **Exchanges:** 4½ Starch, ½ Other Carbohydrate, 3 Medium-Fat Meat, 1 Fat • **Carbohydrate Choices:** 5

# Fiesta Taco Salad

1 lb lean (at least 80%) ground beef

½ cup taco sauce

6 cups bite-size pieces lettuce

1 medium green bell pepper, cut into strips

2 medium tomatoes, cut into wedges

½ cup pitted ripe olives, drained

1 cup corn chips

1 cup shredded Cheddar cheese (4 oz)

½ cup Thousand Island dressing

1 In 10-inch skillet, cook beef over medium heat 8 to 10 minutes, stirring occasionally, until brown; drain. Stir in taco sauce. Cook 2 to 3 minutes, stirring occasionally, until heated.

2 In large bowl, toss lettuce, bell pepper, tomatoes, olives and corn chips. Spoon hot beef mixture over lettuce mixture; toss. Sprinkle with cheese. Serve immediately with dressing.

**5 servings**

**1 Serving:** Calories 410; Total Fat 30g (Saturated Fat 11g; Trans Fat 1g); Cholesterol 85mg; Sodium 710mg; Total Carbohydrate 11g (Dietary Fiber 3g) • **Exchanges:** ½ Other Carbohydrate, 1 Vegetable, 3 Medium-Fat Meat, 3 Fat • **Carbohydrate Choices:** 1

# Beef and Bean Tortilla Bake

Prep Time **20 Minutes**
Start to Finish **55 Minutes**

1 lb extra-lean (at least 90%) ground beef

1 can (15 oz) black beans, rinsed, drained

1 can (15 to 16 oz) pinto beans, rinsed, drained

1 can (14.5 oz) no-salt-added stewed tomatoes, undrained

1 envelope (1 oz) 40%-less-sodium taco seasoning mix

⅔ cup water

¾ cup shredded reduced-fat sharp Cheddar cheese (3 oz)

3 spinach-flavor flour tortillas (8 inch), cut in half, then cut crosswise into ½-inch-wide strips

**1** Heat oven to 350°F. In 12-inch skillet, cook beef over medium heat 8 to 10 minutes, stirring occasionally, until brown; drain. Stir in black beans, pinto beans, tomatoes, taco seasoning mix and water. Cook 2 to 4 minutes, stirring occasionally, until heated through. Stir in ½ cup of the cheese.

**2** In 8-inch square (2-quart) glass baking dish, spread 2 cups of the beef mixture. Top with half of the tortilla strips. Spoon half of the remaining beef mixture over tortilla strips. Add remaining tortilla strips; top with remaining beef mixture.

**3** Bake uncovered about 30 minutes or until bubbly and heated through. Sprinkle with remaining ¼ cup cheese. Bake about 5 minutes longer or until cheese is melted. Cut into squares.

**6 servings**

## Budget Smart

*Mixing ground beef and beans is a great way to add more fiber to your meals without giving up the beef, plus it saves money. If you can't find spinach-flavor flour tortillas, substitute another flavor or use plain white.*

**1 Serving:** Calories 410; Total Fat 9g (Saturated Fat 3.5g, Trans Fat 0.5g); Cholesterol 45mg; Sodium 910mg; Total Carbohydrate 56g (Dietary Fiber 13g) • **Exchanges:** 3 Starch, 1 Vegetable, 3 Very Lean Meat, 1 Fat • **Carbohydrate Choices:** 4

# Fiesta Taco Casserole

Prep Time **15 Minutes**
Start to Finish **45 Minutes**

1 lb lean (at least 80%) ground beef

1 can (15 to 16 oz) spicy chili beans in sauce, undrained

1 cup chunky-style salsa

2 cups coarsely broken tortilla chips

¾ cup sour cream

4 medium green onions, sliced (¼ cup)

1 medium tomato, chopped (¾ cup)

1 cup shredded Cheddar cheese (4 oz)

Shredded lettuce, if desired

Additional salsa, if desired

1 Heat oven to 350°F. In 10-inch skillet, cook beef over medium heat 8 to 10 minutes, stirring occasionally, until thoroughly cooked; drain. Stir in beans and 1 cup salsa. Heat to boiling, stirring occasionally.

2 In ungreased 2-quart casserole, place broken tortilla chips. Top with beef mixture. Spread with sour cream. Sprinkle with onions, tomato and cheese.

3 Bake uncovered 20 to 30 minutes or until hot and bubbly. Serve with lettuce and additional salsa.

**Lighten Up Fiesta Taco Casserole:** *Substitute ground turkey breast for the ground beef, and use reduced-fat sour cream and reduced-fat Cheddar cheese for 21 grams of fat and 520 calories per serving.*

**4 servings**

## Make it a Meal

*Mexican made easy! This family-pleasing taco bake uses staple ingredients like ground beef, salsa and canned beans, so you may already have some of these on hand. If not, stocking up on these foods is a good idea if you like Mexican flavors: Use any remaining ingredients in recipes like Beef and Bean Tortilla Bake (page 163) or Taco Supper Skillet (page 160).*

**1 Serving:** Calories 650; Total Fat 38g (Saturated Fat 17g, Trans Fat 1.5g); Cholesterol 130mg; Sodium 1550mg; Total Carbohydrate 42g (Dietary Fiber 7g) • **Exchanges:** 2 Starch, 1 Other Carbohydrate, 4½ Lean Meat, 4 Fat • **Carbohydrate Choices:** 3

# Cheesy Beef Hash

1 lb lean (at least 80%) ground beef

1 teaspoon salt

5 cups frozen potatoes O'Brien with onions and peppers (from 28-oz bag)

1 medium green bell pepper, chopped (1 cup)

½ medium red onion, chopped (½ cup)

1 container (8 oz) Cheddar cold-pack cheese food or cheese spread

1 cup shredded Cheddar cheese (4 oz)

1 In 12-inch nonstick skillet, cook beef and salt over medium-high heat 5 to 7 minutes, stirring occasionally, until brown; drain.

2 Stir potatoes into beef; reduce heat to medium-low. Cover; cook about 10 minutes, stirring occasionally, until potatoes are almost tender.

3 Stir in bell pepper and onion. Cover; cook 5 to 10 minutes, stirring occasionally, until tender. Stir in cold-pack cheese food. Cook 1 to 2 minutes, stirring occasionally, until thoroughly heated. Top with shredded cheese.

**4 servings (1½ cups each)**

## Instant
## Success!

*Give new flavors of cold-pack cheese food a whirl in this hearty supper dish. Try sharp Cheddar with bacon, sharp Cheddar with garlic, sharp Cheddar with toasted onion, Cheddar with horseradish or even Swiss with roasted almonds!*

**1 Serving:** Calories 700: Total Fat 35g (Saturated Fat 19g; Trans Fat 1.5g); Cholesterol 145mg; Sodium 1760mg; Total Carbohydrate 56g (Dietary Fiber 6g) • **Exchanges:** 3 Starch, ½ Other Carbohydrate, 4½ Medium-Fat Meat, 2 Fat • **Carbohydrate Choices:** 4

# Beefy Rice Skillet

1 lb lean (at least 80%) ground beef

2 ½ cups hot water

¾ cup ready-to-eat baby-cut carrots, cut lengthwise in half

1 tablespoon butter or margarine

¼ teaspoon pepper

1 package (6.4 oz) four-cheese rice and pasta blend

1 ½ cups broccoli florets

½ cup cherry or grape tomatoes, cut in half

1 In 12-inch skillet, cook beef over medium–high heat 5 to 7 minutes, stirring occasionally, until thoroughly cooked; drain.

2 Stir water, carrots, butter, pepper, rice mixture and contents of seasoning packet into beef. Heat to boiling; reduce heat. Cover and cook about 15 minutes or until rice and carrots are almost tender, stirring occasionally.

3 Stir in broccoli. Cover and cook 5 minutes or until crisp–tender. Stir in tomatoes. Cook uncovered about 1 minute or until heated.

**4 servings**

## Budget
Smart

*This simple skillet dinner is a fast and frugal way to get kids to eat their fresh veggies! For extra savings, use ¾ cup chopped carrots instead of baby-cut and a chopped plum (Roma) tomato instead of cherry tomatoes. The prep time will increase only slightly.*

**1 Serving:** Calories 420; Total Fat 20g (Saturated Fat 9g, Trans Fat 1); Cholesterol 80mg; Sodium 690mg; Total Carbohydrate 35g (Dietary Fiber 2g) • **Exchanges:** 2 Starch, 1 Vegetable, 2½ Medium-Fat Meat, 1 Fat • **Carbohydrate Choices:** 2

# Spinach and Beef Enchiladas

Prep Time **25 Minutes**

Start to Finish **1 Hour 10 Minutes**

1 lb lean (at least 80%) ground beef

1 medium onion, chopped (½ cup)

1 box (9 oz) frozen spinach

1 can (4.5 oz) chopped green chiles, undrained

½ teaspoon ground cumin

½ teaspoon garlic-pepper blend

½ cup sour cream

2 cups shredded Colby–Monterey Jack cheese blend (8 oz)

1 can (10 oz) enchilada sauce

1 package (11.5 oz) flour tortillas (8 tortillas)

½ cup chunky-style salsa

1 Heat oven to 350°F. Spray 13 × 9-inch (3-quart) glass baking dish with cooking spray. In 12-inch nonstick skillet, cook beef and onion over medium-high heat 5 to 7 minutes, stirring occasionally, until beef is brown.

2 Stir in spinach; cook, stirring frequently, until thawed. Stir in green chiles, cumin, garlic-pepper blend, sour cream and 1 cup of the cheese.

3 Spread about 1 teaspoon enchilada sauce on each tortilla. Top each with about ½ cup beef mixture. Roll up tortillas; place seam sides down in baking dish. In small bowl, mix remaining enchilada sauce and the salsa; spoon over enchiladas. Sprinkle with remaining 1 cup cheese.

4 Spray sheet of foil with cooking spray; cover baking dish with foil. Bake 40 to 45 minutes or until thoroughly heated.

**8 enchiladas**

## Instant Success!

*Who can resist a hot, bubbly pan of enchiladas? And these are so easy to make! Buying ground beef in bulk will save you even more money—just remember to divide it into smaller portions before freezing so you can defrost just the amount you need.*

1 Enchilada: Calories 400; Total Fat 23g (Saturated Fat 11g, Trans Fat 0.5g); Cholesterol 70mg; Sodium 860mg; Total Carbohydrate 28g (Dietary Fiber 0g) • **Exchanges:** 2 Starch, 2 High-Fat Meat, 1 Fat • **Carbohydrate Choices:** 2

Prep Time **15 Minutes**

Start to Finish **6 Hours 50 Minutes**

# Italian Meatballs with Marinara Sauce

¾ lb ground beef

¾ lb ground pork

1 small onion, chopped (¼ cup)

2 cloves garlic, finely chopped

2 teaspoons Italian seasoning

¼ cup Italian-style dry bread crumbs

1 egg, slightly beaten

1 jar (28 oz) marinara sauce

**1** Heat oven to 375°. Line jelly roll pan, 15 × 10 × 1 inch, with foil; spray with cooking spray. In large bowl, mix all ingredients except marinara sauce. Shape mixture into twenty-four 1½-inch balls. Place in pan. Bake 30 to 35 minutes or until no longer pink in center.

**2** Place meatballs in 3½- to 4-quart slow cooker. Pour marinara sauce over meatballs.

**3** Cover and cook on Low heat setting 6 to 7 hours to blend and develop flavors.

**6 servings (4 meatballs each)**

## Make it a Meal

*The juiciness of the ground pork makes these meatballs especially tender. Serve the meatballs and sauce (or any reheated leftovers) over a bowl of hot cooked pasta.*

**1 Serving:** Calories 390; Total Fat 20g (Saturated Fat 6g, Trans Fat 0); Cholesterol 105mg; Sodium 780mg; Total Carbohydrate 29g (Dietary Fiber 2g) • **Exchanges:** ½ Starch, 1 Other Carbohydrate, 1 Vegetable, 3 Medium-Fat Meat, 1 Fat • **Carbohydrate Choices:** 2

Betty Crocker Supper in a Snap

# Creamy Beef Fold-Over Pie

1 lb lean (at least 80%) ground beef

1 small onion, chopped (¼ cup)

1 can (10¾ oz) condensed cream of mushroom soup

1½ cups frozen mixed vegetables, thawed

1 tablespoon ketchup

2 cups Original Bisquick® mix

½ cup boiling water

¼ cup shredded Cheddar cheese (1 oz)

1 Move oven rack to lowest position. Heat oven to 375°F. Spray 12-inch pizza pan with cooking spray.

2 In 10-inch skillet, cook beef and onion over medium-high heat 5 to 7 minutes, stirring occasionally, until beef is thoroughly cooked; drain. Stir in soup, vegetables and ketchup. Cook 3 to 4 minutes, stirring occasionally, until thoroughly heated.

3 In medium bowl, stir Bisquick mix and boiling water until soft dough forms. Place dough on surface sprinkled with Bisquick mix; gently roll in Bisquick mix to coat. Shape dough into a ball; knead about 5 times or until smooth. Roll dough into 14-inch circle; place on pizza pan.

4 Spoon beef mixture over dough to within 2 inches of edge. Fold edge of dough up over beef mixture. Bake 24 to 27 minutes or until crust is golden brown. Top with cheese. Bake 3 to 4 minutes longer or until cheese is melted. Let stand 5 minutes before cutting.

**6 servings**

**1 Serving:** Calories 390; Total Fat 19g (Saturated Fat 6g, Trans Fat 1.5g); Cholesterol 55mg; Sodium 1030mg; Total Carbohydrate 35g (Dietary Fiber 3g) • **Exchanges:** 2 Starch, ½ Other Carbohydrate, 2 Medium-Fat Meat, 1½ Fat • **Carbohydrate Choices:** 2

# Mexi Shells

Prep Time **15 Minutes**
Start to Finish **55 Minutes**

18 uncooked jumbo pasta shells

4 cans (8 oz each) no-salt-added tomato sauce

2 tablespoons all-purpose flour

1 teaspoon chili powder

3 teaspoons ground cumin

¾ lb extra-lean (at least 90%) ground beef

1 small onion, chopped (¼ cup)

1 tablespoon chopped fresh cilantro

1 can (4.5 oz) chopped green chiles, drained

1 can (15 or 16 oz) chili beans in sauce, undrained

1 cup shredded part-skim mozzarella cheese (4 oz)

## Make it a Meal

*These deeply delicious stuffed shells have a Mexican accent, thanks to the cumin, chili powder, cilantro and green chiles. Serve these with a lightly dressed salad.*

1 Heat oven to 350°F. Cook pasta shells as directed on package.

2 Meanwhile, in medium bowl, mix tomato sauce, flour, chili powder and 2 teaspoons of the cumin; set aside.

3 In 2-quart saucepan, cook beef and onion over medium heat 8 to 10 minutes, stirring occasionally, until beef is brown; drain. Stir in remaining 1 teaspoon cumin, the cilantro, green chiles and chili beans.

4 Drain pasta shells. In ungreased 13 × 9-inch glass baking dish, spread 1 cup of the tomato sauce mixture. Spoon about 1½ tablespoons beef mixture into each pasta shell. Place filled sides up on sauce in dish. Pour remaining tomato sauce mixture over shells. Sprinkle with cheese.

5 Cover with foil and bake 30 minutes. Uncover and let stand 10 minutes before serving.

**6 servings**

**1 Serving:** Calories 380; Total Fat 10g (Saturated Fat 4.5g, Trans Fat 0g); Cholesterol 70mg; Sodium 1020mg; Total Carbohydrate 46g (Dietary Fiber 7g) • **Exchanges:** 3 Starch, 2½ Very Lean Meat, ½ Fat • **Carbohydrate Choices:** 3

# Pan-Fried Ravioli in Vodka Sauce

Prep Time **30 Minutes**
Start to Finish **30 Minutes**

1 bag (25 oz) frozen beef-filled ravioli

3 tablespoons extra-virgin olive oil

1 tablespoon butter or margarine

2 cloves garlic, finely chopped

3 plum (Roma) tomatoes, seeded, chopped

1 jar (25 to 26 oz) vodka pasta sauce

¾ cup shredded Parmesan or Asiago cheese (3 oz)

1 In 6-quart Dutch oven, heat 4 quarts water to boiling. Add ravioli. Cook 3 minutes; drain.

2 In 12-inch nonstick skillet, heat 1 tablespoon of the oil and half of the butter over medium heat. Add half of the drained ravioli. Cook 3 to 4 minutes, stirring once or twice, until golden brown. Remove to large serving platter; cover to keep warm. Repeat with 1 tablespoon oil, the remaining butter and ravioli. Remove to platter.

3 To same skillet, add remaining 1 tablespoon oil and the garlic. Cook over medium heat 30 to 60 seconds, stirring occasionally, until garlic is tender. Stir in tomatoes. Cook 1 to 2 minutes, stirring constantly, until hot. Stir in pasta sauce. Cook 2 to 3 minutes, stirring once, until thoroughly heated.

4 Pour sauce over ravioli. Sprinkle with cheese.

**6 servings**

## Instant Success!

*If you can't find that yummy vodka pasta sauce at your grocery store, make your own by combining 1 jar (26 oz) tomato pasta sauce, ½ cup whipping cream and 2 tablespoons vodka.*

**1 Serving:** Calories 500; Total Fat 24g (Saturated Fat 8g; Trans Fat 0g); Cholesterol 155mg; Sodium 1730mg; Total Carbohydrate 50g (Dietary Fiber 4g) • **Exchanges:** 2 Starch, 1 Other Carbohydrate, 2 High-Fat Meat, 1 ½ Fat • **Carbohydrate Choices:** 3

# Grilled Chili-Rubbed Pork Tenderloin

2 teaspoons packed brown sugar

1½ teaspoons chili powder

1 teaspoon salt

1 teaspoon ground cumin

⅛ teaspoon ground red pepper (cayenne)

1 clove garlic, finely chopped

1 pork tenderloin (about 1 lb)

1 teaspoon vegetable oil

1 Heat gas or charcoal grill. In small bowl, mix all ingredients except pork and oil. Brush pork with oil. Rub and press spice mixture on all sides of pork.

2 Place pork on grill. Cover grill; cook over medium heat 17 to 20 minutes, turning several times, until pork has slight blush of pink in center and meat thermometer inserted in center reads 155°F. Cover pork; let stand about 5 minutes or until thermometer reads 160°F. Cut pork into slices.

**4 servings**

## Easy
### Add-On

*Imagine lively seasoned butter melting over this tender grilled pork! Just mix up a little extra of the seasoning rub mixture and stir it into softened butter. Pass it around to top the pork.*

**1 Serving:** Calories 170; Total Fat 6g (Saturated Fat 1.5g; Trans Fat 0g); Cholesterol 70mg; Sodium 650mg; Total Carbohydrate 3g (Dietary Fiber 0g) • **Exchanges:** 3 ½ Very Lean Meat, 1 Fat • **Carbohydrate Choices:** 0

# Rosemary Pork Roast with Carrots

Olive oil cooking spray

1 boneless pork center loin roast (about 2½ lb)

2 teaspoons dried rosemary leaves, crushed

1 teaspoon salt

¼ teaspoon pepper

2 lb ready-to-eat baby-cut carrots

1 large sweet onion, cut into 16 wedges

½ teaspoon garlic powder

1 Heat oven to 400°F. Spray 15 × 10 × 1-inch pan with olive oil cooking spray. Remove fat from pork. Spray pork with cooking spray; sprinkle with 1 teaspoon of the rosemary, ½ teaspoon of the salt and the pepper. Place in center of pan.

2 In large bowl, mix carrots, onion, garlic powder, the remaining teaspoon rosemary and ½ teaspoon salt. Arrange vegetable mixture around pork; spray vegetables with cooking spray.

3 Roast uncovered 1 hour to 1 hour 30 minutes or until meat thermometer inserted into center of pork reads 155°F and vegetables are tender. Remove from heat; cover with foil and let stand 10 minutes until thermometer reads 160°F. Slice pork; serve with vegetables.

**10 servings**

**1 Serving:** Calories 240; Total Fat 10g (Saturated Fat 3.5g, Trans Fat 0g); Cholesterol 70mg; Sodium 340mg; Total Carbohydrate 10g (Dietary Fiber 3g) • **Exchanges:** 2 Vegetable, 3 Lean Meat, ½ Fat • **Carbohydrate Choices:** ½

# Speedy Pork Dinner

4 pork loin or rib chops, ½ inch thick
    (1 to 1¼ lb)

½ cup beef-flavored or chicken broth
    (from 32-oz carton)

3 medium potatoes, quartered

4 small carrots, cut into 1-inch pieces

2 medium onions, quartered

¾ teaspoon salt

¼ teaspoon pepper

Chopped fresh parsley, if desired

1 Heat 12-inch nonstick skillet over medium-high heat. Cook pork in skillet about 5 minutes, turning once, until brown.

2 Add broth, potatoes, carrots and onions to skillet.

3 Sprinkle with salt and pepper. Heat to boiling; reduce heat. Cover and simmer about 30 minutes or until vegetables are tender and pork is no longer pink in center. Sprinkle with parsley.

**4 servings**

## Instant Success!

*Once the veggies are prepped, this pork dinner comes together pretty quickly! The mix of budget-friendly winter vegetables cook alongside the chops to yield a one-dish meal.*

**1 Serving:** Calories 290; Total Fat 9g (Saturated Fat 3g, Trans Fat 0g); Cholesterol 70mg; Sodium 640mg; Total Carbohydrate 28g (Dietary Fiber 4g) • **Exchanges:** 1½ Starch, 1 Vegetable, 3 Lean Meat • **Carbohydrate Choices:** 2

# Ginger-Peach Pork Medallions

1 tablespoon butter or margarine

1 pork tenderloin (1 lb), cut into ½-inch slices

¼ teaspoon salt

1 large peach, peeled, sliced

2 tablespoons packed brown sugar

1 teaspoon grated gingerroot

⅔ cup chicken broth

2 teaspoons cornstarch

**1** In 10-inch skillet, melt butter over medium–high heat. Sprinkle pork with salt; add to skillet. Cook about 4 minutes, turning pork once, until browned.

**2** Stir in peach slices, brown sugar and gingerroot. Cook 2 minutes, stirring once or twice, until peach slices are tender.

**3** In small bowl, mix broth and cornstarch; stir into pork and peach mixture. Reduce heat to medium–low. Cook 2 minutes, stirring once or twice, until thickened.

**4 servings**

## Make it a Meal

*The sweet and gingery flavor of this pork dish would go well with mashed sweet potatoes or seasoned sweet potato wedges or fries. Garnish the pork mixture with chopped fresh chives or parsley.*

**1 Serving:** Calories 220; Total Fat 8g (Saturated Fat 3.5g; Trans Fat 0g); Cholesterol 80mg; Sodium 390mg; Total Carbohydrate 12g (Dietary Fiber 0g) • **Exchanges:** ½ Other Carbohydrate, 4 Very Lean Meat, 1 Fat • **Carbohydrate Choices:** 1

# Hearty Pork Stew

Prep Time **35 Minutes**
Start to Finish **7 Hours
20 Minutes**

1 tablespoon vegetable oil

1½ lb boneless pork loin roast, cut into 1-inch cubes

3 medium carrots, cut into ¼-inch slices (1½ cups)

1 medium onion, chopped (½ cup)

2 cups ½-inch cubes peeled parsnips

1½ cups 1-inch cubes peeled butternut squash

4 cups chicken broth

1 tablespoon chopped fresh or 1 teaspoon dried sage leaves

2 teaspoons chopped fresh or ¾ teaspoon dried thyme leaves

½ teaspoon salt

½ teaspoon pepper

3 tablespoons all-purpose flour

3 tablespoons butter or margarine, softened

**1** In 10-inch skillet, heat oil over medium–high heat. Cook pork in oil 6 to 8 minutes, stirring occasionally, until browned on all sides.

**2** In 3-quart slow cooker, mix pork and remaining ingredients except flour and butter.

**3** Cover; cook on Low heat setting 6 to 7 hours.

**4** In small bowl, mix flour and butter; gradually stir into stew until blended. Increase heat setting to High. Cover; cook 30 to 45 minutes, stirring occasionally, until thickened.

**6 servings (1½ cups each)**

## Easy
### Add-On

*The aromas created by this stew will have your mouth watering the moment you enter your home for dinner. If you have additional carrots on hand, use those instead of parsnips.*

**1 Serving:** Calories 340; Total Fat 16g (Saturated Fat 6g, Trans Fat 0g); Cholesterol 90mg; Sodium 980mg; Total Carbohydrate 20g (Dietary Fiber 4g) • **Exchanges:** 1 Starch, ½ Other Carbohydrate, 4 Lean Meat, ½ Fat • **Carbohydrate Choices:** 1

# Pork Lo Mein

Prep Time **25 Minutes**

Start to Finish **25 Minutes**

½ lb boneless pork loin

2 ½ cups sugar snap peas

1 ½ cups ready-to-eat baby-cut carrots, cut lengthwise into ¼-inch sticks

½ package (9-oz size) refrigerated linguine, cut into 2-inch pieces

⅓ cup chicken broth

1 tablespoon soy sauce

2 teaspoons cornstarch

1 teaspoon sugar

2 teaspoons finely chopped gingerroot

2 to 4 cloves garlic, finely chopped

2 teaspoons canola oil

½ cup thinly sliced red onion

Toasted sesame seed, if desired (see page 65)

1 Trim fat from pork. Cut pork with grain into 2 × 1-inch strips; cut strips across grain into ⅛-inch slices (pork is easier to cut if partially frozen, about 1½ hours). Remove strings from peas.

2 In 3-quart saucepan, heat 2 quarts water to boiling. Add peas, carrots and linguine; heat to boiling. Boil 2 to 3 minutes or just until linguine is tender; drain.

3 In small bowl, mix broth, soy sauce, cornstarch, sugar, gingerroot and garlic.

4 In 12-inch nonstick skillet or wok, heat oil over medium-high heat. Add pork and onion; stir-fry about 2 minutes or until pork is no longer pink. Stir broth mixture; stir into pork mixture. Stir in peas, carrots and linguine. Cook 2 minutes, stirring occasionally. Sprinkle with sesame seed.

**4 servings**

## Budget
### Smart

*Make your own Chinese takeout! Many common Chinese seasonings, like soy sauce and fresh gingerroot, are inexpensive and keep well. For other Chinese-style recipes that use similar seasonings, see Asian Hoisin Ribs (page 192) and Chicken Sesame Stir-Fry (page 74).*

**1 Serving:** Calories 270; Total Fat 8g (Saturated Fat 2g, Trans Fat 0g); Cholesterol 35mg; Sodium 440mg; Total Carbohydrate 31g (Dietary Fiber 3g) • **Exchanges:** 1 Starch, ½ Other Carbohydrate, 1 Vegetable, 2 Lean Meat, ½ Fat • **Carbohydrate Choices:** 2

Prep Time **15 Minutes**

Start to Finish **15 Minutes**

**Easy**
Add-On

*Sometimes a quick rub is all it takes to jazz up the taste of pork chops! Try it on grilled chicken breasts for another Cuban-style dinner.*

# Cuban Pork Chops

### CUBAN RUB

1 clove garlic

2 tablespoons grated lime peel

1 tablespoon cracked black pepper

1 tablespoon cumin seed

2 tablespoons olive or vegetable oil

½ teaspoon salt

### PORK

4 boneless pork loin or rib chops, about 1 inch thick (about 2 lb), trimmed of fat

### GARNISH, IF DESIRED

Mango slices

1 Heat gas or charcoal grill. In small bowl, mix rub ingredients; rub evenly on both sides of pork.

2 Place pork on grill over medium heat. Cover grill; cook 8 to 10 minutes, turning frequently, until pork is no longer pink and meat thermometer inserted in center reads 160°F. Garnish with mango slices.

**4 servings**

**1 Serving:** Calories 420; Total Fat 24g (Saturated Fat 7g, Trans Fat 0g); Cholesterol 140mg; Sodium 380mg; Total Carbohydrate 2g (Dietary Fiber 0g) • **Exchanges:** 7 Lean Meat, 1 Fat • **Carbohydrate Choices:** 0

# Pork Chops and Apples

1 medium unpeeled apple, such as
Braeburn, Rome Beauty or Granny
Smith, quartered

2 tablespoons packed brown sugar

¼ teaspoon ground cinnamon

2 pork rib chops, ½ to ¾ inch thick
(about ¼ lb each)

1 Heat oven to 350°F. Cut each apple quarter into 3 or 4 wedges. Place
wedges in 1½-quart casserole. Sprinkle with brown sugar and cinnamon.

2 Remove fat from pork chops, if necessary, and discard. Spray 8-inch or
10-inch skillet with cooking spray, and heat over medium heat 1 to
2 minutes. Cook pork chops in hot skillet about 5 minutes, turning once,
until light brown.

3 Place pork in single layer on apples. Cover with lid or foil; bake about
45 minutes or until the pork is no longer pink in center and apples are
tender when pierced with a fork. (For pork chops that are ¾ inch thick,
meat thermometer inserted in center should read 160°F.)

**2 servings**

Instant
## Success!

*Pork chops and apples
make a perfect pair
in this easy dinner
that's just enough
for two. Nice side
dish choices would be
sautéed or steamed
green beans or broccoli,
along with mashed
or baked potatoes.*

**1 Serving:** Calories 260; Total Fat 9g (Saturated Fat 3g, Trans Fat 0g); Cholesterol 65mg; Sodium 45mg; Total Carbohydrate 23g
(Dietary Fiber 2g) • **Exchanges:** ½ Fruit, 1 Other Carbohydrate, 3 Lean Meat • **Carbohydrate Choices:** 1½

# Southwestern Grilled Pork Chops with Peach Salsa

Prep Time **25 Minutes**
Start to Finish **25 Minutes**

SALSA

3 ripe medium peaches, peeled, chopped (about 1½ cups)

¼ cup finely chopped red bell pepper

2 tablespoons finely chopped red onion

1 tablespoon chopped fresh cilantro

2 teaspoons packed brown sugar

2 teaspoons fresh lime juice

¼ teaspoon finely chopped serrano or jalapeño chile

PORK CHOPS

1 tablespoon chili powder

4 bone-in pork loin chops, ½ inch thick (4 oz each)

1  Heat gas or charcoal grill. In medium bowl, mix salsa ingredients; set aside.

2  Rub chili powder on both sides of each pork chop. Place pork on grill over medium heat. Cover grill; cook 6 to 9 minutes, turning once, until pork is no longer pink in center. Serve pork chops topped with salsa, or serve salsa on the side.

**4 servings**

## Easy Add-On

*These restaurant-style pork chops are easy to grill up in your backyard, and the fresh peach salsa takes just minutes to make. Serve extra salsa with a bowl of tortilla chips, or spoon over baguette slices spread with cream cheese for an easy appetizer.*

**1 Serving:** Calories 180; Total Fat 7g (Saturated Fat 2g, Trans Fat 0g); Cholesterol 50mg; Sodium 50mg; Total Carbohydrate 11g (Dietary Fiber 2g) • **Exchanges:** 1 Other Carbohydrate, 2½ Lean Meat • **Carbohydrate Choices:** 1

# Barbecued Ribs

RIBS

4 ½ lb pork spareribs

SPICY BARBECUE SAUCE

⅓ cup butter or margarine

2 tablespoons white vinegar

2 tablespoons water

1 teaspoon granulated sugar

½ teaspoon garlic powder

½ teaspoon onion powder

½ teaspoon pepper

Dash of ground red pepper (cayenne)

1 Heat oven to 325°F. Cut ribs into 6 serving pieces. Place ribs, meaty sides down, in shallow roasting pan, about 13 × 9 inches. Bake uncovered 1 hour.

2 Meanwhile, in 1-quart saucepan, heat sauce ingredients over medium heat, stirring frequently, until butter is melted. (Or microwave sauce ingredients in 1-cup microwavable measuring cup on High about 30 seconds or until butter is melted.)

3 Brush sauce over ribs, using pastry brush. Turn ribs over, using tongs. Brush meaty sides of ribs with sauce.

4 Bake uncovered about 45 minutes longer, brushing frequently with sauce, until ribs are tender and no longer pink next to bones. To serve any remaining sauce with ribs, heat sauce to boiling, stirring constantly, then continue to boil and stir 1 minute.

**6 servings**

**Slow Cooker Barbecued Ribs:** *Use 3½ lb spareribs and cut into 2- or 3-rib portions. Place ribs in 5- to 6-quart slow cooker. Sprinkle with ½ teaspoon salt and ¼ teaspoon pepper; add ½ cup water. Cover; cook on Low heat setting 8 to 9 hours or until tender. Remove ribs. Drain and discard liquid from slow cooker. Dip ribs into sauce to coat. Place ribs in slow cooker. Pour any remaining sauce over ribs. Cover; cook on Low heat setting 1 hour.*

## Easy
### Add-On

*The tangy barbecue sauce for these ribs takes just a few minutes to make from items you may already have in your pantry. If you want a spicier sauce, add a few dashes of your favorite hot sauce.*

**1 Serving:** Calories 610; Total Fat 51g (Saturated Fat 21g, Trans Fat 0.5g); Cholesterol 190mg; Sodium 200mg; Total Carbohydrate 1g (Dietary Fiber 0g) • **Exchanges:** 5½ High-Fat Meat, 1½ Fat • **Carbohydrate Choices:** 0

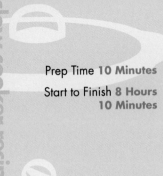

# Asian Hoisin Ribs

3 lbs pork bone-in country-style ribs

1 medium onion, sliced

½ cup hoisin sauce

⅓ cup seasoned rice vinegar

¼ cup soy sauce

1 tablespoon grated gingerroot or
1 teaspoon ground ginger

2 teaspoons sesame oil, if desired

Fresh cilantro leaves, if desired

1 Place ribs in 3½- to 4-quart slow cooker. Cover with onion slices. In small bowl, mix remaining ingredients except cilantro; pour over ribs and onion.

2 Cover and cook on Low heat setting 8 to 10 hours or until ribs are tender.

3 Remove ribs to serving platter; keep warm. Skim fat from surface of juices in cooker. Serve ribs with sauce; sprinkle with cilantro.

**4 servings**

**Simple Swaps:** *The sesame oil adds a nice subtle sesame flavor to the ribs. However, if you don't have sesame oil, sprinkle the ribs with toasted sesame seed (page 65) before serving.*

## Instant
## Success!

*Hoisin sauce is available bottled in the Asian aisle of most supermarkets, as is sesame oil. Country-style ribs are the meatiest ribs of all, and they are often on sale.*

**1 Serving:** Calories 450; Total Fat 23g (Saturated Fat 8g, Trans Fat 0g); Cholesterol 120mg; Sodium 1490mg; Total Carbohydrate 18g (Dietary Fiber 1g) • **Exchanges:** 1 Other Carbohydrate, 6 Lean Meat, 1 Fat • **Carbohydrate Choices:** 1

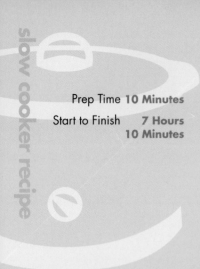

Prep Time **10 Minutes**

Start to Finish **7 Hours 10 Minutes**

# Saucy Barbecued Ribs

3½ lb pork loin back ribs or pork spareribs

½ teaspoon salt

¼ teaspoon pepper

½ cup water

1⅓ cups barbecue sauce

Chopped green onions, if desired

1 Spray inside of 5- to 6-quart slow cooker with cooking spray. Cut ribs into 2- or 3-rib portions. Place ribs in cooker. Sprinkle with salt and pepper. Pour water into cooker.

2 Cover and cook on Low heat setting 6 to 7 hours. Remove ribs from cooker; place in shallow baking pan. Drain and discard liquid from cooker.

3 Brush both sides of ribs with barbecue sauce. Return ribs to cooker. Pour any remaining sauce over ribs. Cover and cook on Low heat setting about 1 hour or until ribs are glazed and sauce is desired consistency. Sprinkle with green onions.

**6 servings**

## Make it a Meal

*These ribs get a double-cooking for twice the flavor. Loin back ribs are a good deal less expensive than baby back ribs or country-style ribs, and they benefit from long, slow cooking. Serve these with potato salad and a green vegetable.*

**1 Serving:** Calories 580; Total Fat 39g (Saturated Fat 14g, Trans Fat 0g); Cholesterol 155mg; Sodium 870mg; Total Carbohydrate 20g (Dietary Fiber 0g) • **Exchanges:** 1 Starch, 1 Vegetable, 4 High-Fat Meat, 1½ Fat • **Carbohydrate Choices:** 1

# Ham Steak with Barbecued Baked Beans

1 teaspoon vegetable oil

1 center-cut fully cooked ham steak (about 1 lb)

1 small green bell pepper, chopped (½ cup)

1 small onion, chopped (¼ cup)

1 can (16 oz) baked beans

¼ cup barbecue sauce

1  In 12-inch nonstick skillet, heat oil over medium heat. Cook ham steak in oil 6 to 8 minutes, turning once, until browned and hot. Remove steak to deep serving platter; cover to keep warm.

2  In same skillet, cook bell pepper and onion over medium heat 2 to 4 minutes, stirring frequently, until crisp-tender. Stir in beans and barbecue sauce. Heat until bubbly. Pour beans over ham.

**4 servings**

## Make it a Meal

*Any leftover ham and beans would be great reheated and served with eggs and toast for a hearty breakfast.*

**1 Serving:** Calories 330; Total Fat 11g (Saturated Fat 3.5g, Trans Fat 0g); Cholesterol 65mg; Sodium 2100mg; Total Carbohydrate 30g (Dietary Fiber 7g) • **Exchanges:** 1½ Starch, 1 Vegetable, 3 Lean Meat, ½ Fat • **Carbohydrate Choices:** 2

# Grilled Mango Ham Steak

1 tablespoon packed brown sugar

1 tablespoon butter or margarine

Dash ground cloves

1 cup refrigerated sliced mango (from 1-lb 8-oz jar), cut into desired thickness

1 ham steak, ½ inch thick (about 1¼ lb)

1 lime, cut into wedges

1 Heat gas or charcoal grill. In 1-quart saucepan, cook brown sugar, butter, cloves and mango over medium heat about 5 minutes, stirring occasionally, until mango is hot. Remove from heat; cover to keep warm.

2 Place ham on grill. Cover grill; cook over medium heat 8 to 10 minutes, turning once, until thoroughly heated.

3 Spoon mango sauce over ham. Garnish with lime wedges.

**4 servings**

## Instant
## Success!

*Mango adds a tropical, sweet flavor that tastes great with salty ham. If fresh mangoes are in season, feel free to use them (see the tip on page 124 for cutting instructions). Papaya, peaches or nectarines are a good substitute.*

**1 Serving:** Calories 320; Total Fat 16g (Saturated Fat 6g; Trans Fat 0g); Cholesterol 90mg; Sodium 2150mg; Total Carbohydrate 12g (Dietary Fiber 1g) • **Exchanges:** ½ Fruit, ½ Other Carbohydrate, 4½ Lean Meat, ½ Fat • **Carbohydrate Choices:** 1

Betty Crocker Supper in a Snap

Prep Time **20 Minutes**
Start to Finish **20 Minutes**

# Grilled Maple-Mustard Ham Steak

⅓ cup maple-flavored syrup

1 tablespoon yellow mustard

2 medium green onions, sliced (2 tablespoons)

1 ham steak, ½ inch thick (about 1¼ lb)

1 Heat gas or charcoal grill. In small bowl, mix syrup, mustard and onions. Reserve 3 tablespoons syrup mixture in separate small microwavable bowl. Brush remaining mixture on ham.

2 Place ham on grill. Cover grill; cook over medium heat 8 to 10 minutes, turning once, until browned. Microwave reserved syrup mixture uncovered on High 20 to 30 seconds or until hot. Place ham on serving platter; pour syrup mixture over ham.

**4 servings**

## Instant
## Success!

*Ham steaks, also called ham slices, are a terrific item to keep on hand for quick meals. They don't need to be gussied up, but this maple syrup and mustard glaze with a little hit of onion really hits the spot.*

**1 Serving:** Calories 290; Total Fat 11g (Saturated Fat 4g; Trans Fat 0g); Cholesterol 70mg; Sodium 1880mg; Total Carbohydrate 21g (Dietary Fiber 0g) • **Exchanges:** 1½ Other Carbohydrate, 4 Lean Meat • **Carbohydrate Choices:** 1½

# Cheesy Scalloped Potatoes with Ham

2 tablespoons butter or margarine

1 clove garlic, finely chopped

2 lb round white potatoes (about 4 medium), peeled, thinly sliced

½ lb fully cooked ham, cut into ½-inch pieces (about 2 cups)

1 cup shredded American-Cheddar cheese blend (4 oz)

3 tablespoons all-purpose flour

¼ teaspoon pepper

1 pint (2 cups) half-and-half

1  In 4-quart Dutch oven, melt butter over medium heat. Cook garlic in butter 1 minute, stirring occasionally, until softened. Remove from heat. Stir in potatoes, ham, cheese, flour and pepper.

2  Pour half-and-half over potato mixture. Heat to boiling over medium-high heat; reduce heat to low. Cover and simmer about 30 minutes, stirring occasionally, until potatoes are tender.

**6 servings (1 cup each)**

## Make it a Meal

*Cooked ham is so handy when you want to add meat to any dish—a little goes a long way! Check out the other recipes that also use cubed ham: Lemon-Basil Pasta with Ham (page 203), Ham and Wild Rice Soup (page 301) and Ham and Swiss Pizza (page 391).*

**1 Serving:** Calories 430; Total Fat 24g (Saturated Fat 13g, Trans Fat 0.5g); Cholesterol 85mg; Sodium 850mg; Total Carbohydrate 34g (Dietary Fiber 3g) • **Exchanges:** 2 Starch, 2 Medium-Fat Meat, 2½ Fat • **Carbohydrate Choices:** 2

# Ham and Cheese Ziti

1 package (16 oz) ziti pasta
(5 cups)

½ cup butter or margarine

2 cloves garlic, finely chopped

½ cup all-purpose flour

1 teaspoon salt

4 cups milk

1 teaspoon Dijon mustard

4 cups shredded Colby cheese (16 oz)

8 oz sliced cooked deli ham, cut into
thin strips

⅔ cup grated Parmesan cheese

**Easy**
Add-On

*This is a cheese lover's dream dish. You can substitute cooked sausage, turkey or chicken for the sliced ham if that's what you have on hand.*

**1** Heat oven to 350°F. Cook and drain pasta as directed on package.

**2** Meanwhile, melt butter in 4-quart saucepan or Dutch oven over low heat. Cook garlic in butter 30 seconds, stirring frequently. Stir in flour and salt, using wire whisk. Cook over medium heat, stirring constantly, until mixture is smooth and bubbly.

**3** Gradually stir in milk. Heat to boiling, stirring constantly. Boil and stir 1 minute. Stir in mustard and Colby cheese. Cook, stirring occasionally, until cheese is melted. Stir pasta and ham into cheese sauce. Pour pasta mixture into ungreased 13 × 9-inch (3-quart) glass baking dish. Sprinkle with Parmesan cheese.

**4** Bake uncovered 20 to 25 minutes or until bubbly.

**8 servings (1⅓ cups each)**

1 **Serving:** Calories 715; Total Fat 38g (Saturated Fat 23g, Trans Fat 1g); Cholesterol 120mg; Sodium 1290mg; Total Carbohydrate 58g (Dietary Fiber 2g) • **Exchanges:** 4 Starch, 2 High-Fat Meat, 3 Fat • **Carbohydrate Choices:** 4

Betty Crocker Supper in a Snap

# Lemon-Basil Pasta with Ham

Prep Time **30 Minutes**
Start to Finish **30 Minutes**

2 cups uncooked rotini pasta (6 oz)

2 cups 1-inch pieces asparagus spears

1 cup diced cooked ham

1 tablespoon grated lemon peel

1 clove garlic, finely chopped

¼ cup olive or vegetable oil

½ cup sliced fresh basil leaves

½ cup shredded Swiss cheese (2 oz)

1 Cook and drain pasta as directed on package, adding asparagus during last 3 to 4 minutes of cooking.

2 Return pasta mixture to saucepan. Stir in ham, lemon peel, garlic and oil. Cook over medium heat, stirring occasionally, until hot. Stir in basil. Sprinkle with cheese.

**4 servings**

## Budget Smart

*If you don't have fresh basil, use ⅓ cup chopped fresh parsley and add 1 teaspoon dried basil leaves. Ham, asparagus and Swiss cheese are natural partners, and the lemon zest brings them together in this appetizing, cost-conscious dish.*

**1 Serving:** Calories 410; Total Fat 22g (Saturated Fat 6g, Trans Fat 0g); Cholesterol 35mg; Sodium 710mg; Total Carbohydrate 37g (Dietary Fiber 4g) • **Exchanges:** 2 Starch, 1 Vegetable, 1½ Lean Meat, 3 Fat • **Carbohydrate Choices:** 2½

# Italian Sausage with Tomatoes and Penne

## Budget
### Smart

*Grape and cherry tomatoes can sometimes be expensive, so feel free to substitute any kind of chopped fresh tomatoes here, or use canned drained tomatoes. Either way, this summertime pasta dish is juicy, meaty and satisfying.*

3 cups uncooked penne pasta (9 oz)

1 lb uncooked Italian sausage links, cut crosswise into ¼-inch slices

½ cup beef broth

1 medium yellow summer squash, cut lengthwise in half, then cut crosswise into ¼-inch slices

2 cups grape or cherry tomatoes, cut lengthwise in half

¼ cup chopped fresh or 1 tablespoon dried basil leaves

6 green onions, cut into ½-inch pieces (½ cup)

2 tablespoons olive or vegetable oil

1  Cook and drain pasta as directed on package.

2  Meanwhile, spray 12-inch skillet with cooking spray; heat over medium-high heat. Cook sausage in skillet 4 to 6 minutes, stirring frequently, until brown. Stir in broth; reduce heat to medium. Cover and cook 5 minutes.

3  Stir in squash, tomatoes and 2 tablespoons of the basil. Heat to boiling; reduce heat to low. Cover and simmer 5 minutes, stirring occasionally. Stir in onions. Simmer uncovered 1 minute.

4  Toss pasta, oil and remaining 2 tablespoons basil. Divide pasta among individual bowls. Top with sausage mixture.

**4 servings**

1 **Serving:** Calories 590; Total Fat 31g (Saturated Fat 9g, Trans Fat 0); Cholesterol 120mg; Sodium 920mg; Total Carbohydrate 51g (Dietary Fiber 4g) • **Exchanges:** 3 Starch, 1 Vegetable, 2 High-Fat Meat, 5 Fat • **Carbohydrate Choices:** 3½

# Barbecued Beans and Polish Sausage

2 cans (15 to 16 oz each) great
   northern beans, rinsed, drained

2 cans (15 oz each) black beans,
   rinsed, drained

1 large onion, chopped (1 cup)

1 cup barbecue sauce

¼ cup packed brown sugar

1 tablespoon ground mustard

1 tablespoon Worcestershire sauce

2 teaspoons chili powder

1 ring (1 to 1¼ lbs) fully cooked smoked
   Polish sausage

1  Spray 3- to 4-quart slow cooker with cooking spray. Mix all ingredients except sausage in cooker. Place sausage ring on bean mixture.

2  Cover and cook on Low heat setting 5 to 6 hours.

**6 servings**

## Instant
## Success!

*This bean-and-sausage pot can be prepped in the time it takes the kids to get ready for school. The hearty flavors of the smoked Polish sausage, also called kielbasa, infuse the beans in this low-cost dish.*

**1 Serving:** Calories 750; Total Fat 23g (Saturated Fat 8g, Trans Fat 0.5g); Cholesterol 45mg; Sodium 1740mg; Total Carbohydrate 102g (Dietary Fiber 19g) • **Exchanges:** 7 Starch, 1½ Medium-Fat Meat • **Carbohydrate Choices:** 7

# Fettuccine with Italian Sausage and Olive Sauce

1 lb bulk Italian pork sausage

2 cans (14.5 oz each) diced tomatoes with basil, garlic and oregano, undrained

1 can (8 oz) tomato sauce

½ cup assorted small pitted olives

1 package (9 oz) refrigerated fettuccine

½ cup shredded Parmesan cheese (2 oz)

1 Heat water for cooking fettuccine to boiling. Meanwhile, in 12-inch skillet, cook sausage over medium-high heat 5 to 7 minutes, stirring occasionally, until no longer pink; drain if necessary.

2 Stir tomatoes, tomato sauce and olives into sausage. Reduce heat to low. Cover; cook 10 to 15 minutes, stirring occasionally, to blend flavors.

3 Cook and drain fettuccine as directed on package. Serve sauce over fettuccine. Sprinkle with cheese.

**4 servings**

## Instant Success!

*Hot Italian sausage is a definite option here and would go especially well with the flavor of the olives, but if you live on the "mild" side, by all means, use the mild sweet version!*

**1 Serving:** Calories 610; Total Fat 29g (Saturated Fat 10g; Trans Fat 0g); Cholesterol 75mg; Sodium 2340mg; Total Carbohydrate 57g (Dietary Fiber 3g) • **Exchanges:** 2½ Starch, 1 Other Carbohydrate, 1 Vegetable, 3 High-Fat Meat, ½ Fat • **Carbohydrate Choices:** 4

# Chile-Sausage Pasta

2 ½ cups uncooked bow-tie (farfalle) pasta (5 oz)

¾ lb mild Italian sausage links, cut into 1-inch pieces

1 can (14.5 oz) diced tomatoes and mild green chiles, undrained

1 can (8 oz) tomato sauce

1 can (15 oz) pinto beans, drained, rinsed

Chopped fresh cilantro or parsley, if desired

1   Cook and drain pasta as directed on package.

2   Meanwhile, in 12-inch nonstick skillet, cook sausage over medium heat 8 to 10 minutes, stirring occasionally, until no longer pink. Stir in tomatoes and tomato sauce. Reduce heat to medium-low. Cover; cook 5 minutes, stirring occasionally.

3   Stir in beans and pasta. Cook uncovered 3 to 5 minutes, stirring occasionally, until thoroughly heated. Sprinkle with cilantro.

**5 servings (1 ½ cups each)**

## Speed it Up

*Ready in less than 30 minutes, this straightforward pasta will delight, and there's an extra serving for a lunch tomorrow. If anyone in your group likes spicy food, put a bottle of hot sauce on the table.*

**1 Serving:** Calories 410; Total Fat 14g (Saturated Fat 4.5g, Trans Fat 0g); Cholesterol 40mg; Sodium 1090mg; Total Carbohydrate 49g (Dietary Fiber 10g) • **Exchanges:** 2 ½ Starch, ½ Other Carbohydrate, 1 Vegetable, 1 ½ High-Fat Meat • **Carbohydrate Choices:** 3

# Mac 'n Cheese Shells with Sausage

**Prep Time 25 Minutes**
**Start to Finish 25 Minutes**

3 cups reduced-sodium chicken broth (from 32-oz carton)

2 cups uncooked small pasta shells (8 oz)

1½ cups frozen baby sweet peas

½ lb smoked sausage, cut in half

lengthwise, then cut into ½-inch pieces

2 cups shredded American-Cheddar cheese blend (8 oz)

3 tablespoons grated Parmesan cheese, if desired

1  In 3-quart saucepan, heat broth to boiling over medium–high heat. Add pasta; heat to boiling. Boil 6 minutes; do not drain. Reduce heat. Stir in peas and sausage. Cover and simmer 3 to 5 minutes or until pasta is tender. Remove from heat.

2  Add American–Cheddar cheese; toss gently until cheese is melted. Sprinkle with Parmesan cheese.

**4 servings (1½ cups each)**

## Easy Add-On

*Frozen peas are not only cheaper than fresh, they're often sweeter since they're usually frozen very soon after being harvested. Keep some on hand to add color and springtime flavor to everything from pasta and rice to meat.*

**1 Serving:** Calories 570; Total Fat 25g (Saturated Fat 14g, Trans Fat 0.5g); Cholesterol 90mg; Sodium 1370mg; Total Carbohydrate 53g (Dietary Fiber 5g) • **Exchanges:** 3½ Starch, 3 High-Fat Meat, 2 Fat • **Carbohydrate Choices:** 3½

# Stove-Top Lasagna

1 lb bulk Italian sausage

1 medium green bell pepper, sliced

1 package (8 oz) sliced mushrooms (3 cups)

1 medium onion, chopped (½ cup)

3 cups uncooked mini lasagna (mafalda) noodles (6 oz)

2½ cups water

½ teaspoon Italian seasoning

1 jar (26 oz) chunky tomato pasta sauce (any variety)

1 cup shredded Italian cheese blend or mozzarella cheese (4 oz)

**1** In 12-inch skillet or 4-quart Dutch oven, cook sausage, bell pepper, mushrooms and onion over medium-high heat, stirring occasionally, until sausage is no longer pink; drain.

**2** Stir in remaining ingredients except cheese. Heat to boiling, stirring occasionally; reduce heat. Simmer uncovered about 10 minutes or until pasta is tender. Sprinkle with cheese.

**6 servings**

## Speed it Up

*Crumble, cook and drain sausage ahead to save time. Cooked and drained ground beef is a quick substitution for the sausage in this easy lasagna.*

**1 Serving:** Calories 500; Total Fat 24g (Saturated Fat 9g; Trans Fat 0g); Cholesterol 60mg; Sodium 1260mg; Total Carbohydrate 50g (Dietary Fiber 5g) • **Exchanges:** 2½ Starch, 1 Other Carbohydrate, 2 High-Fat Meat, 1 Fat • **Carbohydrate Choices:** 3

# 4 fish & seafood

## Add Dessert

*A dish of ice cream can satisfy, but for nearly effortless "oohs and aahs," express yourself in a new way. Here's how.*

1 **Brownie Volcanoes:** Cut brownies into 1- to 1½-inch squares and mound in individual shallow serving bowls to resemble a volcano. Drizzle with ice cream toppings, and top with whipped topping and a cherry.

2 **Double-Chocolate Truffles:** Drizzle warm hot fudge topping in a zigzag pattern on very small individual serving plates; place a purchased truffle in the center of the plate. Garnish with a few fresh raspberries or slices of strawberry if desired, or dust very, very lightly with unsweetened baking cocoa or powdered sugar.

3 **Puddin' Parfaits:** Alternate layers of purchased ready-to-eat pudding with crushed cookie crumbs and whipped topping. Top with gummy worms for extra fun.

4 **Yogurt, Fruit and Granola Parfaits:** Alternate layers of yogurt with fresh or canned fruit and granola or crushed cereal.

5 **Elegant Orange-Kiwifruit:** On a serving platter or individual serving plates, arrange sliced oranges and kiwifruit; drizzle with warm caramel or chocolate topping, and sprinkle with toasted sliced almonds.

6 **Heavenly Angel Food:** Make a box of regular (not instant) vanilla pudding with half-and-half or whipping cream instead of milk. Serve warm over purchased angel food cake slices; garnish with fresh fruit if desired.

7 **Caramel Apple Pie with Toasted Pecans:** Serve warm slices of purchased apple pie with warmed caramel topping and toasted pecan halves. Add vanilla or cinnamon ice cream if you must! If you're baking a frozen pie or warming a prebaked pie, toast the pecans at the same time; they take about 6 to 10 minutes.

8 **Sorbet Trio:** Purchase three different kinds of sorbet, like mango, raspberry and lemon. Place scoop of each flavor in small individual serving bowls; serve with fancy store-bought cookies like pirouettes.

9 **Paradise Pineapple:** In a shallow baking dish, arrange fresh or canned pineapple slices (look for peeled and cored whole fresh pineapple in the produce aisle); pat dry with paper towels. Sprinkle with brown sugar and a little cinnamon. Broil with tops 4 to 6 inches from heat just until brown sugar becomes bubbly. Sprinkle with coconut. Serve with whipped cream or vanilla ice cream if desired.

10 **Lemon Shortcake Cups:** Mix equal amounts of whipped topping or whipped cream with canned lemon pie filling; spoon into purchased sponge-type shortcake cups. Top with fresh blueberries.

# Basil Salmon and Julienne Vegetables

1 tablespoon butter or margarine

1 bag (1 lb) frozen bell pepper and onion stir-fry

1 medium zucchini, cut into julienne (matchstick-size) strips

1½ lb salmon fillets, about ½ inch thick, cut into 4 serving pieces

2 tablespoons chopped fresh basil leaves

½ teaspoon seasoned salt

1 teaspoon lemon-pepper seasoning

¼ cup chicken broth

1 In 12-inch nonstick skillet, melt butter over medium heat. Add bell pepper mixture. Cook and stir 2 minutes. Stir in zucchini.

2 Place fish, skin side down, in skillet, pushing down into vegetables if necessary. Sprinkle fish and vegetables with basil, seasoned salt and lemon-pepper seasoning. Pour broth over fish and vegetables.

3 Cover; cook over medium-low heat 8 to 10 minutes or until fish flakes easily with fork. Remove fish and vegetables from skillet with slotted spoon.

**4 servings**

## Instant
## Success!

*Make short work of cutting up the zucchini with this technique. Cut the whole "zuke" crosswise into 2- to 3-inch sections. Then, stand a section on its end and cut it from top to bottom into ⅛-inch slices. Next, lay the slices flat, stack them, and cut the stack lengthwise into ⅛-inch match-like sticks.*

**1 Serving:** Calories 320; Total Fat 13g (Saturated Fat 4.5g; Trans Fat 0g); Cholesterol 120mg; Sodium 450mg; Total Carbohydrate 12g (Dietary Fiber 2g) • **Exchanges:** ½ Other Carbohydrate, 1 Vegetable, 5 Lean Meat • **Carbohydrate Choices:** 1

# Grilled Salmon with Nectarine Salsa

2 lb salmon fillets, about ½ inch thick, cut into 6 serving pieces

½ cup lemon juice

4 medium nectarines or peaches,

chopped

½ cup chopped fresh cilantro

2 teaspoons chopped jalapeño chile

1 Heat gas or charcoal grill.

2 Place fish, skin side down, on grill; drizzle with ¼ cup lemon juice Cover grill; cook over medium heat 10 to 20 minutes or until fish flakes easily with fork.

3 In medium bowl, mix remaining ingredients and remaining ¼ cup lemon juice. Serve nectarine salsa over fish.

**6 servings**

## Make it a Meal

*An easy spinach salad goes perfectly with this sweet 'n' succulent dish. Just open a bag of washed fresh baby spinach leaves, toss in some raisins, sliced mushrooms and maybe a few chopped nuts, and voilà!*

**1 Serving:** Calories 260; Total Fat 9g (Saturated Fat 2.5g; Trans Fat 0g); Cholesterol 100mg; Sodium 95mg; Total Carbohydrate 11g (Dietary Fiber 2g) • **Exchanges:** ½ Fruit, 4½ Lean Meat • **Carbohydrate Choices:** 1

Betty Crocker Supper in a Snap

# Baked Salmon with Cilantro

Prep Time **5 Minutes**

Start to Finish **25 Minutes**

Cooking spray

¼ cup butter or margarine, slightly softened

1 tablespoon chopped fresh cilantro

½ teaspoon grated lemon peel

1½ lb salmon, red snapper or other medium-firm fish fillets, about 1 inch thick, cut into 4 serving pieces

¼ teaspoon salt

¼ teaspoon ground cumin

1 tablespoon lemon juice

1 Heat oven to 425°F. Line 13 × 9-inch pan with foil; spray foil with cooking spray. In small bowl, mix butter, cilantro and lemon peel. Cover butter; refrigerate while preparing fish.

2 Place fish, skin side down, in pan. Sprinkle with salt and cumin. Drizzle with lemon juice.

3 Bake 15 to 20 minutes or until fish flakes easily with fork. Carefully lift fish from skin with pancake turner. Top each serving of fish with butter mixture.

**4 servings**

## Make it a Meal

*Having people over? The recipe is easy to double. Serve the salmon on a bed of angel hair pasta or skin-on mashed potatoes (look for the new refrigerated ready-to-eat varieties) on a pretty serving platter. Garnish the platter with cilantro sprigs and slices of lemon.*

**1 Serving:** Calories 340; Total Fat 21g (Saturated Fat 10g; Trans Fat 0.5g); Cholesterol 140mg; Sodium 330mg; Total Carbohydrate 0g (Dietary Fiber 0g) • **Exchanges:** 5 Lean Meat, 1½ Fat • **Carbohydrate Choices:** 0

# Grilled Maple-Dijon Salmon and Asparagus Salad

DRESSING

⅓ cup maple-flavored syrup

2 tablespoons Dijon mustard

2 tablespoons olive or vegetable oil

SALAD

1 lb asparagus spears

1½ lb salmon fillets, about ½ inch thick,
    cut into 4 serving pieces

4 cups fresh baby salad greens

1 cup shredded carrots (about 2 medium)

2 hard-cooked eggs, cut into 8 wedges

Freshly ground pepper, if desired

1 Heat gas or charcoal grill. In small bowl, mix all dressing ingredients with wire whisk.

2 Break off tough ends of asparagus as far down as stalks snap easily. Brush fish with 1 tablespoon of the dressing. In 11 × 7-inch glass baking dish, toss asparagus and 1 tablespoon of the dressing. Place asparagus in grill basket (grill "wok").

3 Place grill basket and fish, skin side down, on grill. Cover grill; cook asparagus over medium heat 7 to 10 minutes, shaking grill basket or turning asparagus occasionally, until crisp-tender; cook fish 10 to 15 minutes or until fish flakes easily with fork.

4 Slide pancake turner between fish and skin to remove each piece from skin. Among 4 plates, divide salad greens, carrots and eggs. Top with fish and asparagus. Sprinkle with pepper. Serve with remaining dressing.

**4 servings**

## Instant
## Success!

*Too hot for a hot salad? Try it cold. Grill the salmon and asparagus, cook the eggs and make the dressing up to one day ahead of time. Cover and refrigerate until serving.*

**1 Serving:** Calories 420; Total Fat 19g (Saturated Fat 4g; Trans Fat 0g); Cholesterol 200mg; Sodium 370mg; Total Carbohydrate 27g (Dietary Fiber 3g) • **Exchanges:** 1 Other Carbohydrate, 2 Vegetable, 4½ Lean Meat, 1 Fat • **Carbohydrate Choices:** 2

# Orange and Dill Pan-Seared Tuna

1 tablespoon butter or margarine

1 tablespoon olive or vegetable oil

1½ lb tuna, swordfish or other firm fish steaks, about ¾ inch thick, cut into 4 serving pieces

1 teaspoon peppered seasoned salt

½ cup thinly sliced red onion

¾ cup orange juice

1 tablespoon chopped fresh or ¼ teaspoon dried dill weed

1 tablespoon butter or margarine

1 teaspoon grated orange peel, if desired

1  In 10-inch nonstick skillet, heat 1 tablespoon butter and the oil over medium-high heat. Sprinkle both sides of fish with peppered seasoned salt. Add fish to skillet; cook about 1 minute on each side until golden brown. Reduce heat to medium-low. Cook 3 to 4 minutes longer, turning once, until fish flakes easily with fork (tuna steaks will also be slightly pink in center). Remove fish from skillet; keep warm.

2  Add onion to skillet. Cook over medium heat 2 minutes, stirring occasionally. Stir in orange juice; cook 2 minutes. Stir in dill weed, 1 tablespoon butter and the orange peel. Cook 1 to 2 minutes or until slightly thickened. Serve sauce over fish.

**4 servings**

## Make it a Meal

*Fresh green beans or asparagus and lightly buttered new potatoes pair well with this citrus-flavored fish. For a stylish, easy garnish, use orange slices and dill sprigs.*

**1 Serving:** Calories 320; Total Fat 18g (Saturated Fat 7g; Trans Fat 0g); Cholesterol 115mg; Sodium 480mg; Total Carbohydrate 7g (Dietary Fiber 0g) • **Exchanges:** ½ Other Carbohydrate, 4½ Very Lean Meat, 3 Fat • **Carbohydrate Choices:** ½

# Grilled Teriyaki Tuna Salad

DRESSING

½ cup pineapple juice

¼ cup teriyaki baste and glaze
(from 12-oz bottle)

1 tablespoon sesame oil

¼ teaspoon ground ginger

SALAD

12 pieces (1½ inches each) fresh
pineapple (2 cups)

1½ lb tuna steaks, about ¾ inch thick,
cut into 4 serving pieces

4 cups bite-size pieces mixed salad
greens

1 cup grape or cherry tomatoes, cut in
half

1 small red onion, sliced and separated
into rings

½ cup sesame oat bran sticks or croutons

1 Spray grill rack with cooking spray. Heat gas or charcoal grill. In small
bowl, mix all dressing ingredients with wire whisk; reserve 2 tablespoons.

2 On each of 2 (10-inch) metal skewers, thread pineapple, leaving ¼-inch
space between each piece. Brush 1 tablespoon of the reserved dressing on
pineapple; brush remaining 1 tablespoon reserved dressing on fish.

3 Place fish on grill. Cover grill; cook over medium heat about
10 minutes, turning once and adding pineapple for last 5 minutes of
grilling, until fish flakes easily with fork.

4 Among 4 plates, divide salad greens, tomatoes and onion. Top with
pineapple and tuna. Sprinkle with sesame sticks. Serve with remaining
dressing.

**4 servings**

## Instant Success!

*Keeping a few bastes
in your pantry
lets you grill at a
moment's notice. One
of the most versatile
is teriyaki baste and
glaze; it has a thick,
syruplike consistency
and shouldn't be
confused with teriyaki
marinade or sauce,
which is more watery.
If you like, use stir-fry
sauce instead, but look
for a thicker brand.*

**1 Serving:** Calories 420; Total Fat 15g (Saturated Fat 3.5g; Trans Fat 0g); Cholesterol 100mg; Sodium 710mg; Total
Carbohydrate 35g (Dietary Fiber 4g) • **Exchanges:** ½ Starch, 1 Fruit, ½ Other Carbohydrate, 1 Vegetable, 4½ Very Lean Meat,
2½ Fat • **Carbohydrate Choices:** 2

# Grilled Lemon-Garlic Halibut Steaks

## **Make** it a **Meal**

*Light and easy is the name of the game here. If you have a grill basket (grill "wok"), grill some snow peas for a crisp refreshing side. Or cook them till crisp-tender in boiling water.*

¼ cup lemon juice

1 tablespoon olive or vegetable oil

¼ teaspoon salt

¼ teaspoon pepper

2 cloves garlic, finely chopped

2 lb halibut or tuna steaks, about ¾ inch thick, cut into 4 serving pieces

¼ cup chopped fresh parsley

1 tablespoon grated lemon peel

1 Brush grill rack with vegetable oil. Heat gas or charcoal grill. In shallow glass or plastic dish or resealable food-storage plastic bag, mix lemon juice, oil, salt, pepper and garlic. Add fish; turn several times to coat. Cover dish or seal bag; refrigerate 10 minutes to marinate.

2 Remove fish from marinade; reserve marinade. Place fish on grill. Cover grill; cook over medium heat 10 to 15 minutes, turning once and brushing with marinade, until fish flakes easily with fork (tuna steaks will also be slightly pink in center). Discard any remaining marinade.

3 Sprinkle fish with parsley and lemon peel.

**4 servings**

**1 Serving:** Calories 240; Total Fat 6g (Saturated Fat 1g; Trans Fat 0g); Cholesterol 120mg; Sodium 340mg; Total Carbohydrate 2g (Dietary Fiber 0g) • **Exchanges:** 6 Very Lean Meat, ½ Fat • **Carbohydrate Choices:** 0

# Grilled Latin Halibut with Green Sauce

2½ lb halibut or sea bass steaks, about ¾ inch thick, cut into 6 serving pieces

1 tablespoon olive or vegetable oil

1 teaspoon seasoned salt

1 jar (16 oz) green salsa (salsa verde) (2 cups)

1 ripe avocado, pitted, peeled and chopped

2 tablespoons chopped ripe olives

Sour cream, if desired

Fresh cilantro leaves, if desired

**1** Heat gas or charcoal grill. Brush fish lightly with oil; sprinkle with seasoned salt.

**2** Place fish on grill. Cover grill; cook over medium-high heat about 10 minutes, turning once, until fish flakes easily with fork.

**3** In medium bowl, mix salsa, avocado and olives. Serve over fish. Garnish with sour cream and cilantro.

**6 servings**

## Instant **Success!**

*Even though green salsa is becoming more mainstream, tomato salsa is readily available and a wonderful alternative. Add olives and fresh avocados to the salsa for extra flair.*

**1 Serving:** Calories 270; Total Fat 10g (Saturated Fat 1.5g; Trans Fat 0g); Cholesterol 100mg; Sodium 480mg; Total Carbohydrate 8g (Dietary Fiber 3g) • **Exchanges:** ½ Other Carbohydrate, 5 Very Lean Meat, 1½ Fat • **Carbohydrate Choices:** ½

# Gremolata-Topped Sea Bass

Cooking spray

¼ cup Italian-style dry bread crumbs

¼ cup chopped fresh parsley

2 teaspoons grated lemon peel

1 tablespoon butter or margarine, melted

1 lb sea bass, mahi-mahi or other medium-firm fish fillets, cut into 4 serving pieces

¼ teaspoon seasoned salt

1 tablespoon lemon juice

1 Heat oven to 425°F. Line 13 × 9-inch pan with foil; spray foil with cooking spray. In small bowl, mix bread crumbs, parsley, lemon peel and butter.

2 Place fish in pan. Sprinkle with seasoned salt. Drizzle with lemon juice. Spoon crumb mixture over each piece; press lightly.

3 Bake 15 to 20 minutes or until fish flakes easily with fork.

**4 servings**

## Instant
## Success!

*It almost takes less time to assemble than it takes to say "gremolata." This zesty citrus-flavored breading also makes a great topping for broiled lamb chops.*

**1 Serving:** Calories 180; Total Fat 8g (Saturated Fat 3g; Trans Fat 0g); Cholesterol 65mg; Sodium 290mg; Total Carbohydrate 6g (Dietary Fiber 0g) • **Exchanges:** ½ Starch, 3 Very Lean Meat, 1 Fat • **Carbohydrate Choices:** ½

# Brown Butter Fish Florentine

¼ cup all-purpose flour

1 lb tilapia fillets, about ½ inch thick, cut into 4 serving pieces

½ teaspoon salt

1 teaspoon lemon-pepper seasoning

¼ cup butter*

1 bag (9 oz) washed fresh baby spinach leaves

½ red bell pepper, cut into thin slivers

¼ cup slivered almonds, toasted**

1  In shallow dish, place flour. Sprinkle fish with salt and lemon-pepper seasoning; dip in flour to coat.

2  In 12-inch nonstick skillet, heat butter over medium heat 3 to 4 minutes, stirring constantly, until light golden brown. Add fish. Cook 6 to 8 minutes, turning once, until outside is browned and fish flakes easily with fork. Remove to plate; cover to keep warm.

3  Add spinach and bell pepper to butter in skillet. Cook 2 to 4 minutes, stirring frequently, until tender. On 4 dinner plates, spoon spinach mixture; top with fish. Sprinkle with almonds.

**4 servings**

*Do not use margarine or spreads.

**To toast nuts, bake uncovered in ungreased shallow pan in 350°F oven 6 to 10 minutes, stirring occasionally, until light brown. Or cook in ungreased heavy skillet over medium heat 5 to 7 minutes, stirring frequently until browning begins, then stirring constantly until golden brown.

## Make it a Meal

*Superb, elegant and extremely simple! The browned butter flavor will knock your socks off. You don't want to waste even a tiny drop of the butter, so serve the fish and vegetables over angel hair pasta to soak it up.*

**1 Serving:** Calories 300; Total Fat 17g (Saturated Fat 8g; Trans Fat 0.5g); Cholesterol 90mg; Sodium 610mg; Total Carbohydrate 11g (Dietary Fiber 3g) • **Exchanges:** ½ Starch, 1 Vegetable, 3 Lean Meat, 1½ Fat • **Carbohydrate Choices:** 1

# Crispy Herbed Fish Fillets

1 lb flounder fillets, about ½ inch thick, cut into 4 serving pieces

2 eggs

1¼ cups panko bread crumbs

1 teaspoon grated lemon peel

1 teaspoon dried marjoram leaves

½ teaspoon salt

¼ teaspoon pepper

¼ cup olive or vegetable oil

1 Dry fish well on paper towels. In shallow dish, beat eggs with fork or wire whisk until well mixed. In another shallow dish, mix bread crumbs, lemon peel, marjoram, salt and pepper.

2 In 12-inch nonstick skillet, heat 2 tablespoons of the oil over medium heat. Dip fish in eggs, then coat well with crumb mixture. Add about half of the fish in single layer to oil. Cook 3 to 4 minutes, carefully turning once, until outside is browned and crisp and fish flakes easily with fork.

3 Remove cooked fish to plate; cover to keep warm. Repeat with remaining oil and fish.

**4 servings**

## Instant
## Success!

*Panko, or Japanese bread crumbs, are coarse in texture. Once you try panko, you'll be hooked—they're crunchier and make a more attractive coating!*

**1 Serving:** Calories 310; Total Fat 17g (Saturated Fat 3g; Trans Fat 0g); Cholesterol 160mg; Sodium 440mg; Total Carbohydrate 14g (Dietary Fiber 0g) • **Exchanges:** 1 Starch, 3 Very Lean Meat, 3 Fat • **Carbohydrate Choices:** 1

# Lemony Fish over Vegetables and Rice

1 box (6 oz) fried rice (rice and vermicelli mix with almonds and Oriental seasonings)

2 tablespoons butter or margarine

2 cups water

½ teaspoon grated lemon peel

1 bag (1 lb) frozen broccoli, corn and peppers (or other combination)

1 lb cod, haddock or other mild-flavored fish fillets, about ½ inch thick, cut into 4 serving pieces

½ teaspoon lemon-pepper seasoning

1 tablespoon lemon juice

Chopped fresh parsley, if desired

1 In 12-inch nonstick skillet, cook rice and butter over medium heat about 3 minutes, stirring occasionally, until rice is golden brown. Stir in water, seasoning packet from rice mix and lemon peel. Heat to boiling; reduce heat to low. Cover; simmer 10 minutes.

2 Stir in frozen vegetables. Heat to boiling over medium-high heat, stirring occasionally. Arrange fish on rice mixture. Sprinkle fish with lemon–pepper seasoning; drizzle with lemon juice.

3 Reduce heat to low. Cover; simmer 8 to 12 minutes or until fish flakes easily with fork and vegetables are tender. Sprinkle with parsley.

**4 servings**

## Make it a Meal

*What could be easier than making a meal in one skillet? (Well, maybe pizza delivery.) Add a salad kit or bagged greens and your favorite dressing and dinner is a go!*

**1 Serving:** Calories 250; Total Fat 8g (Saturated Fat 4g; Trans Fat 0g); Cholesterol 75mg; Sodium 620mg; Total Carbohydrate 19g (Dietary Fiber 3g) • **Exchanges:** 1 Starch, 1 Vegetable, 3 Very Lean Meat, 1 Fat • **Carbohydrate Choices:** 1

# Grilled Herbed Seafood

8 oz uncooked thin spaghetti or vermicelli

Cooking spray

½ lb bay scallops

½ lb orange roughy fillets, cut into 1-inch pieces

½ lb uncooked deveined peeled large shrimp, thawed if frozen, tail shells removed

2 tablespoons chopped fresh or 2 teaspoons dried marjoram leaves

½ teaspoon grated lemon peel

⅛ teaspoon white pepper

3 tablespoons butter or margarine, melted

2 tablespoons lemon juice

1 Heat gas or charcoal grill. Cook and drain spaghetti as directed on package.

2 Meanwhile, cut 18-inch square of heavy-duty foil; spray with cooking spray. On center of foil square, arrange scallops, fish and shrimp, placing shrimp on top. Sprinkle with marjoram, lemon peel and white pepper. Drizzle with butter and lemon juice. Bring corners of foil up to center and seal loosely.

3 Place packet on grill. Cover grill; cook over medium heat 8 to 10 minutes, rotating packet ½ turn after 5 minutes, until scallops are white, fish flakes easily with fork and shrimp are pink. Serve seafood mixture over spaghetti.

**4 servings**

## Instant
## Success!

*Cooking rice in chicken broth instead of water gives it lots of extra flavor without adding extra time or effort; in fact, "chicken rice" is a great alternative to white rice anytime. And the trick works for other starches, too, like couscous.*

**1 Serving:** Calories 420; Total Fat 11g (Saturated Fat 6g; Trans Fat 0.5g); Cholesterol 150mg; Sodium 510mg; Total Carbohydrate 46g (Dietary Fiber 3g) • **Exchanges:** 3 Starch, 3½ Very Lean Meat, 1½ Fat • **Carbohydrate Choices:** 3

# Seafood Rice Skillet

1 tablespoon olive or vegetable oil

1 medium onion, chopped (½ cup)

1 can (14 oz) chicken broth

1 cup uncooked medium or long-grain white rice

1 cup ready-to-eat baby-cut carrots, cut in half lengthwise

½ cup water

½ teaspoon garlic-pepper blend

2 cups washed fresh baby spinach leaves

1 package (8 oz) refrigerated imitation crabmeat chunks

¼ cup shredded Parmesan cheese (1 oz)

1 In 12-inch nonstick skillet, heat oil over medium-high heat. Cook onion in oil 2 to 3 minutes, stirring occasionally, until crisp-tender. Stir in broth; heat to boiling. Stir in rice; reduce heat. Cover; simmer 10 minutes without stirring.

2 Stir in carrots, water and garlic-pepper blend. Cover; simmer 8 to 10 minutes without stirring until rice is tender.

3 Stir in spinach until wilted. Stir in imitation crabmeat and cheese.

**4 servings**

## Instant
## Success!

*Cooking rice in chicken broth instead of water gives it lots of extra flavor without adding extra time or effort; in fact, "chicken rice" is a great alternative to white rice anytime. And the trick works for other starches, too, like couscous.*

**1 Serving:** Calories 340; Total Fat 7g (Saturated Fat 2g; Trans Fat 0g); Cholesterol 25mg; Sodium 1060mg; Total Carbohydrate 50g (Dietary Fiber 2g) • **Exchanges:** 3 Starch, 1 Vegetable, 1 Very Lean Meat, 1 Fat • **Carbohydrate Choices:** 3

# Caesar Shri

4 cups uncooked medium p
(10 oz)

1 cup shredded Parm

1 cup reduced-fa
dressing

8 mediu

Prep Time **25 Minutes**
Start to Finish **25 Minutes**

# mp Salad

...asta shells

...esan cheese (4 oz)

...creamy Caesar

...green onions, sliced (½ cup)

1 ½ lb frozen cooked deveined peeled shrimp, thawed, drained and tail shells removed

1 bag (10 oz) ready-to-eat romaine lettuce (7 cups)

2 cups Caesar-flavored croutons

**1** Cook and drain pasta as directed on package. Rinse with cold water; drain.

**2** In very large (4-quart) bowl, place pasta, cheese, dressing, onions and shrimp; toss. Just before serving, add lettuce and croutons; toss.

**8 servings (2 cups each)**

## Make it a Meal

*Crisp breadsticks are perfect with this salad. The cracker aisle usually has plain and flavored versions that are either long and skinny or shorter and a bit wider.*

**1 Serving:** Calories 370; Total Fat 9g (Saturated Fat 3.5g; Trans Fat 0.5g); Cholesterol 180mg; Sodium 1000mg; Total Carbohydrate 42g (Dietary Fiber 4g) • **Exchanges:** 2 Starch, ½ Other Carbohydrate, 1 Vegetable, 3 Very Lean Meat, 1 Fat • **Carbohydrate Choices:** 3

# Scampi with Fettuccine

8 oz uncooked fettuccine

2 tablespoons olive or vegetable oil

1½ lb uncooked deveined peeled medium shrimp, thawed if frozen, tail shells removed

2 medium green onions, thinly sliced (2 tablespoons)

2 cloves garlic, finely chopped

1 tablespoon chopped fresh or ½ teaspoon dried basil leaves

1 tablespoon chopped fresh parsley

2 tablespoons lemon juice

¼ teaspoon salt

**1** Cook and drain fettuccine as directed on package. Meanwhile, in 10-inch skillet, heat oil over medium heat. Cook remaining ingredients in oil 2 to 3 minutes, stirring frequently, until shrimp are pink; remove from heat.

**2** Toss fettuccine with shrimp mixture in skillet.

**4 servings**

## Speed it Up

*Peeling and deveining shrimp is time consuming—and unnecessary! Luckily for us, somebody else has done this laborious task. Look for fresh or frozen shrimp that has already been peeled and deveined.*

**1 Serving:** Calories 380; Total Fat 10g (Saturated Fat 1.5g; Trans Fat 0g); Cholesterol 290mg; Sodium 670mg; Total Carbohydrate 38g (Dietary Fiber 2g) • **Exchanges:** 2½ Starch, 3½ Very Lean Meat, 1½ Fat • **Carbohydrate Choices:** 2½

# Marinara Shrimp and Vegetable Bowls

8 oz uncooked vermicelli

1 tablespoon olive or vegetable oil

2 cloves garlic, finely chopped

½ cup red onion wedges

1 medium zucchini, cut into 2 × ¼-inch strips

1 medium yellow summer squash, cut into 2 × ¼-inch strips

¼ teaspoon salt

1 lb uncooked deveined peeled medium or large shrimp, thawed if frozen, tail shells removed

1 cup marinara sauce

2 tablespoons chopped fresh or ½ teaspoon dried basil leaves

1 Cook and drain vermicelli as directed on package. Meanwhile, in 10-inch skillet, heat oil over medium heat. Cook garlic and onion in oil 2 to 3 minutes, stirring frequently, until onion is crisp-tender. Stir in zucchini, yellow squash and salt. Cook 2 to 3 minutes, stirring frequently, just until squash is tender; remove vegetables from skillet.

2 Add shrimp to skillet. Cook over medium heat 1 to 2 minutes, stirring frequently, until shrimp are pink. Meanwhile, in 1-quart saucepan, heat marinara sauce over medium heat, stirring occasionally, until hot.

3 Among 4 bowls, divide vermicelli; toss each serving with about 2 tablespoons marinara sauce. Top with vegetables and shrimp. Drizzle with remaining marinara sauce. Sprinkle with basil.

**4 servings**

## Speed it Up

*Here's a recipe where dovetailing—that is, making several parts of the recipe at once—saves loads of time. While the pasta water comes to a boil, start chopping the veggies. Then while the pasta cooks, start the shrimp and heat the marinara sauce. Dinner will be ready 1-2-3!*

**1 Serving:** Calories 430; Total Fat 8g (Saturated Fat 1g; Trans Fat 0g); Cholesterol 160mg; Sodium 880mg; Total Carbohydrate 63g (Dietary Fiber 6g) • **Exchanges:** 3½ Starch, ½ Other Carbohydrate, 1 Vegetable, 2 Very Lean Meat, 1 Fat • **Carbohydrate Choices:** 4

Prep Time **20 Minutes**

Start to Finish **20 Minutes**

# Shrimp Alfredo Primavera

3 cups uncooked bow-tie (farfalle) pasta (6 oz)

2 slices bacon, cut into ½-inch pieces

1½ cups frozen sweet peas (from 1-lb bag)

¼ cup water

1 lb uncooked deveined peeled medium shrimp, thawed if frozen, tail shells removed

¾ cup refrigerated Alfredo sauce (from 10-oz container)

2 tablespoons chopped fresh chives

## Instant
## Success!

*Using refrigerated Alfredo sauce is only one option—the jarred version can be used instead, or lighten up if you wish by using the reduced-fat version of this creamy, cheesy sauce.*

1 Cook and drain pasta as directed on package.

2 Meanwhile, in 12-inch nonstick skillet, cook bacon over medium heat 4 to 5 minutes, stirring occasionally, until crisp. Stir in peas; cook 2 minutes, stirring occasionally. Add water; cover and cook 3 to 5 minutes or until peas are tender and water has evaporated. Add shrimp; cook 2 to 3 minutes, stirring occasionally, until shrimp are pink.

3 Stir in Alfredo sauce and pasta. Cook over medium-low heat, stirring occasionally, until thoroughly heated. Sprinkle with chives.

**4 servings**

**1 Serving:** Calories 450; Total Fat 18g (Saturated Fat 10g; Trans Fat 0.5g); Cholesterol 210mg; Sodium 650mg; Total Carbohydrate 43g (Dietary Fiber 4g) • **Exchanges:** 2 Starch, 1 Other Carbohydrate, 3 Very Lean Meat, 3 Fat • **Carbohydrate Choices:** 3

# Linguine with Tuna and Tomatoes

8 oz uncooked linguine

½ cup crumbled feta cheese (2 oz)

2 cups cherry tomatoes, quartered, or coarsely chopped tomatoes

1 can (12 oz) water-packed white tuna, drained, flaked

2 tablespoons chopped fresh parsley

2 tablespoons olive, canola or soybean oil

1 clove garlic, finely chopped

¼ teaspoon salt

1   In 3-quart saucepan, cook linguine to desired doneness as directed on package. Drain; return to saucepan.

2   Reserve 2 tablespoons of the feta cheese for garnish. Add remaining feta cheese and remaining ingredients to linguine; toss to mix. Sprinkle with reserved feta cheese.

**4 servings (1½ cups each)**

## Instant
## Success!

*This tasty pasta comes together in a jiffy. Think of it as a kind of inside-out tuna noodle casserole, but lighter and more flavorful. In a pinch, use canned diced tomatoes instead of fresh, although the cherry tomatoes add a nice punch of freshness.*

**1 Serving:** Calories 440; Total Fat 12g (Saturated Fat 3.5g, Trans Fat 0g); Cholesterol 35mg; Sodium 780mg; Total Carbohydrate 54g (Dietary Fiber 4g) • **Exchanges:** 3 Starch, 1 Vegetable, 2½ Lean Meat, ½ Fat • **Carbohydrate Choices:** 3½

# Florentine Tuna Tetrazzini

Prep Time **20 Minutes**

Start to Finish **1 Hour
5 Minutes**

1 package (9 oz) refrigerated linguine, cut into thirds

1 can (10¾ oz) condensed cream of celery soup

1 box (10 oz) frozen creamed spinach, thawed

¾ cup milk

2 cans (6 oz each) albacore tuna in water, drained

¼ cup sliced drained roasted red bell peppers (from 7-oz jar)

¼ cup Italian-style dry bread crumbs

2 tablespoons grated Parmesan cheese

1 tablespoon butter or margarine, melted

1 Heat oven to 350°F. Spray 8-inch square (2-quart) glass baking dish with cooking spray. Cook and drain linguine as directed on package.

2 In baking dish, mix soup, spinach and milk. Stir in tuna, bell peppers and linguine. In small bowl, mix bread crumbs, cheese and butter; sprinkle over tuna mixture.

3 Bake uncovered 40 to 45 minutes or until bubbly around edges and top is golden brown.

**4 servings (1½ cups each)**

**Simple Swap:** *Chopped pimientos make a good substitution for the roasted red bell peppers.*

## Instant
## Success!

*If it says "Florentine," chances are there's spinach involved. To make this recipe truly "straight-from-the-pantry," substitute dried linguine for the fresh.*

**1 Serving:** Calories 540; Total Fat 14g (Saturated Fat 5g, Trans Fat 1g); Cholesterol 45mg; Sodium 1220mg; Total Carbohydrate 69g (Dietary Fiber 5g) • **Exchanges:** 4 Starch, ½ Other Carbohydrate, 1 Vegetable, 3½ Lean Meat • **Carbohydrate Choices:** 4½

# 5 meatless meals

## Salads on the Side

*Go beyond a bag of lettuce or a complete salad mix with one of these simple taste sensations!*

**1 Hearts of Palm:** Drain and slice canned or jarred hearts of palm; drizzle with your favorite vinaigrette dressing.

**2 Cukes and Tomatoes:** On a serving platter or individual salad plates, arrange cucumber chunks or slices with tomato wedges or slices. Sprinkle with salt and pepper; drizzle with your favorite dressing or add a splash of vinegar.

**3 Mediterranean Vegetable Salad:** On a serving platter, arrange sliced tomatoes and sliced bell peppers; drizzle with your favorite vinaigrette dressing. Top with pitted kalamata olives or small whole pitted ripe olives; sprinkle with crumbled feta cheese.

**4** Artichokes and Greens: Toss prewashed bagged salad greens, jarred marinated artichoke hearts (undrained) and Caesar-flavored croutons.

**5** Cheddar, Bacon and Smoked Almond Salad: Toss prewashed bagged salad greens with shredded Cheddar cheese and purchased precooked bacon bits. Sprinkle with smoked whole almonds; serve with your favorite dressing.

**6** Easy Fried Cheese and Mixed-Greens Salad: Heat frozen breaded mozzarella cheese sticks as directed on package; cut each stick into fourths. Top salad greens with cheese stick pieces and halved cherry tomatoes; serve with your favorite dressing.

**7** Mango-Avocado-Raspberry Salad: On a serving platter or individual serving plates, arrange ripe avocado and jarred mango slices; drizzle with purchased raspberry vinaigrette. Serve with freshly ground pepper.

**8** Pineapple and Honey-Nut Coleslaw: Stir canned pineapple tidbits (drained) and honey-roasted peanuts into purchased creamy coleslaw.

**9** Melon and Berries with Vanilla Sauce: On a serving platter, arrange sliced cantaloupe and honeydew melon; top with raspberries or blackberries. Mix together vanilla yogurt and milk until it has a saucy consistency; drizzle over fruit.

**10** Sunny Lime Fruit Salad: Drizzle a variety of cut-up fruits with thawed frozen limeade concentrate. Toss in poppy seed or slivered almonds if desired.

**This icon means:** 🕐 20 minutes or less

# Quinoa with Black Beans

1 cup uncooked quinoa

2 cups vegetable or chicken broth

1 cup black beans (from 15-oz can), drained, rinsed

½ cup frozen whole kernel corn, thawed

1 small tomato, chopped (½ cup)

¼ cup chopped fresh cilantro

4 medium green onions, chopped (¼ cup)

1 tablespoon fresh lime juice

1 clove garlic, finely chopped

¼ teaspoon salt

1 Rinse quinoa thoroughly by placing in a fine-mesh strainer and holding under cold running water until water runs clear; drain well.

2 In 2-quart saucepan, heat broth to boiling. Add quinoa; reduce heat to low. Cover; simmer 15 to 20 minutes or until liquid is absorbed.

3 Fluff quinoa with fork. Stir in remaining ingredients. Cook uncovered about 3 minutes, stirring occasionally, until thoroughly heated.

**4 servings (1 cup each)**

## Make it a Meal

*Go whole-grain with quinoa, pronounced "KEEN-wa." A nutty tasting whole grain, quinoa contains all the amino acids, making it a complete protein like meat. That makes it a great grain to use in vegetarian dishes when you want some protein. Leftovers would make an easy lunch for tomorrow.*

**1 Serving:** Calories 260; Total Fat 3.5g (Saturated Fat 0.5g, Trans Fat 0g); Cholesterol 0mg; Sodium 660mg; Total Carbohydrate 45g (Dietary Fiber 8g) • **Exchanges:** 3 Starch, ½ Lean Meat • **Carbohydrate Choices:** 3

# Curry Lentil and Brown Rice Casserole

1 medium dark-orange sweet potato, peeled, cut into ½- to ¾-inch pieces (2 cups)

¾ cup dried lentils (6 oz), sorted, rinsed

½ cup uncooked natural whole-grain brown rice

½ cup chopped red bell pepper

½ cup raisins

2 ½ cups water

2 tablespoons soy sauce

2 teaspoons curry powder

2 tablespoons slivered almonds, if desired

1 Heat oven to 375°F. In ungreased 2- or 2½-quart casserole, mix all ingredients except almonds.

2 Cover and bake 1 hour to 1 hour 15 minutes or until rice and lentils are tender. Uncover and stir mixture. Let stand 5 minutes before serving. Sprinkle with almonds.

**4 servings (1½ cups each)**

## Instant Success!

*Mild, hearty lentils and brown rice get zing from the curry powder and a touch of sweetness from the raisins. Cut the remaining red bell pepper into strips and serve them with ranch dressing to satisfy any hungry mouths while the casserole is baking.*

**1 Serving:** Calories 270; Total Fat 1.5g (Saturated Fat 0g, Trans Fat 0g); Cholesterol 0mg; Sodium 470mg; Total Carbohydrate 63g (Dietary Fiber 12g) • **Exchanges:** 2 Starch, 2 Other Carbohydrate, 1 Very Lean Meat • **Carbohydrate Choices:** 4

Betty Crocker Supper in a Snap

# Peppers Stuffed with Broccoli, Beans and Rice

2 large bell peppers, cut in half lengthwise, seeded

⅔ cup water

½ cup uncooked instant brown rice

1 cup chopped fresh broccoli

2 tablespoons chopped onion

½ cup canned red beans, drained, rinsed

⅓ cup chunky-style salsa

¼ cup shredded reduced-fat Cheddar cheese (1 oz)

2 tablespoons chopped fresh cilantro

1 In 8- or 9-inch square microwavable dish, place peppers, cut sides down. Cover dish with plastic wrap, folding back one edge or corner ¼ inch to vent steam. Microwave on High about 4 minutes or until tender.

2 Meanwhile, in 1-quart saucepan, heat water to boiling over high heat. Stir in rice, broccoli and onion. Reduce heat to low; cover and simmer about 10 minutes or until water is absorbed. Stir in beans and salsa.

3 Spoon hot rice mixture into pepper halves. Place filled sides up in microwavable dish. Sprinkle each pepper half with 1 tablespoon of the cheese.

4 Cover dish with plastic wrap, folding back one edge or corner ¼ inch to vent steam. Microwave on High about 1 minute or until cheese is melted. Sprinkle with cilantro. Let stand 1 to 2 minutes before serving.

**2 servings**

**1 Serving:** Calories 260; Total Fat 2.5g (Saturated Fat 1g, Trans Fat 0g); Cholesterol 0mg; Sodium 430mg; Total Carbohydrate 46g (Dietary Fiber 8g) • **Exchanges:** 2 Starch, ½ Other Carbohydrate, 2 Vegetable, ½ Lean Meat • **Carbohydrate Choices:** 3

# Rice and Bean Bake

Prep Time **10 Minutes**

Start to Finish **1 Hour 15 Minutes**

1 cup uncooked regular long-grain rice

1 ½ cups boiling water

1 tablespoon vegetable or chicken bouillon granules

1 ½ teaspoons chopped fresh or ½ teaspoon dried marjoram leaves

1 medium onion, chopped (½ cup)

1 can (15 to 16 oz) kidney beans, undrained

1 box (9 oz) frozen baby lima beans, thawed, drained

½ cup shredded Cheddar cheese (2 oz)

1 Heat oven to 350°F. In ungreased 2-quart casserole, mix all ingredients except cheese.

2 Cover and bake 1 hour to 1 hour 5 minutes or until liquid is absorbed; stir. Sprinkle with cheese.

**4 servings (1⅔ cups each)**

## Instant Success!

*Gotta love canned and frozen beans—they're healthy, cheap and convenient! This easy rice and bean bake, for example, requires only 10 minutes of prep work, then dinner's in the oven.*

**1 Serving:** Calories 430; Total Fat 6g (Saturated Fat 3.5g, Trans Fat 0g); Cholesterol 15mg; Sodium 1330mg; Total Carbohydrate 80g (Dietary Fiber 12g) • **Exchanges:** 5 Starch, ½ Other Carbohydrate, 1 Very Lean Meat • **Carbohydrate Choices:** 4½

# Spanish Rice Bake

Prep Time **20 Minutes**

Start to Finish **1 Hour 25 Minutes**

2 tablespoons canola oil

1 cup uncooked long-grain brown rice

1 medium onion, chopped (½ cup)

1 small green bell pepper, chopped (½ cup)

1 cup frozen whole kernel corn (from 1-lb bag), thawed, drained

1 can (10¾ oz) condensed tomato soup

2½ cups boiling water

1 tablespoon chopped fresh cilantro, if desired

1 teaspoon chili powder

¼ teaspoon salt

1½ cups shredded reduced fat Colby–Monterey Jack cheese blend (6 oz)

1 Heat oven to 375°F. Spray 2-quart casserole with cooking spray. In 10-inch skillet, heat oil over medium heat. Cook brown rice, onion and bell pepper in oil 6 to 8 minutes, stirring frequently, until rice is light brown and onion is tender. Stir in corn.

2 In casserole, mix remaining ingredients except cheese. Stir in rice mixture and 1 cup of the cheese.

3 Cover; bake 20 minutes. Stir mixture. Cover; bake about 30 minutes longer or until rice is tender. Stir mixture; sprinkle with remaining ½ cup cheese. Bake uncovered 2 to 3 minutes or until cheese is melted. Let stand 10 minutes before serving.

**4 servings (1 cup each)**

## Easy Add-On

*Jazz it up! If you've got 'em, offer sides of salsa, sour cream and chopped avocado or guacamole. How about crushed red pepper flakes, too?*

**1 Serving:** Calories 460; Total Fat 18g (Saturated Fat 6g, Trans Fat 0g); Cholesterol 20mg; Sodium 960mg; Total Carbohydrate 59g (Dietary Fiber 8g) • **Exchanges:** 3 Starch, 1 Other Carbohydrate, 1 High-Fat Meat, 1½ Fat • **Carbohydrate Choices:** 4

# Asparagus Risotto

3 cups vegetable broth or reduced-sodium chicken broth (from 32-oz carton)

3 cups water

1 tablespoon olive or canola oil

1 medium onion, chopped (½ cup)

¼ cup shredded carrot

2 cloves garlic, finely chopped

¼ cup dry white wine, vegetable broth or reduced-sodium chicken broth (from 32-oz carton)

1 package (12 oz) uncooked Arborio or other short-grain rice

½ teaspoon coarse (kosher or sea) salt

1 box (9 oz) frozen asparagus cuts, thawed

2 tablespoons pine nuts, toasted*

2 oz shredded Parmesan cheese (½ cup)

1  In 3- to 4-quart saucepan, heat broth and water to boiling. Reduce heat; simmer while preparing risotto.

2  In 10-inch skillet, heat oil over medium heat. Cook and stir onion, carrot and garlic in oil 2 to 3 minutes or until onion and carrot are tender. Stir in wine; cook 1 minute or until wine boils. Stir in rice, salt and 1 cup simmering liquid. Cook until liquid is absorbed into rice, stirring frequently. Continue to add liquid, 1 cup at a time, cooking until liquid is absorbed, stirring frequently.

3  When 4 cups liquid have been absorbed, stir in asparagus. Test rice for doneness, and continue adding ½ cup liquid at a time until rice is tender but still firm and creamy (process takes 15 to 20 minutes).

4  Remove skillet from heat. Stir in pine nuts and cheese. Serve immediately.

*\*To toast pine nuts: In ungreased heavy skillet, cook over medium-low heat 5 to 7 minutes, stirring frequently until browning begins, then stirring constantly until golden brown.*

**5 servings (1¼ cups each)**

**1 Serving:** Calories 360; Total Fat 8g (Saturated Fat 2.5g, Trans Fat 0g); Cholesterol 10mg; Sodium 760mg; Total Carbohydrate 58g (Dietary Fiber 1g) • **Exchanges:** 3 Starch, ½ Other Carbohydrate, 1 Vegetable, 1½ Fat • **Carbohydrate Choices:** 4

# Farmers' Market Barley Risotto

Prep Time **1 Hour**
**15 Minutes**

Start to Finish **1 Hour**
**15 Minutes**

1 tablespoon olive oil

1 medium onion, chopped (½ cup)

1 medium bell pepper, coarsely
    chopped (1 cup)

2 cups chopped fresh mushrooms (4 oz)

1 cup frozen whole kernel corn

1 cup uncooked pearl barley

¼ cup dry white wine or chicken broth

2 cups roasted vegetable stock or
    chicken broth

3 cups water

1½ cups grape tomatoes, cut in half (if
    large, cut into quarters)

⅔ cup shredded Parmesan cheese

3 tablespoons chopped fresh or
    1 teaspoon dried basil leaves

½ teaspoon pepper

**1** In 4-quart Dutch oven, heat oil over medium heat. Cook onion, bell pepper, mushrooms and corn in oil about 5 minutes, stirring frequently, until onion is crisp-tender. Add barley, stirring about 1 minute to coat.

**2** Stir in wine and ½ cup of the vegetable stock. Cook 5 minutes, stirring frequently, until liquid is almost absorbed. Repeat with remaining stock and 3 cups water, adding ½ to ¾ cup of stock or water at a time and stirring frequently, until absorbed.

**3** Stir in tomatoes, ⅓ cup of the cheese, the basil and pepper. Cook until hot. Sprinkle with remaining ⅓ cup cheese.

**4 servings (1½ cups each)**

## Budget Smart

*Here's a farmers' market shopping secret: Many farmers will give a discount near the end of the day to help sell remaining food. It's the perfect time to snag those pricey heirloom tomatoes, which you could substitute for the grape tomatoes in this risotto (use 1½ cups coarsely chopped tomatoes).*

**1 Serving:** Calories 370; Total Fat 9g (Saturated Fat 4g, Trans Fat 0g); Cholesterol 15mg; Sodium 820mg; Total Carbohydrate 56g (Dietary Fiber 11g) • **Exchanges:** 2½ Starch, ½ Other Carbohydrate, 2 Vegetable, ½ Medium-Fat Meat, 1 Fat • **Carbohydrate Choices:** 4

# Sage and Garlic Vegetable Bake

Prep Time **25 Minutes**
Start to Finish **1 Hour
40 Minutes**

1 medium butternut squash, peeled, cut into 1-inch pieces (3 cups)

2 medium parsnips, peeled, cut into 1-inch pieces (2 cups)

2 cans (14 oz each) stewed tomatoes, undrained

2 cups frozen cut green beans

½ cup coarsely chopped onion

½ cup uncooked quick-cooking barley

½ cup water

1 teaspoon dried sage leaves

½ teaspoon seasoned salt

2 cloves garlic, finely chopped

1 Heat oven to 375°F. In ungreased 3-quart casserole, mix all ingredients, breaking up large pieces of tomatoes.

2 Cover and bake 1 hour to 1 hour 15 minutes or until vegetables and barley are tender.

**4 servings (2 cups each)**

## Budget Smart

*Butternut squash plays a starring role in this fall vegetable casserole. If you've never bought a whole squash, you'll be amazed at how inexpensive they can be. It takes a few minutes to peel the skin and scoop out the stringy center, but as a bonus you get all the seeds, which you can roast just like pumpkin seeds!*

**1 Serving:** Calories 250; Total Fat 1g (Saturated Fat 0g, Trans Fat 0g); Cholesterol 0mg; Sodium 730mg; Total Carbohydrate 60g (Dietary Fiber 11g) • **Exchanges:** 2½ Starch, 1 Other Carbohydrate, 1 Vegetable • **Carbohydrate Choices:** 4

# Vegetable Curry with Couscous

1 tablespoon vegetable oil

1 medium red bell pepper, cut into thin strips

¼ cup vegetable or chicken broth

1 tablespoon curry powder

1 teaspoon salt

1 bag (1 lb) frozen broccoli, carrots and cauliflower (or other combination)

½ cup raisins

⅓ cup chutney

2 cups hot cooked couscous or rice

¼ cup chopped peanuts

**1** In 12-inch skillet, heat oil over medium–high heat. Cook bell pepper in oil 4 to 5 minutes, stirring frequently, until tender.

**2** Stir in broth, curry powder, salt and vegetables. Heat to boiling. Boil about 4 minutes, stirring frequently, until vegetables are crisp-tender.

**3** Stir in raisins and chutney. Serve over couscous. Sprinkle with peanuts.

**4 servings**

## Easy
### Add-On

*This vegetable curry is equally good over couscous or rice, so use whichever you prefer or have on hand! Try using any extra chutney in sandwiches instead of mayo or mustard.*

**1 Serving:** Calories 330; Total Fat 9g (Saturated Fat 1.5g, Trans Fat 0g); Cholesterol 0mg; Sodium 730mg; Total Carbohydrate 53g (Dietary Fiber 7g) • **Exchanges:** 3 Starch, 2 Vegetable, ½ Fat • **Carbohydrate Choices:** 3½

# Vegetables and Tofu Skillet Supper

Prep Time **45 Minutes**
Start to Finish **45 Minutes**

2 tablespoons olive or vegetable oil

½ cup coarsely chopped red onion

4 or 5 small red potatoes, sliced (2 cups)

1 cup frozen cut green beans (from 12-oz bag)

½ teaspoon Italian seasoning

½ teaspoon garlic salt

½ package (14-oz size) firm tofu, cut into ½-inch cubes

2 plum (Roma) tomatoes, thinly sliced

1 Hard-Cooked Egg, chopped

**Easy** Add-On

*This delicious main course is low-calorie and low-cost. Add a fresh touch by sprinkling each serving with a little chopped cilantro or chives if you have some. Serve any leftovers for a tasty lunch the next day.*

1 In 12-inch skillet, heat oil over medium–high heat. Cook onion in oil 2 minutes, stirring frequently. Stir in potatoes; reduce heat to medium-low. Cover and cook 10 to 12 minutes, stirring occasionally, until potatoes are tender.

2 Stir in green beans, Italian seasoning and garlic salt. Cover and cook 6 to 8 minutes, stirring occasionally, until beans are tender and potatoes are light golden brown.

3 Stir in tofu and tomatoes. Cook 3 to 5 minutes, stirring occasionally and gently, just until hot. Sprinkle each serving with egg.

**4 servings**

**Hard-Cooked Eggs:** *In saucepan, place eggs in single layer. Add cold water to at least 1 inch above eggs. Cover and heat to boiling. Remove from heat; let stand covered 15 minutes. Drain. Immediately place eggs in cold water with ice cubes, or run cold water over eggs until completely cooled. To remove shell, crackle it by tapping gently all over, roll between hands to loosen. Peel, starting at large end. If shell is hard to peel, hold egg in cold water while peeling.*

**1 Serving:** Calories 230; Total Fat 9g (Saturated Fat 1.5g, Trans Fat 0g); Cholesterol 55mg; Sodium 330mg; Total Carbohydrate 31g (Dietary Fiber 5g) • **Exchanges:** 2 Starch, 1 Fat • **Carbohydrate Choices:** 2

# Southwestern Bean Skillet

1 cup fresh corn kernels or frozen whole kernel corn

2 tablespoons chopped fresh cilantro

½ teaspoon salt

1 small green bell pepper, chopped (½ cup)

1 small onion, chopped (¼ cup)

1 can (15 oz) chili beans in sauce, undrained

1 can (15 oz) black beans, drained, rinsed

1 cup shredded Cheddar–Monterey Jack cheese blend with jalapeño peppers (4 oz)

2 medium tomatoes, chopped (1½ cups)

1 In 12-inch skillet, mix all ingredients except cheese and tomatoes. Heat to boiling; reduce heat. Cover and simmer 5 minutes.

2 Uncover and simmer 5 to 10 minutes, stirring occasionally, until vegetables are tender. Stir in cheese and tomatoes until cheese is melted.

**4 servings**

## Budget Smart

*This super-easy skillet dish is also super-fast. Going with beans really cuts down on the cost and gives you a fiber boost! Serve with white or yellow rice flavored with additional chopped fresh cilantro if you have any remaining.*

**1 Serving:** Calories 425; Total Fat 11g (Saturated Fat 6g, Trans Fat 0g); Cholesterol 30mg; Sodium 1660mg; Total Carbohydrate 57g (Dietary Fiber 13g) • **Exchanges:** 3 Starch, 2 Vegetable, 1 Fat • **Carbohydrate Choices:** 4

# Couscous, Corn and Lima Bean Sauté

1 tablespoon butter or margarine

1 large onion, chopped (1 cup)

1 clove garlic, finely chopped

1 box (12 oz) whole wheat couscous

1 box (9 oz) frozen whole kernel corn, thawed

2 boxes (9 oz each) frozen baby lima beans, thawed

2 cups water

1 tablespoon chopped fresh or 1 teaspoon dried thyme leaves

1 teaspoon salt

⅓ cup slivered almonds, toasted*

1 In 12-inch skillet, melt butter over medium-high heat. Add onion and garlic; cook about 2 minutes, stirring occasionally, until onion is crisp-tender.

2 Stir in remaining ingredients except almonds. Heat to boiling over high heat. Remove from heat; let stand 5 minutes. Fluff before serving. Sprinkle with almonds.

*To toast almonds, sprinkle in ungreased heavy skillet. Cook over medium heat 5 to 7 minutes, stirring frequently until almonds begin to brown, then stirring constantly until light brown.

**8 servings (1¼ cups each)**

**Simple Swap:** *If you're not partial to lima beans, substitute frozen shelled edamame.*

**1 Serving:** Calories 390; Total Fat 6g (Saturated Fat 1.5g, Trans Fat 0g); Cholesterol 5mg; Sodium 470mg; Total Carbohydrate 69g (Dietary Fiber 11g) • **Exchanges:** 4 Starch, 2 Vegetable, ½ Fat • **Carbohydrate Choices:** 4½

# Mediterranean Couscous Salad

1 cup vegetable or chicken broth (from 32-oz carton)

¾ cup uncooked couscous

3 medium plum (Roma) tomatoes, cubed (1 cup)

1 small unpeeled cucumber, cubed (1 cup)

½ cup halved pitted kalamata olives

4 medium green onions, chopped (¼ cup)

¼ cup chopped fresh or 1 tablespoon dried dill weed

2 tablespoons lemon juice

2 tablespoons olive or vegetable oil

⅛ teaspoon salt

2 tablespoons crumbled feta cheese

1 In 2-quart saucepan, heat broth to boiling. Stir in couscous; remove from heat. Cover; let stand 5 minutes.

2 In large bowl, place tomatoes, cucumber, olives, onions and dill weed. Stir in couscous.

3 In small bowl, beat lemon juice, oil and salt with wire whisk until well blended; pour over vegetable mixture and toss. Cover; refrigerate 1 hour to blend flavors.

4 Just before serving, sprinkle with cheese.

**5 servings (1½ cup each)**

**1 Serving:** Calories 380; Total Fat 16g (Saturated Fat 3g, Trans Fat 0g); Cholesterol 5mg; Sodium 790mg; Total Carbohydrate 49g (Dietary Fiber 5g) • **Exchanges:** 2½ Starch, ½ Other Carbohydrate, 1 Vegetable, 3 Fat • **Carbohydrate Choices:** 3

# Spicy Chipotle–Peanut Noodle Bowls

Prep Time **30 Minutes**
Start to Finish **30 Minutes**

½ cup creamy peanut butter

½ cup apple juice

2 tablespoons soy sauce

2 chipotle chiles in adobo sauce (from 7-oz can), seeded, chopped

1 teaspoon adobo sauce from can of chiles

¼ cup chopped fresh cilantro

4 cups water

2 medium carrots, cut into julienne strips (1½ × ¼ × ¼ inch)

1 medium red bell pepper, cut into julienne strips (1½ × ¼ × ¼ inch)

1 package (8 to 10 oz) Chinese curly noodles

2 tablespoons chopped peanuts

## Make it a Meal

*Put peanut butter to work for dinner with these lightly spicy peanut noodles. They're also good cold, so consider making a double batch and having some for lunch.*

1 In small bowl, mix peanut butter, apple juice, soy sauce, chiles and adobo sauce until smooth. Stir in cilantro.

2 In 2-quart saucepan, heat water to boiling. Add carrots and bell pepper; cook 1 minute. Remove carrots and bell pepper from water with slotted spoon. Add noodles to water; cook and drain as directed on package.

3 Toss noodles with peanut butter mixture; divide noodles among 4 bowls. Top with carrots and bell pepper. Sprinkle with peanuts.

**4 servings**

**1 Serving:** Calories 500; Total Fat 20g (Saturated Fat 4g, Trans Fat 0g); Cholesterol 0mg; Sodium 800mg; Total Carbohydrate 62g (Dietary Fiber 7g) • **Exchanges:** 3½ Starch, 2 Vegetable, ½ High-Fat Meat, 3 Fat • **Carbohydrate Choices:** 4

# Asian Noodle Bowl

Prep Time **25 Minutes**
Start to Finish **25 Minutes**

¼ cup barbecue sauce

2 tablespoons hoisin sauce or barbecue sauce

1 tablespoon peanut butter

Dash of ground red pepper (cayenne), if desired

1 tablespoon vegetable oil

1 small onion, cut into thin wedges

¼ cup chopped red bell pepper

2 cups fresh broccoli florets or 2 cups frozen (thawed) broccoli florets

½ cup water

1 package (10 oz) Chinese curly noodles

1 can (14 to 15 oz) baby corn nuggets, drained

¼ cup salted peanuts, coarsely chopped

1 In small bowl, mix barbecue sauce, hoisin sauce, peanut butter and ground red pepper; set aside.

2 In 12-inch skillet, heat oil over medium heat 1 to 2 minutes. Add onion and bell pepper. Cook 2 minutes, stirring frequently. Stir in broccoli and water. Cover with lid; cook 2 to 4 minutes, stirring occasionally, until broccoli is crisp-tender.

3 Meanwhile, cook and drain noodles as directed on package.

4 While noodles are cooking, stir corn and sauce mixture into vegetable mixture. Cook uncovered 3 to 4 minutes, stirring occasionally, until mixture is hot and bubbly.

5 Divide noodles among 4 individual serving bowls. Spoon vegetable mixture over noodles. Sprinkle with peanuts.

**4 servings**

## Instant
## Success!

*Once the vegetables and sauce are prepped, this dish comes together quickly. To avoid waste, serve the remaining ¾ red bell pepper cut into strips with a dip as a quick appetizer. If you're using fresh broccoli, buy a whole broccoli rather than precut florets. It's usually cheaper per pound and you can use the stem, peeled and sliced into ¼-inch slices, with the florets.*

**1 Serving:** Calories 520; Total Fat 13g (Saturated Fat 2g, Trans Fat 0g); Cholesterol 0mg; Sodium 590mg; Total Carbohydrate 83g (Dietary Fiber 8g) • **Exchanges:** 4 Starch, 1 Other Carbohydrate, 1 Vegetable, ½ High-Fat Meat, 1½ Fat • **Carbohydrate Choices:** 5½

# Spinach Pasta Salad

3 cups uncooked bow-tie (farfalle) pasta (6 oz)

1 small tomato, quartered

½ cup basil pesto

¼ teaspoon salt

¼ teaspoon pepper

4 cups bite-size pieces spinach leaves

2 medium carrots, thinly sliced (1 cup)

1 small red onion, thinly sliced

1 can (14 oz) quartered artichoke hearts, drained, rinsed

1 Cook and drain pasta as directed on package. Rinse with cold water; drain.

2 Meanwhile, in food processor or blender, place tomato, pesto, salt and pepper. Cover; process 30 seconds.

3 Toss pasta, pesto mixture and remaining ingredients.

**6 servings**

## Easy
Add-On

*This vegetarian pasta salad is brimming with flavors! If you bought a large container of pesto, why not double the recipe to use it up? The leftovers will be great served cold.*

**1 Serving:** Calories 290; Total Fat 12g (Saturated Fat 2.5g, Trans Fat 0g); Cholesterol 0mg; Sodium 560mg; Total Carbohydrate 35g (Dietary Fiber 6g) • **Exchanges:** 1½ Starch, ½ Other Carbohydrate, 1 Vegetable, 2½ Fat • **Carbohydrate Choices:** 2

# Lo Mein Noodle Salad

### SALAD

1 package (8 oz) lo mein noodles

1 bag (10 oz) frozen shelled edamame (green) soybeans

1 large red bell pepper, chopped (1½ cups)

4 medium green onions, sliced (¼ cup)

### DRESSING

⅓ cup rice vinegar

⅓ cup peanut butter

¼ cup soy sauce

2 tablespoons packed brown sugar

2 tablespoons vegetable oil

¼ teaspoon crushed red pepper flakes

1 Break lo mein noodles into thirds. Cook as directed on package. Rinse with cold water; drain.

2 Cook edamame as directed on bag; drain.

3 In medium bowl, place bell pepper, onions, noodles and edamame.

4 In small bowl, beat dressing ingredients with wire whisk until well blended. Spoon over noodle mixture; toss to coat. Serve immediately, or cover and refrigerate until serving time.

**6 servings (1½ cups each)**

## Instant
## Success!

*Here's a fun use for the peanut butter in your pantry—a cold noodle salad that's healthy and not at all costly. It's a great dish to serve either at room temperature or chilled.*

**1 Serving:** Calories 400; Total Fat 15g (Saturated Fat 2.5g, Trans Fat 0g); Cholesterol 0mg; Sodium 820mg; Total Carbohydrate 48g (Dietary Fiber 6g) • **Exchanges:** 2 Starch, 1 Other Carbohydrate, 1 Vegetable, 1 High-Fat Meat, 1 Fat • **Carbohydrate Choices:** 3

# Creamy Mushroom Tortelloni

2 packages (9 oz each) refrigerated portabello mushroom–filled tortelloni

2 tablespoons butter or margarine

¼ cup Italian-style dry bread crumbs

1 container (8 oz) chive-and-onion cream cheese spread

1 cup half-and-half

2 tablespoons chopped fresh parsley

2 tablespoons chopped fresh basil leaves

½ teaspoon salt

1 In 4-quart saucepan or Dutch oven, cook and drain tortelloni as directed on package.

2 Meanwhile, in 8-inch skillet, melt butter over medium heat. Cook bread crumbs in butter 3 to 5 minutes, stirring occasionally, until golden brown; remove from heat.

3 Return drained tortelloni to saucepan. Reduce heat to medium-low. Gently stir in cream cheese spread, half-and-half, parsley, basil and salt until cheese is melted and mixture is hot, about 3 to 5 minutes. Spoon into individual serving dishes. Sprinkle buttered bread crumbs over tortelloni. Serve immediately.

**5 servings**

## Instant
## Success!

*Don't keep dry bread crumbs in your pantry? Two slices of bread can be crumbled by hand, or for a finer texture, whirled in a food processor.*

**1 Serving:** Calories 560; Total Fat 30g (Saturated Fat 18g; Trans Fat 1g); Cholesterol 105mg; Sodium 1120mg; Total Carbohydrate 54g (Dietary Fiber 3g) • **Exchanges:** 2½ Starch, 1 Other Carbohydrate, 1½ High-Fat Meat, 3½ Fat • **Carbohydrate Choices:** 3½

Betty Crocker Supper in a Snap

# Spaghetti with Squash

1 medium spaghetti squash (about 3 lb)

4 oz uncooked spaghetti, broken in half

¼ cup chopped fresh parsley

2 tablespoons grated Parmesan cheese

2 tablespoons butter or margarine, melted

1 tablespoon chopped fresh or
    1 teaspoon dried oregano leaves

½ teaspoon garlic salt

1 Prick squash with fork; place on microwavable paper towel in microwave oven. Microwave on High 8 minutes; turn squash over. Microwave 8 to 11 minutes longer or until tender. Let stand 10 minutes.

2 Meanwhile, cook and drain spaghetti as directed on package; return spaghetti to saucepan.

3 Cut squash lengthwise in half; remove seeds and fibers. Reserve one half for another use. From other half, remove spaghetti-like strands with 2 forks; reserve shell. Add squash and remaining ingredients to spaghetti in saucepan; toss. Return spaghetti mixture to squash shell to serve.

**6 servings**

## Budget
### Smart

*If you've never tried spaghetti squash, you're in for a fun surprise: once cooked, it separates into yellow spaghetti-like strands! It's a fun way to add vegetables to your pasta, and like all winter squash it costs little per pound. The remaining squash would make a great side dish to any roast or stewed meat, maybe with some grated Parmesan cheese on top.*

**1 Serving:** Calories 170; Total Fat 5g (Saturated Fat 2.5g, Trans Fat 0g); Cholesterol 10mg; Sodium 260mg; Total Carbohydrate 28g (Dietary Fiber 4g) • **Exchanges:** 2 Starch, 1 Fat • **Carbohydrate Choices:** 2

# Garden Vegetable Spaghetti

Prep Time **25 Minutes**
Start to Finish **25 Minutes**

1 package (16 oz) spaghetti

2 tablespoons olive or vegetable oil

2 medium carrots, sliced (1 cup)

1 medium onion, diced (½ cup)

2 medium zucchini, cut into ½-inch slices (4 cups)

2 cloves garlic, finely chopped

3 medium tomatoes, cut into 1-inch pieces

½ cup frozen sweet peas (from 12-oz bag), cooked and drained

1 tablespoon chopped fresh or 1 teaspoon dried basil leaves

½ teaspoon salt

¼ teaspoon pepper

⅔ cup grated Parmesan cheese

## Instant Success!

*Chock full of vegetables, this pasta dish is like summer in a bowl! If you don't have basil, try parsley or thyme.*

1 Cook and drain spaghetti as directed on package.

2 Meanwhile, in 10-inch skillet, heat oil over medium–high heat. Cook carrots, onion, zucchini and garlic in oil, stirring frequently, until vegetables are crisp-tender.

3 Stir in remaining ingredients except cheese; cook until hot. Serve vegetable mixture over spaghetti. Sprinkle with cheese.

**6 servings**

**Simple Swap:** *Substitute 1 small eggplant (about 12 oz), peeled and diced (3½ cups), for the zucchini.*

**1 Serving:** Calories 440; Total Fat 10g (Saturated Fat 3g, Trans Fat 0g); Cholesterol 10mg; Sodium 430mg; Total Carbohydrate 71g (Dietary Fiber 7g) • **Exchanges:** 4 Starch, 2 Vegetable, 1½ Fat • **Carbohydrate Choices:** 5

# Rigatoni with Basil Pesto

RIGATONI

3 cups uncooked rigatoni pasta (8 oz)

BASIL PESTO

1 cup firmly packed fresh basil leaves

2 cloves garlic

⅓ cup grated Parmesan cheese

⅓ cup olive or vegetable oil

2 tablespoons pine nuts or walnut pieces

Additional grated Parmesan cheese, if desired

1 Cook pasta as directed on package.

2 Meanwhile, in food processor or blender, place the basil leaves, garlic, cheese, oil and pine nuts. Cover and process, stopping occasionally to scrape sides, until smooth.

3 Drain pasta. Place in large serving bowl or back in Dutch oven. Immediately pour pesto over hot pasta, and toss until pasta is well coated. Serve with additional grated Parmesan cheese.

**4 servings**

## Easy
### Add-On

*Store-bought pesto may be convenient, but it's also convenient (and cheaper) to have homemade pesto stored in your freezer. For freezing, in step 2 process everything but the cheese, scrape into a freezer container and store in the freezer up to 6 months. Thaw in the refrigerator and add the cheese just before serving. Pine nuts also keep well tightly sealed in the freezer, so if you bought a large package of nuts, you can store the remainder for up to 2 years to use as needed.*

**1 Serving:** Calories 470; Total Fat 25g (Saturated Fat 4.5g, Trans Fat 0g); Cholesterol 5mg; Sodium 135mg; Total Carbohydrate 50g (Dietary Fiber 3g) • **Exchanges:** 3½ Starch, 4½ Fat • **Carbohydrate Choices:** 3

# Gemelli with Fresh Green and Yellow Wax Beans

Prep Time **25 Minutes**

Start to Finish **1 Hour**
**25 Minutes**

2 cups uncooked gemelli pasta (8 oz)

4 oz fresh green beans, cut into 2-inch
    pieces (1 cup)

4 oz fresh yellow wax beans, cut into
    2-inch pieces (1 cup)

1 pint (2 cups) grape or cherry
    tomatoes, halved

¼ cup vegetable oil

¼ cup tarragon vinegar or white wine
    vinegar

½ teaspoon salt

¾ cup shaved Parmesan cheese (3 oz)

¼ teaspoon freshly ground black pepper

## Easy Add-On

*This refreshing and inexpensive springtime pasta dish would make a side dish at a barbecue or a nice lunch. Use frozen peas instead of one or both of the beans if you want.*

1 Cook pasta as directed on package, adding green and yellow beans for last 5 minutes of cooking time; drain. Rinse with cold water to cool; drain well.

2 In large bowl, mix pasta, beans and tomatoes.

3 In small bowl, beat oil, vinegar and salt with wire whisk until well blended; stir into pasta mixture. Stir in ½ cup of the cheese. Cover; refrigerate at least 1 hour to blend flavors.

4 Just before serving, stir salad; top with remaining ¼ cup cheese and sprinkle with pepper.

**6 servings**

**1 Serving:** Calories 320; Total Fat 14g (Saturated Fat 4g, Trans Fat 0g); Cholesterol 10mg; Sodium 580mg; Total Carbohydrate 37g (Dietary Fiber 3g) • **Exchanges:** 2 Starch, 1 Vegetable, ½ Medium-Fat Meat, 2 Fat • **Carbohydrate Choices:** 2½

# Fettuccine Alfredo

8 oz uncooked fettuccine

½ cup butter or margarine

½ cup whipping cream

¾ cup grated Parmesan cheese

½ teaspoon salt

Dash of pepper

Chopped fresh parsley, if desired

1 Cook and drain pasta as directed on package.

2 Meanwhile, in 2-quart saucepan, heat butter and whipping cream over low heat, stirring constantly, until butter is melted. Stir in cheese, salt and dash of pepper until mixture is smooth.

3 Pour sauce over hot fettuccine, and stir until fettuccine is well coated. Sprinkle with parsley.

**Lighten Up Fettuccine Alfredo:** *For 24 grams of fat and 440 calories per serving, decrease butter to ⅓ cup and substitute fat-free half-and-half for the whipping cream.*

**Chicken Fettuccine Alfredo:** *In step 2, stir in 2 cups chopped cooked chicken or turkey with the cheese.*

**4 servings**

## Instant **Success!**

*Fettuccine Alfredo is simple to make and delightfully rich. If you want to pick up a nice hunk of Parmesan to freshly grate, this is the recipe for it—it really shows off the flavor of the cheese. Pregrated Parmesan costs less and cuts down on prep, so choose what works best for you.*

**1 Serving:** Calories 580; Total Fat 41g (Saturated Fat 24g, Trans Fat 1.5g); Cholesterol 155mg; Sodium 760mg; Total Carbohydrate 39g (Dietary Fiber 2g) • **Exchanges:** 2½ Starch, 1 Lean Meat, 7 Fat • **Carbohydrate Choices:** 2½

# Mom's Macaroni and Cheese

Prep Time **10 Minutes**
Start to Finish **40 Minutes**

1½ cups uncooked elbow macaroni (5 oz)

2 tablespoons butter or margarine

1 small onion, chopped (¼ cup)

¼ cup all-purpose flour

½ teaspoon salt

¼ teaspoon pepper

1¾ cups milk

6 oz American cheese loaf (from 8-oz package), cut into ½-inch cubes

1 Heat oven to 375°F. Cook and drain pasta as directed on package.

2 Meanwhile, in 3-quart saucepan, melt butter over medium heat. Add onion. Cook about 2 minutes, stirring occasionally, until onion is softened. Stir in flour, salt and pepper. Cook 1 to 2 minutes, stirring constantly, until smooth and bubbly. Remove from heat. Stir in milk with wire whisk. Return saucepan to medium heat and heat to boiling, stirring constantly. Continue boiling and stirring 1 minute.

4 Remove saucepan from heat again. Stir in cheese until melted and smooth. Stir macaroni into cheese sauce.

5 Into ungreased 1½-quart casserole, spoon macaroni mixture. Bake uncovered about 30 minutes or until bubbly and light brown.

**5 servings**

## Budget Smart–

*Everybody loves macaroni and cheese! The boxed kind may be a budget pantry staple, but this simple homemade version is a lot more delicious, and still pretty economical at $0.63 per serving. If you want to replicate the traditional orange color, use the yellow cheese loaf rather than white. To give this a crunchy crust, sprinkle crushed corn flake cereal or similar cereal on top for the last 15 minutes of baking.*

**1 Serving:** Calories 360; Total Fat 18g (Saturated Fat 11g, Trans Fat 0.5g); Cholesterol 50mg; Sodium 810mg; Total Carbohydrate 35g (Dietary Fiber 2g) • **Exchanges:** 1½ Starch, 1 Other Carbohydrate, 1½ High-Fat Meat, 1 Fat • **Carbohydrate Choices:** 2

# Penne with Spicy Sauce

Prep Time **30 Minutes**
Start to Finish **30 Minutes**

1 package (16 oz) penne pasta

1 can (28 oz) Italian-style peeled whole tomatoes, undrained

2 tablespoons olive or vegetable oil

2 cloves garlic, finely chopped

1 teaspoon crushed red pepper flakes

2 tablespoons chopped fresh parsley

1 tablespoon tomato paste (from 6-oz can)

½ cup freshly grated or shredded Parmesan cheese

1 Cook and drain pasta as directed on package. Meanwhile, in food processor or blender, place tomatoes with juice. Cover; process until coarsely chopped.

2 In 12-inch skillet, heat oil over medium-high heat. Cook garlic, red pepper flakes and parsley in oil about 5 minutes, stirring frequently, until garlic just begins to turn golden. Stir in chopped tomatoes and tomato paste. Heat to boiling; reduce heat. Cover; simmer about 10 minutes, stirring occasionally, until slightly thickened.

3 Add pasta and ¼ cup of the cheese to mixture in skillet. Cook about 3 minutes, tossing gently, until pasta is evenly coated. Sprinkle with remaining ¼ cup cheese.

**6 servings**

## Instant
## Success!

*Not in the mood for a meatless red sauce? Add sliced pepperoni with the chopped tomatoes in step 2 for a new taste sensation.*

**1 Serving:** Calories 400; Total Fat 9g (Saturated Fat 2.5g; Trans Fat 0g); Cholesterol 5mg; Sodium 640mg; Total Carbohydrate 66g (Dietary Fiber 6g) • **Exchanges:** 4 Starch, 1 Vegetable, 1½ Fat • **Carbohydrate Choices:** 4½

# Tagliatelle Pasta with Asparagus and Gorgonzola Sauce

1 lb asparagus

8 oz uncooked tagliatelle pasta
   or fettuccine

2 tablespoons olive or vegetable oil

4 medium green onions, sliced (¼ cup)

¼ cup chopped fresh parsley

1 clove garlic, finely chopped

1 cup crumbled Gorgonzola cheese
   (4 oz)

½ teaspoon freshly cracked pepper

1 Break off tough ends of asparagus as far down as stalks snap easily. Cut asparagus into 1-inch pieces. Cook pasta as directed on package, adding asparagus during last 5 minutes of cooking; drain.

2 Meanwhile, in 12-inch skillet, heat oil over medium-high heat. Cook onions, parsley and garlic in oil about 5 minutes, stirring occasionally, until onions are tender. Reduce heat to medium.

3 Add pasta, asparagus and cheese to mixture in skillet. Cook about 3 minutes, tossing gently, until cheese is melted and pasta is evenly coated. Sprinkle with pepper.

**4 servings**

## Speed it Up

*Let your ingredients join forces! Adding vegetables to pasta water during the last minutes of cooking saves a major step (and saves you extra pans).*

**1 Serving:** Calories 370; Total Fat 17g (Saturated Fat 7g; Trans Fat 0g); Cholesterol 70mg; Sodium 640mg; Total Carbohydrate 40g (Dietary Fiber 3g) • **Exchanges:** 2 Starch, ½ Other Carbohydrate, 1 Vegetable, 1 High-Fat Meat, 1½ Fat • **Carbohydrate Choices:** 2½

# Impossibly Easy Vegetable Pie

2 cups chopped fresh broccoli or sliced fresh cauliflower florets

⅓ cup chopped onion

⅓ cup chopped green bell pepper

1 cup shredded Cheddar cheese (4 oz)

½ cup Original Bisquick mix

1 cup milk

½ teaspoon salt

¼ teaspoon pepper

2 eggs

1 Heat oven to 400°F. Spray bottom and side of 9-inch glass pie plate with cooking spray. In 2-quart saucepan, heat 1 inch water (salted if desired) to boiling. Add broccoli; cover and return to boiling. Cook about 5 minutes or until broccoli is almost tender; drain thoroughly.

2 In pie plate, mix broccoli, onion, bell pepper and cheese. In small bowl, stir remaining ingredients until blended. Pour into pie plate.

3 Bake 30 to 35 minutes or until golden brown and knife inserted in center comes out clean. Let stand 5 minutes before cutting.

**6 servings**

**Impossibly Easy Spinach Pie:** *Use a 9-oz package of frozen spinach, thawed and squeezed to drain, in place of the broccoli; do not cook. Omit bell pepper. Substitute Swiss cheese for the Cheddar cheese. Add ¼ teaspoon ground nutmeg with the pepper. Bake about 30 minutes.*

**1 Serving:** Calories 160; Total Fat 10g (Saturated Fat 5g, Trans Fat 0g); Cholesterol 95mg; Sodium 420mg; Total Carbohydrate 9g (Dietary Fiber 1g) • **Exchanges:** 2 Vegetable, ½ Medium-Fat Meat, 1½ Fat • **Carbohydrate Choices:** ½

# Easy Garden Bake

Prep Time **15 Minutes**

Start to Finish **55 Minutes**

1 cup chopped zucchini

1 large tomato, chopped (1 cup)

1 medium onion, chopped (1 cup)

⅓ cup grated Parmesan cheese

½ cup Bisquick Heart Smart mix

1 cup fat-free (skim) milk

½ cup fat-free egg product or 2 eggs

½ teaspoon salt

⅛ teaspoon pepper

1 Heat oven to 400°F. Lightly grease 8-inch square baking dish or 9-inch pie plate. Sprinkle zucchini, tomato, onion and cheese in baking dish.

2 In small bowl, stir remaining ingredients until blended. Pour over vegetables and cheese.

3 Bake uncovered about 35 minutes or until knife inserted in center comes out clean. Cool 5 minutes.

**4 servings**

## Budget
### Smart

*Zucchini and onions are some of the least expensive vegetables in the whole supermarket. Learn to like zucchini—it has nice delicate flavors and is a highly versatile vegetable.*

**1 Serving:** Calories 210; Total Fat 6g (Saturated Fat 3g, Trans Fat 0g); Cholesterol 15mg; Sodium 830mg; Total Carbohydrate 21g (Dietary Fiber 2g) • **Exchanges:** ½ Starch, ½ Other Carbohydrate, 1 Vegetable, 2 Lean Meat • **Carbohydrate Choices:** 1 ½

# 6 soup, sandwiches & pizza

## Quick Ideas for Bread

*Any way you slice it, bread can make the meal—kick it way up by topping it with one of these great options.*

**1** **Ranch–Parmesan Cheese Toasts:** Spread cut sides of hot dog buns with ranch dressing; sprinkle with grated Parmesan cheese. Broil with tops 4 to 6 inches from heat 1 to 2 minutes or until topping begins to bubble.

**2** **Cheddar and Garlic "Saucers":** Spread cut sides of hamburger buns with softened butter; sprinkle with garlic powder or garlic salt and shredded Cheddar cheese. Broil with tops 4 to 6 inches from heat 1 to 2 minutes or until cheese is melted.

**3** **Smoked Cheddar and Almond Focaccia:** Heat oven to 375°F. On an ungreased cookie sheet, place 12-inch prebaked thin Italian pizza crust. Spread crust lightly with honey mustard; sprinkle with shredded smoked Cheddar or Gouda cheese and sliced almonds. Bake 15 to 20 minutes or until cheese is melted.

**4** **Soft Italian Breadsticks:** Brush purchased soft breadsticks with olive oil; sprinkle with Italian seasoning and grated Parmesan cheese. Heat in oven as directed on breadstick package.

**5** **Spinach Dip Crostini:** On an ungreased cookie sheet, place 1-inch slices of French bread. Broil with tops 4 to 6 inches from heat 30 to 60 seconds or until lightly toasted. Spread each slice with purchased spinach dip; sprinkle with shredded mozzarella or Asiago cheese. Broil 1 to 2 minutes longer or until cheese is melted.

**6** **Pesto-Parmesan Loaf:** Cut a 1-pound loaf of French bread horizontally in half; place with cut sides up on an ungreased cookie sheet. Broil with tops 4 to 6 inches from heat about 1 minute or until lightly toasted. Spread toasted sides with basil pesto; sprinkle with shredded Parmesan cheese. Broil 1 to 2 minutes longer or until cheese is melted.

**7** **Singing-the-Blues Garlic Bread:** Sprinkle bottom half of a purchased garlic bread loaf with crumbled blue cheese; replace the top. Heat as directed on package.

**8** **Texas Toast:** Spread one side of Texas toast bread or thickly sliced bread (about 1 inch) with softened butter; sprinkle with barbecue seasoning. Broil with tops 4 to 6 inches from heat 30 to 60 seconds or until lightly toasted.

**9** **Corn Muffins with Maple Butter:** Beat ½ cup softened butter with electric mixer until light and fluffy; beat in ½ cup maple syrup until well mixed and creamy. Serve with heated corn muffins or cornbread squares.

**10** **Warm Tortillas with Lime Butter:** Mix melted butter with grated lime peel; brush over warm tortillas. Fold tortillas in half and then in half again, or roll them up.

**This icon means:** 20 minutes or less

**This icon means:** slow-cooker recipe

# After-Work Chicken Noodle Soup

2 cups cut-up rotisserie or other cooked chicken

2 medium stalks celery, chopped (1 cup)

2 medium carrots, sliced (1 cup)

1 medium onion, chopped (½ cup)

1 tablespoon chopped fresh parsley or 1 teaspoon parsley flakes

1 teaspoon dried thyme leaves

¼ teaspoon pepper

2 cloves garlic, finely chopped

4 cans (14 oz each) chicken broth

1 cup uncooked wide egg noodles (2 oz)

1 In 3-quart saucepan, heat all ingredients except noodles to boiling. Stir in noodles. Heat to boiling; reduce heat.

2 Simmer uncovered 8 to 10 minutes, stirring occasionally, until noodles and vegetables are tender.

**4 servings**

## Speed it Up

*This recipe is pretty streamlined, but here are a couple of tricks to make it even quicker. Use about 2 tablespoons plus 1 teaspoon chicken bouillon granules and 4 cups of water instead of getting out the can opener for the canned chicken broth. And substitute ¼ to ½ teaspoon garlic powder to skip chopping fresh garlic.*

**1 Serving:** Calories 260; Total Fat 8g (Saturated Fat 2g; Trans Fat 0g); Cholesterol 70mg; Sodium 2070mg; Total Carbohydrate 17g (Dietary Fiber 2g) • **Exchanges:** 1 Starch, 4 Very Lean Meat, 1 Fat • **Carbohydrate Choices:** 1

# Turkey–Wild Rice Soup

2 tablespoons butter or margarine

½ cup all-purpose flour

2 cans (14 oz each) fat-free chicken broth with 33% less sodium

1 package (8 oz) 98% fat-free oven-roasted turkey breast, cubed (about 2 cups)

2 cups water

2 tablespoons dried chopped onion

1 package (6 oz) original-flavor long-grain and wild rice mix

2 cups original-flavored soymilk or fat-free (skim) milk

1 In 5-quart Dutch oven, melt butter over medium heat. Stir in flour with wire whisk until well blended. Slowly stir in broth with wire whisk.

2 Stir in turkey, water, onion, rice and contents of seasoning packet. Heat to boiling over high heat, stirring occasionally. Reduce heat to medium-low; cover and simmer about 25 minutes or until rice is tender.

3 Stir in soymilk; heat just to boiling.

**6 servings (1½ cups each)**

## Instant
## Success!

*Wild rice is not really rice at all, but the seed of an aquatic grass. Here, the wild rice adds a delicious nutty flavor and slightly chewy texture to this quick and tasty soup. Wild rice can be expensive, but a little goes a long way, so look for it mixed with other rices, as in the long-grain and wild rice mix called for here.*

**1 Serving:** Calories 260; Total Fat 6g (Saturated Fat 3g, Trans Fat 0g); Cholesterol 45mg; Sodium 720mg; Total Carbohydrate 33g (Dietary Fiber 0g) • **Exchanges:** 1½ Starch, ½ Other Carbohydrate, 2 Very Lean Meat, 1 Fat • **Carbohydrate Choices:** 2

# Chicken Cordon Bleu Chowder

2 cans (18.8 oz each) ready-to-serve creamy potato with roasted garlic soup

1 cup cut-up rotisserie or other cooked chicken

1 cup diced cooked ham

1 cup shredded Swiss cheese (4 oz)

1 tablespoon chopped fresh chives

1  In 3-quart saucepan, heat soup, chicken and ham over medium heat 5 minutes, stirring occasionally.

2  Slowly stir in cheese. Cook about 2 minutes, stirring frequently, until cheese is melted. Serve topped with chives.

**4 servings**

## Instant
## Success!

*Chicken or veal cordon bleu is a traditional dish that rolls chicken breasts or veal around Swiss cheese and ham. This lively trio has been morphed into a hearty chowder that's so good! Use all ham or all chicken if that's what you have on hand.*

**1 Serving:** Calories 460; Total Fat 29g (Saturated Fat 11g; Trans Fat 0g); Cholesterol 100mg; Sodium 1640mg; Total Carbohydrate 19g (Dietary Fiber 2g) • **Exchanges:** 1½ Starch, 4 Lean Meat, 3 Fat • **Carbohydrate Choices:** 1

# Italian Chicken Noodle Soup

1 tablespoon olive or canola oil

½ lb boneless skinless chicken breasts, cut into ½-inch pieces

1 medium onion, chopped (½ cup)

2 cans (14 oz each) chicken broth

2 cups water

3 medium carrots, sliced (1½ cups)

2 cups fresh broccoli florets

1½ cups uncooked medium egg noodles

1 teaspoon dried basil leaves

½ teaspoon garlic-pepper blend

¼ cup shredded Parmesan cheese (1 oz)

1 In 4-quart saucepan, heat oil over medium heat. Add chicken; cook 4 to 6 minutes, stirring occasionally, until no longer pink in center. Stir in onion. Cook 2 to 3 minutes, stirring occasionally, until onion is tender.

2 Stir in broth, water and carrots. Heat to boiling. Cook 5 minutes over medium heat.

3 Stir in broccoli, noodles, basil and garlic-pepper blend. Heat to boiling. Reduce heat; simmer uncovered 8 to 10 minutes, stirring occasionally, until vegetables and noodles are tender. Top each serving with cheese.

**6 servings (1½ cups each)**

## Make it a Meal

*The vegetables in this Italian take on comforting chicken noodle soup give it a nice, fresh flavor.*

**1 Serving:** Calories 170; Total Fat 6g (Saturated Fat 2g, Trans Fat 0g); Cholesterol 35mg; Sodium 730mg; Total Carbohydrate 14g (Dietary Fiber 2g) • **Exchanges:** ½ Other Carbohydrate, 1 Vegetable, 2 Very Lean Meat, 1 Fat • **Carbohydrate Choices:** 1

# Southwestern Pork Soup

2 teaspoons vegetable oil

1 lb pork boneless loin, trimmed of fat, cut into ½-inch cubes

4 medium green onions, sliced (¼ cup)

1 small jalapeño chile, seeded, finely chopped

1 clove garlic, finely chopped

2 cans (14 oz each) 33%-less-sodium chicken broth

2 cans (15 to 16 oz each) great northern beans, rinsed, drained

½ cup loosely packed chopped fresh cilantro

¼ cup loosely packed chopped fresh parsley

1 In 3-quart nonstick saucepan, heat oil over medium-high heat. Add pork; cook 3 to 5 minutes, stirring occasionally, until browned. Add onions, chile and garlic; cook and stir 1 minute.

2 Add broth and beans. Heat to boiling; reduce heat. Cover and simmer about 10 minutes or until pork is no longer pink in center. Stir in cilantro and parsley; cook until heated through.

**5 servings (1¼ cups each)**

**Simple Swap:** *One pound of pork boneless loin chops, cut into cubes, would also work well for this recipe.*

## Make it a Meal

*A blend of Southwestern flavors paired with pork loin and beans makes for a substantial soup with a fun kick. There's plenty of meat, but the beans add even more body to the soup while keeping the costs low. This soup would be absolutely delicious—and serve even more people— ladled over white rice (a great idea if you've got any leftovers).*

**1 Serving:** Calories 400; Total Fat 11g (Saturated Fat 3g, Trans Fat 0g); Cholesterol 60mg; Sodium 380mg; Total Carbohydrate 45g (Dietary Fiber 11g) • **Exchanges:** 3 Starch, 4½ Very Lean Meat, ½ Fat • **Carbohydrate Choices:** 3

# Asian Pork and Noodle Soup

1 lb boneless pork sirloin or loin, cut into ½-inch pieces

2 cloves garlic, finely chopped

2 teaspoons finely chopped gingerroot

2 cans (14 oz each) chicken broth

2 cups water

2 tablespoons soy sauce

2 cups uncooked fine egg noodles (4 oz)

1 medium carrot, sliced (½ cup)

1 small red bell pepper, chopped (½ cup)

2 cups fresh spinach leaves

1 Spray 3-quart saucepan with cooking spray; heat over medium-high heat. Add pork, garlic and gingerroot; cook 3 to 5 minutes, stirring frequently, until pork is brown.

2 Stir in broth, water and soy sauce. Heat to boiling; reduce heat. Simmer uncovered 5 minutes. Stir in noodles, carrot and bell pepper. Simmer uncovered about 10 minutes or until noodles are tender.

3 Stir in spinach; cook until thoroughly heated.

**5 servings**

## Speed it Up

*There always seems to be a way to make things faster! For this recipe, instead of cutting up the pork yourself, buy pork chow mein meat, which is already cut up and ready to go.*

**1 Serving:** Calories 260; Total Fat 9g (Saturated Fat 3g; Trans Fat 0g); Cholesterol 75mg; Sodium 1100mg; Total Carbohydrate 19g (Dietary Fiber 2g) • **Exchanges:** 1 Starch, 1 Vegetable, 3 Lean Meat • **Carbohydrate Choices:** 1

# Ham and Wild Rice Soup

Prep Time **10 Minutes**
Start to Finish **8 Hours
25 Minutes**

2 cups diced cooked ham

¾ cup uncooked wild rice

1 medium onion, chopped (½ cup)

1 bag (12 oz) frozen mixed vegetables, thawed, drained

1 can (14 oz) chicken broth

1 can (10¾ oz) cream of celery soup

¼ teaspoon pepper

3 cups water

½ cup half-and-half

1 In 3- to 4-quart slow cooker, mix all ingredients except half-and-half.

2 Cover; cook on Low heat setting 8 to 9 hours.

3 Stir in half-and-half. Increase heat setting to High. Cover; cook 10 to 15 minutes longer or until hot.

**8 servings (1 cup each)**

## Instant
## Success!

*Rich and creamy, with the nutty flavor of wild rice, this soup would make the perfect dinner appetizer or weekend lunch.*

**1 Serving:** Calories 210; Total Fat 6g (Saturated Fat 2.5g, Trans Fat 0g); Cholesterol 25mg; Sodium 920mg; Total Carbohydrate 25g (Dietary Fiber 4g) • **Exchanges:** 1½ Starch, 1 Vegetable, 1 Lean Meat, ½ Fat • **Carbohydrate Choices:** 1½

# Beef 'n Veggie Soup with Mozzarella

1 lb lean (at least 80%) ground beef

1 large onion, chopped (1 cup)

2 cups frozen mixed vegetables (from 1-lb bag)

1 can (14.5 oz) diced tomatoes with green pepper, celery and onions (or other variety), undrained

4 cups water

5 teaspoons beef bouillon granules

1½ teaspoons Italian seasoning

¼ teaspoon pepper

1 cup shredded mozzarella cheese (4 oz)

1  In 4-quart Dutch oven, cook beef and onion over medium-high heat 5 to 7 minutes, stirring occasionally, until beef is brown; drain.

2  Stir in remaining ingredients except cheese. Heat to boiling; reduce heat. Simmer uncovered 6 to 8 minutes, stirring occasionally, until vegetables are tender.

3  Sprinkle about 2 tablespoons cheese in each of 8 soup bowls; fill bowls with soup.

**8 servings**

## Make it a Meal

*Add some hearty rustic sourdough or Italian rolls for dipping into the soup and a Caesar salad kit for chilly, crunchy goodness and that, my friend, is supper!*

**1 Serving:** Calories 200; Total Fat 9g (Saturated Fat 4.5g; Trans Fat 0g); Cholesterol 45mg; Sodium 790mg; Total Carbohydrate 13g (Dietary Fiber 3g) • **Exchanges:** ½ Other Carbohydrate, 1 Vegetable, 2 Medium-Fat Meat • **Carbohydrate Choices:** 1

# Italian Tomato Soup with Pesto-Cheese Toasts

1 cup water

2 cans (14 oz each) diced tomatoes with Italian herbs, undrained

1 can (11.5 oz) tomato juice

4 slices rosemary, Italian or French bread, ½ inch thick

2 tablespoons basil pesto

2 tablespoons shredded Parmesan cheese

1 In 3-quart saucepan, heat water, tomatoes and tomato juice to boiling.

2 Set oven control to broil. Place bread on ungreased cookie sheet. Spread with pesto; sprinkle with cheese. With tops 4 to 6 inches from heat, broil 1 to 2 minutes or until edges of bread are golden brown.

3 Into 4 soup bowls, ladle soup. Top each serving with bread slice.

**4 servings**

## Instant Success!

*This super-fast soup gets a boost of flavor from the quick pesto-cheese toasts. Basil pesto is often available in small containers in the supermarket's refrigerator section. Better yet, make pesto and freeze it in small portions (see the tip on page 276); then just pull some out to use in this recipe. If you don't have rosemary, Italian or French bread, use bread you have on hand, such as whole wheat.*

**1 Serving:** Calories 260; Total Fat 7g (Saturated Fat 2g, Trans Fat 0g); Cholesterol 0mg; Sodium 910mg; Total Carbohydrate 39g (Dietary Fiber 4g) • **Exchanges:** 1½ Starch, ½ Other Carbohydrate, 2 Vegetable, 1½ Fat • **Carbohydrate Choices:** 2½

# Chunky Vegetable Chowder

1 tablespoon butter

1 medium green bell pepper, coarsely chopped (1 cup)

1 medium red bell pepper, coarsely chopped (1 cup)

8 medium green onions, sliced (½ cup)

3 cups water

¾ lb small red potatoes, cut into 1-inch pieces (2 ½ cups)

1 tablespoon chopped fresh or 1 teaspoon dried thyme leaves

½ teaspoon salt

1 cup fat-free half-and-half

⅛ teaspoon pepper

2 cans (14.75 oz each) cream-style corn

1 In 4-quart Dutch oven, melt butter over medium heat. Add bell peppers and onions; cook 3 minutes, stirring occasionally.

2 Stir in water, potatoes, thyme and salt. Heat to boiling. Reduce heat to low; cover and simmer about 10 minutes or until potatoes are tender.

3 Stir in remaining ingredients; cook about 1 minute or until hot (do not boil).

**6 servings**

## Budget
### Smart

*You can cut the cost of this soup even more by using 2 green bell peppers instead of 1 green and 1 red. The soup won't be as colorful, but it will taste just as good.*

**1 Serving:** Calories 240; Total Fat 4g (Saturated Fat 2g, Trans Fat 0g); Cholesterol 5mg; Sodium 570mg; Total Carbohydrate 43g (Dietary Fiber 5g) • **Exchanges:** 2 Starch, ½ Other Carbohydrate, 1 Vegetable, ½ Fat • **Carbohydrate Choices:** 3

# Fire-Roasted Tomato Basil Soup

| | |
|---|---|
| 1 tablespoon olive or vegetable oil | 2 cans (14 oz each) chicken broth |
| 1 large onion, chopped (1 cup) | 1 cup water |
| 2 medium carrots, chopped (1 cup) | 1 teaspoon red pepper sauce |
| 2 cans (14.5 oz each) fire-roasted diced tomatoes, undrained | ½ cup uncooked orzo pasta |
| | 1 teaspoon dried basil leaves |

1 In 4-quart saucepan, heat oil over medium heat. Add onion and carrots. Cook 2 to 3 minutes, stirring occasionally, until softened.

2 Stir in tomatoes, broth, water and pepper sauce. Heat to boiling. Stir in pasta. Heat to boiling; reduce heat to medium. Cook uncovered 10 to 15 minutes, stirring occasionally, until pasta and carrots are tender.

3 Stir in basil. Cook about 1 minute, stirring constantly.

**5 servings (1½ cups each)**

## Make it a Meal

*Starting with fire-roasted diced tomatoes is an easy and inexpensive way to add extra flavor to this 30-minute soup. They have a lightly smoky flavor and cost only a few cents per serving more than plain diced tomatoes. If you have any leftover cooked short- or small-type pasta, add it at the end to make this dish yield even more servings. Add leftover cooked chicken and top with grated Parmesan.*

**1 Serving:** Calories 160; Total Fat 4g (Saturated Fat 0.5g, Trans Fat 0g); Cholesterol 0mg; Sodium 990mg; Total Carbohydrate 23g (Dietary Fiber 4g) • **Exchanges:** 1 ½ Starch, 1 Vegetable, ½ Fat • **Carbohydrate Choices:** 1 ½

# Cheddar Cheese and Broccoli Soup

Prep Time **30 Minutes**
Start to Finish **30 Minutes**

2 cans (10¾ oz each) condensed
   Cheddar cheese soup

2 cups water

5 cups frozen broccoli florets

2 cups milk

½ teaspoon ground mustard

¼ teaspoon salt

¼ teaspoon garlic powder

⅛ teaspoon pepper

2 cups shredded Cheddar cheese (8 oz)

1  In 4-quart saucepan, mix soup and water. Heat over high heat, stirring constantly, until boiling and smooth.

2  Add broccoli. Heat to boiling; reduce heat to medium. Cover; cook 8 to 10 minutes, stirring occasionally, until broccoli is tender.

3  Stir in milk, mustard, salt, garlic powder and pepper. Cook uncovered 3 to 5 minutes, stirring occasionally, until thoroughly heated. Stir in cheese until melted.

**6 servings (1⅓ cups each)**

## Budget Smart

*Broccoli and cheddar cheese are such a great flavor combination, not to mention a great way to get picky eaters to eat their green vegetables! If you love this combo, look for the 24-pack of soup to save money on the case price.*

1 **Serving:** Calories 340; Total Fat 22g (Saturated Fat 13g, Trans Fat 1.5g); Cholesterol 60mg; Sodium 1300mg; Total Carbohydrate 16g (Dietary Fiber 2g) • **Exchanges:** ½ Starch, ½ Other Carbohydrate, 2½ High-Fat Meat, ½ Fat • **Carbohydrate Choices:** 1

# Southwest Cheese Soup

1 loaf (1 lb) prepared cheese product, cut into cubes

1 can (15.25 oz) whole kernel corn, drained

1 can (15 oz) black beans, drained, rinsed

1 can (10 oz) diced tomatoes with green chiles, undrained

1 cup milk

Fresh cilantro sprigs, if desired

1 In 4-quart saucepan, mix all ingredients except cilantro.

2 Cook over medium-low heat 10 to 15 minutes, stirring frequently, until cheese is melted and soup is hot. Garnish each serving with cilantro.

**4 servings**

## Make it a Meal

*Enjoy this unbelievably easy cheese soup with warm cornbread.*

**1 Serving:** Calories 610; Total Fat 28g (Saturated Fat 17g; Trans Fat 0.5g); Cholesterol 95mg; Sodium 2130mg; Total Carbohydrate 59g (Dietary Fiber 9g) • **Exchanges:** 2½ Starch, 1½ Other Carbohydrate, 3½ Medium-Fat Meat, 1½ Fat • **Carbohydrate Choices:** 4

# Tortellini Soup

2 tablespoons butter or margarine

1 medium stalk celery, chopped (½ cup)

1 medium carrot, chopped (½ cup)

1 small onion, chopped (¼ cup)

1 clove garlic, finely chopped

6 cups water

2 extra-large vegetarian vegetable bouillon cubes

2½ cups dried cheese-filled tortellini (10 oz)

1 tablespoon chopped fresh parsley

½ teaspoon ground nutmeg

¼ teaspoon pepper

Freshly grated Parmesan cheese, if desired

1 In 4-quart Dutch oven, melt butter over medium heat. Add celery, carrot, onion and garlic; cook, stirring frequently, until crisp-tender.

2 Stir in water and bouillon cubes. Heat to boiling. Reduce heat to low; stir in tortellini. Cover; simmer about 20 minutes, stirring occasionally, until tortellini are tender.

3 Stir in parsley, nutmeg and pepper. Sprinkle individual servings with cheese.

**5 servings**

## Budget
Smart

*Dried tortellini is less expensive than frozen fresh tortellini, and it works very well in this hearty wholesome soup. The celery, carrot, onion and garlic will enhance the flavor of the vegetable bouillon cubes; you can also use chicken bouillon if you like.*

**1 Serving:** Calories 280; Total Fat 10g (Saturated Fat 5g, Trans Fat 0g); Cholesterol 55mg; Sodium 1420mg; Total Carbohydrate 38g (Dietary Fiber 2g) • **Exchanges:** 2½ Starch, ½ High-Fat Meat, 1 Fat • **Carbohydrate Choices:** 2½

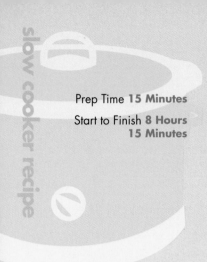

Prep Time **15 Minutes**

Start to Finish **8 Hours 15 Minutes**

# Lentil Soup

1 lb smoked ham shanks

8 cups chicken broth

1 package (16 oz) dried lentils (2¼ cups), sorted, rinsed

4 medium stalks celery, chopped (2 cups)

4 medium carrots, chopped (2 cups)

3 tablespoons chopped fresh parsley

3 cloves garlic, finely chopped

2 cups shredded fresh spinach

1 In 5- to 6-quart slow cooker, mix all ingredients except spinach.

2 Cover and cook on Low heat setting 8 to 9 hours or until lentils are tender.

3 Remove ham from cooker; place on cutting board. Pull meat from bones, using 2 forks; discard bones and skin. Stir ham and spinach into soup. Stir well before serving.

**8 servings**

## Instant
## Success!

*This classic, rustic soup is easy on the wallet and healthy to boot. If you don't have the spinach, it's fine to omit.*

**1 Serving:** Calories 205; Total Fat 3g (Saturated Fat 1g, Trans Fat 0g); Cholesterol 5mg; Sodium 810mg; Total Carbohydrate 37g (Dietary Fiber 14g) • **Exchanges:** 2 Starch, 1 Vegetable, 1 Very Lean Meat • **Carbohydrate Choices:** 2½

# Three-Bean Beer Pot

8 slices uncooked bacon, cut into small pieces

1 large onion, chopped (1 cup)

1 cup barbecue sauce

¾ cup regular or nonalcoholic dark beer

¼ cup packed brown sugar

2 cans (15 oz each) black beans, drained, rinsed

2 cans (15 oz each) pinto beans, drained

1 can (19 oz) cannellini beans, drained

1 In 10-inch skillet, cook bacon and onion over medium heat 7 to 10 minutes, stirring occasionally, until bacon is crisp; drain.

2 Spray 3- to 4-quart slow cooker with cooking spray. In cooker, place bacon mixture and remaining ingredients; mix well.

3 Cover; cook on Low heat setting 4 to 6 hours.

**16 servings (½ cup each)**

## Budget
### Smart

*Sometimes it only takes a little meat to flavor a huge pot of beans, which helps keep the cost per serving small but the flavor big. The dark beer and sugar give the beans a wonderful caramel flavor that will make these the hit of your next outdoor potluck.*

**1 Serving:** Calories 270; Total Fat 2.5g (Saturated Fat 0.5g, Trans Fat 0g); Cholesterol 0mg; Sodium 650mg; Total Carbohydrate 47g (Dietary Fiber 13g) • **Exchanges:** 2 Starch, 1 Other Carbohydrate, 1 Lean Meat • **Carbohydrate Choices:** 3

soup, sandwiches & pizza

# Lentil-Tofu Soup

1 tablespoon canola oil

1 small onion, chopped (¼ cup)

1½ teaspoons curry powder

½ teaspoon ground cumin

1 clove garlic, finely chopped

⅓ cup dried lentils, sorted, rinsed

2½ cups fat-free vegetable broth with
⅓ less sodium (from 32-oz carton)

4 oz firm tofu (from 12-oz package)

¾ cup coarsely chopped fresh broccoli

2 tablespoons chopped fresh parsley

1 In 2-quart saucepan, heat oil over medium heat. Add onion, curry powder, cumin and garlic; cook, stirring occasionally, 4 to 6 minutes or until onion is tender. Stir in lentils and broth. Heat to boiling. Reduce heat; cover and simmer 10 minutes.

2 Meanwhile, cut tofu into ½-inch pieces.

3 Stir tofu, broccoli and parsley into simmering lentil mixture. Cook over medium heat about 5 to 8 minutes, stirring occasionally, until broccoli is crisp-tender.

**2 servings (about 1¼ cups each)**

## Instant
## Success!

*Sometimes it's nice not to have any leftovers! This soup makes just enough for two (or just one if you want a second helping), so you're using up only the amount of ingredients you really need.*

**1 Serving:** Calories 270; Total Fat 10g (Saturated Fat 1g, Trans Fat 0g); Cholesterol 0mg; Sodium 370mg; Total Carbohydrate 31g (Dietary Fiber 7g) • **Exchanges:** 2 Starch, 1½ Medium-Fat Meat • **Carbohydrate Choices:** 2

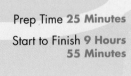

Prep Time **25 Minutes**

Start to Finish **9 Hours 55 Minutes**

# Mixed-Bean and Sausage Minestrone

1 package (20 oz) 15-dried-bean soup mix, sorted, rinsed

8 cups water

12 oz bulk Italian sausage

1 medium onion, chopped (½ cup)

2 medium carrots, chopped (1 cup)

2 cans (14 oz each) beef broth

2 cups water

2 cans (14.5 oz each) Italian-style stewed tomatoes, undrained, large pieces cut up

½ cup uncooked small pasta shells

¼ cup shredded Parmesan cheese

2 tablespoons chopped fresh parsley

**Budget** Smart

*If you see bulk sausage on sale, pick up more than you need and freeze some in small portions for future recipes.*

1 If bean soup mix comes with seasoning mix, save for another use. In 4-quart saucepan, heat beans and 8 cups water to boiling; reduce heat to low. Simmer uncovered 10 minutes; remove from heat. Cover and let stand 1 hour.

2 In 10-inch nonstick skillet, cook sausage and onion over medium heat, stirring occasionally, until sausage is no longer pink; drain if necessary.

3 Drain beans and discard water. In 5- to 6-quart slow cooker, mix beans, sausage mixture, carrots, broth and 2 cups water.

4 Cover and cook on Low heat setting 8 to 9 hours.

5 Stir in tomatoes and pasta. Increase heat setting to High. Cover and cook about 30 minutes longer or until pasta is tender. Sprinkle individual servings with cheese and parsley.

**8 servings (1¾ cups each)**

**1 Serving:** Calories 440; Total Fat 10g (Saturated Fat 3.5g, Trans Fat 0g); Cholesterol 25mg; Sodium 1400mg; Total Carbohydrate 64g (Dietary Fiber 9g) • **Exchanges:** 4 Starch, 1 Vegetable, 1 Lean Meat • **Carbohydrate Choices:** 4

# Skillet Nacho Chili

1 lb lean (at least 80%) ground beef

1 medium onion, chopped (½ cup)

1 can (19 oz) hearty tomato soup

1 can (15 oz) spicy chili beans in sauce, undrained

1 can (4.5 oz) chopped green chiles, undrained

1 cup frozen whole kernel corn

1 cup shredded Cheddar cheese (4 oz)

2 cups corn chips

**1** Spray 12-inch skillet with cooking spray; heat over medium-high heat. Cook beef and onion in skillet 5 to 7 minutes, stirring occasionally, until beef is thoroughly cooked and onion is tender; drain.

**2** Stir soup, chili beans, green chiles and corn into beef mixture. Heat to boiling; reduce heat to medium. Cook 8 to 10 minutes, stirring occasionally, until sauce is slightly thickened and corn is cooked.

**3** Sprinkle each serving with cheese. Serve with corn chips.

**4 servings**

**Simple Swap:** *Substitute ground turkey for the ground beef.*

## Budget Smart

*This quick, easy and cheap-to-make chili is a big hit with kids. Have a bowl of regular or low-fat sour cream on the table in case the chili is too spicy for some eaters. Dairy quickly cuts spiciness.*

**1 Serving:** Calories 585; Total Fat 29g (Saturated Fat 11g, Trans Fat 1g); Cholesterol 95mg; Sodium 1790mg; Total Carbohydrate 45g (Dietary Fiber 8g) • **Exchanges:** 3 Starch, 4 Medium-Fat Meat, 1 Fat • **Carbohydrate Choices:** 3

# Easy Chili Mole

1 lb extra-lean (at least 90%) ground
   beef

1 medium onion, chopped  (½ cup)

1 package (1.25 oz) Tex-Mex chili
   seasoning mix

1 can (28 oz) diced tomatoes,
   undrained

1 can (28 oz) crushed tomatoes

1 can (15 oz) spicy chili beans,
   undrained

1 oz unsweetened baking chocolate,
   coarsely chopped

8 soft corn tortillas (6 inch)

1  In 4-quart Dutch oven, cook beef and onion over medium heat, stirring occasionally, until beef is brown; drain.

2  Stir in seasoning mix, both tomatoes and beans. Heat to boiling over high heat. Reduce heat to low; cover and cook 15 minutes, stirring occasionally, to blend flavors. Stir in chocolate just until melted. Serve with tortillas.

**8 servings (about 1 cup each)**

## Instant
## **Success!**

*If you've never tasted mole, you're in for a treat! Mole is a rich Mexican sauce flavored with a "secret" ingredient of unsweetened chocolate. This is the perfect way to use up any extra unsweetened chocolate you may have on hand from making brownies.*

**1 Serving:** Calories 270; Total Fat 8g (Saturated Fat 3g, Trans Fat 0g); Cholesterol 35mg; Sodium 830mg; Total Carbohydrate 32g (Dietary Fiber 7g) • **Exchanges:** 1½ Starch, ½ Other Carbohydrate, 1 Vegetable, 1½ Lean Meat, ½ Fat • **Carbohydrate Choices:** 2

Betty Crocker Supper in a Snap

# Chili

Prep Time **30 Minutes**

Start to Finish **1 Hour 50 Minutes**

1 lb lean (at least 80%) ground beef

1 large onion, chopped (1 cup)

2 cloves garlic, finely chopped, or
⅟₄ teaspoon garlic powder

1 tablespoon chili powder

2 teaspoons chopped fresh or
1 teaspoon dried oregano leaves

1 teaspoon ground cumin

½ teaspoon salt

½ teaspoon red pepper sauce

1 can (14.5 oz) diced tomatoes,
undrained

1 can (15 to 16 oz) red kidney beans,
undrained

1 In 3-quart saucepan, cook beef, onion and garlic over medium heat 8 to 10 minutes, stirring occasionally, until beef is thoroughly cooked. Place strainer or colander in large bowl; line strainer with double thickness of paper towels. Pour beef mixture into strainer to drain. Return beef mixture to saucepan; discard paper towels and any juices in bowl.

2 Into beef, stir remaining ingredients except beans.

3 Heat mixture to boiling over high heat. Once mixture is boiling, reduce heat just enough so mixture bubbles gently. Cover; cook 1 hour, stirring occasionally.

4 Stir in beans. Heat to boiling over high heat. Once mixture is boiling, reduce heat just enough so mixture bubbles gently. Cook uncovered about 20 minutes, stirring occasionally, until desired thickness.

**4 servings**

**Lighten Up Chili:** *Use 1 lb lean ground turkey for the ground beef for chili with 7 grams of fat and 320 calories per serving.*

**Cincinnati-Style Chili:** *For each serving, spoon about ¾ cup beef mixture over 1 cup hot cooked spaghetti. Sprinkle each serving with ¼ cup shredded Cheddar cheese and 2 tablespoons chopped onion. Top with sour cream if desired.*

## Budget Smart

*There are as many different kinds of chili as there are states in America—and probably more! The Cincinnati-Style Chili variation, for example, serves the chili over spaghetti— making it a super kid-pleaser and a money-saver, too. Chili freezes well, so make a double batch the next time you see ground beef on sale.*

**1 Serving:** Calories 360; Total Fat 14g (Saturated Fat 5g, Trans Fat 1g); Cholesterol 70mg; Sodium 720mg; Total Carbohydrate 31g (Dietary Fiber 8g) • **Exchanges:** 2 Starch, 3 Lean Meat, 1 Fat • **Carbohydrate Choices:** 2

# Chili with Cornbread Dumplings

1½ lb ground beef

1 large onion, chopped (¾ cup)

1 can (15.25 oz) whole kernel corn, undrained

1 can (14.5 oz) stewed tomatoes, undrained

1 can (16 oz) tomato sauce

2 tablespoons chili powder

1 teaspoon red pepper sauce

1⅓ cups Original Bisquick mix

⅔ cup cornmeal

⅔ cup milk

3 tablespoons chopped fresh cilantro or parsley, if desired

1 In 4-quart Dutch oven, cook beef and onion over medium heat, stirring occasionally, until beef is brown; drain. Reserve ½ cup of the corn. Stir remaining corn with liquid, tomatoes, tomato sauce, chili powder and pepper sauce into beef mixture. Heat to boiling; reduce heat. Cover and simmer 15 minutes.

2 In medium bowl, mix Bisquick mix and cornmeal. Stir in milk, cilantro and reserved ½ cup corn just until moistened.

3 Heat chili to boiling. Drop dough by rounded tablespoonfuls onto chili; reduce heat to low. Cook uncovered 10 minutes. Cover and cook about 10 minutes longer or until dumplings are dry.

**6 servings**

## Instant **Success!**

*This fun twist on chili and cornbread combines them into a one-dish meal. What could be better to serve up on a cold winter night?*

**1 Serving:** Calories 500; Total Fat 18g (Saturated Fat 6g, Trans Fat 2); Cholesterol 75mg; Sodium 1200mg; Total Carbohydrate 57g (Dietary Fiber 5g) • **Exchanges:** 3 Starch, ½ Other Carbohydrate, 1 Vegetable, 2 Medium-Fat Meat, 1½ Fat • **Carbohydrate Choices:** 4

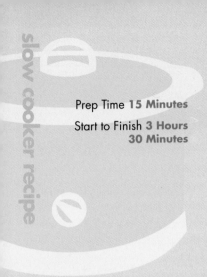

Prep Time **15 Minutes**

Start to Finish **3 Hours 30 Minutes**

# Mediterranean Bulgur and Lentils

1 cup uncooked bulgur wheat or cracked wheat

½ cup dried lentils, sorted, rinsed

1 teaspoon ground cumin

¼ teaspoon salt

3 cloves garlic, finely chopped

1 can (15.25 oz) whole kernel corn, drained

2 cans (14 oz each) vegetable or chicken broth

2 medium tomatoes, chopped (1½ cups)

½ cup drained pitted kalamata olives

1 cup crumbled reduced-fat Feta cheese (4 oz)

**1** In 3- to 4-quart slow cooker, mix all ingredients except tomatoes, olives and cheese.

**2** Cover; cook on Low heat setting 3 to 4 hours or until lentils are tender.

**3** Stir in tomatoes and olives. Increase heat setting to High. Cover; cook 15 minutes longer. Top with cheese.

**8 servings**

## Instant Success!

*Bulgur—wheat kernels that have been boiled, dried, and crushed—and lentils are an integral and beloved part of the Mediterranean and Middle Eastern cooking. Both are fairly inexpensive, but yield a vegetarian stew that's hearty.*

**1 Serving:** Calories 210; Total Fat 4g (Saturated Fat 1.5g, Trans Fat 0g); Cholesterol 0mg; Sodium 880mg; Total Carbohydrate 33g (Dietary Fiber 7g) • **Exchanges:** 2 Starch, ½ Very Lean Meat, ½ Fat • **Carbohydrate Choices:** 2

Betty Crocker Supper in a Snap

# Creole Jambalaya

Prep Time **10 Minutes**

Start to Finish **7 Hours
40 Minutes**

2 medium stalks celery, chopped (1 cup)

4 cloves garlic, finely chopped

2 cans (14.5 oz each) diced tomatoes with green pepper and onion, undrained

½ cup chopped fully cooked smoked sausage

½ teaspoon dried thyme leaves

¼ teaspoon pepper

¼ teaspoon red pepper sauce

12 oz uncooked deveined peeled medium (26 to 30 count) shrimp, thawed if frozen, tail shells removed

⅔ cup uncooked long-grain white rice

1⅓ cups water

1  In 3- to 3½-quart slow cooker, mix all ingredients except shrimp, rice and water.

2  Cover; cook on Low heat setting 7 to 8 hours or until vegetables are tender.

3  Stir in shrimp. Cover; cook on Low heat setting about 30 minutes longer or until shrimp are pink. Meanwhile, cook rice in water as directed on package, omitting butter and salt. Serve jambalaya with rice.

**4 servings (about 1 cup each)**

## Easy
### Add-On

*You don't have to wait till Fat Tuesday (Mardi Gras) to cook this fabulous jambalaya. For the most authentic stew, try to find cooked Cajun andouille sausage, generally available in large supermarkets. Any extra sausage will keep very well, refrigerated, for snacking purposes, or chop and mix it with scrambled eggs.*

**1 Serving:** Calories 300; Total Fat 6g (Saturated Fat 2g, Trans Fat 0g); Cholesterol 130mg; Sodium 910mg; Total Carbohydrate 43g (Dietary Fiber 3g) • **Exchanges:** 1½ Starch, 1 Other Carbohydrate, 1 Vegetable, 2 Lean Meat • **Carbohydrate Choices:** 3

# Vegetarian Chili

2 medium unpeeled white or red potatoes, cut into ½-inch cubes

1 medium onion, chopped (½ cup)

1 small bell pepper (any color), chopped

1 can (15 to 16 oz) garbanzo beans, drained, rinsed

1 can (15 to 16 oz) kidney beans, drained, rinsed

2 cans (14.5 oz each) diced tomatoes, undrained

1 can (8 oz) tomato sauce

1 tablespoon chili powder

1 teaspoon ground cumin

1 medium zucchini, cut into ½-inch slices, then cut in half

1 In 4-quart Dutch oven, place all ingredients except zucchini. Heat to boiling over high heat, stirring occasionally.

2 Once chili is boiling, reduce heat just enough so chili bubbles gently. Cover; cook 10 minutes.

3 Stir zucchini into chili. Cover; cook 5 to 7 minutes longer, stirring occasionally, until potatoes and zucchini are tender when pierced with fork.

**6 servings**

## Budget Smart

*With all the flavors from the beans, vegetables and spices in this vegetarian chili, you won't miss the beef one bit! Leftovers are possibly even more delicious the next day.*

**1 Serving:** Calories 280; Total Fat 2.5g (Saturated Fat 0g, Trans Fat 0g); Cholesterol 0mg; Sodium 650mg; Total Carbohydrate 51g (Dietary Fiber 12g) • **Exchanges:** 2½ Starch, ½ Other Carbohydrate, 1 Vegetable, ½ Very Lean Meat • **Carbohydrate Choices:** 3½

# Caesar Chicken Paninis

Prep Time **30 Minutes**
Start to Finish **30 Minutes**

4 boneless skinless chicken breasts
  (about 1 ¼ lb)

4 hard rolls (about 5 × 3 inches), split

4 slices red onion

1 large tomato, sliced

⅓ cup Caesar dressing

¼ cup shredded Parmesan cheese
  (1 oz)

4 leaves romaine lettuce

1  Between pieces of plastic wrap or waxed paper, place each chicken breast smooth side down; gently pound with flat side of meat mallet or rolling pin until about ¼ inch thick.

2  Spray 8- or 10-inch skillet with cooking spray; heat over medium-high heat. Cook chicken in skillet 10 to 15 minutes, turning once, until chicken is no longer pink in center. Remove chicken from skillet; keep warm.

3  In skillet, place rolls, cut sides down. Cook over medium heat about 2 minutes or until toasted. Place chicken on bottom halves of rolls. Top with onion, tomato, dressing, cheese, lettuce and tops of rolls.

**4 sandwiches**

## Instant
## Success!

*For kid-friendly crispy chicken paninis, nix the boneless skinless chicken breasts and steps 1 and 2, and instead, heat frozen breaded chicken patties per package directions and continue with the recipe in step 3.*

**1 Sandwich:** Calories 500; Total Fat 20g (Saturated Fat 4.5g; Trans Fat 1g); Cholesterol 90mg; Sodium 750mg; Total Carbohydrate 37g (Dietary Fiber 3g) • **Exchanges:** 2 Starch, 1 Vegetable, 4½ Very Lean Meat, 3½ Fat • **Carbohydrate Choices:** 2½

# Montana Paninis

12 slices turkey bacon

1 small avocado, pitted, peeled

¼ cup ranch dressing

12 slices sourdough bread, ½ inch thick

3 tablespoons butter or margarine, softened

¾ lb thinly sliced cooked turkey (from deli)

1 large tomato, sliced

6 slices (1 oz each) Colby–Monterey Jack cheese blend

**1** In 10-inch skillet, cook bacon over medium heat 8 to 10 minutes, turning occasionally, until crisp and brown. Remove from skillet; drain on paper towels. Break bacon slices in half.

**2** In small bowl, mash avocado. Stir in dressing.

**3** Spread one side of each bread slice with butter. Place 6 bread slices with buttered sides down; top with turkey, bacon, tomato, cheese and avocado mixture. Top with remaining bread slices, buttered sides up.

**4** In 12-inch skillet, place sandwiches. Cover; cook over medium heat 4 to 5 minutes, turning once, until bread is crisp and cheese is melted.

**6 sandwiches**

## Instant
## Success!

*Slash a little fat by trying turkey bacon. It has the same smoky flavor as pork bacon but much less fat. One slice of regular bacon weighs in at about 6 grams of fat per slice, versus turkey bacon at roughly ½ gram of fat per slice.*

**1 Sandwich:** Calories 630; Total Fat 36g (Saturated Fat 14g; Trans Fat 1.5g); Cholesterol 100mg; Sodium 2020mg; Total Carbohydrate 43g (Dietary Fiber 4g) • **Exchanges:** 2 Starch, 1 Other Carbohydrate, 3½ Lean Meat, 5 Fat • **Carbohydrate Choices:** 3

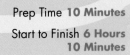
Prep Time **10 Minutes**

Start to Finish **6 Hours
10 Minutes**

# Teriyaki Barbecued Chicken Sandwiches

2 packages (20 oz each) boneless, skinless chicken thighs (about 24 thighs)

1 envelope (1 oz) stir-fry seasoning mix

½ cup ketchup

¼ cup stir-fry sauce

2½ cups coleslaw mix

10 kaiser rolls

1 Place chicken in 3½- to 4-quart slow cooker. In small bowl, mix seasoning mix (dry), ketchup and stir-fry sauce; pour over chicken.

2 Cover and cook on Low heat setting 6 to 7 hours or until juice of chicken is no longer pink when centers of thickest pieces are cut and chicken is tender.

3 Pull chicken into shreds, using 2 forks. Stir well to mix chicken with sauce. To serve, place ¼ cup coleslaw mix on roll and top with chicken. Chicken mixture will hold on Low heat setting up to 2 hours.

**10 sandwiches**

## Instant
## Success!

*Try these teriyaki sandwiches at your next outdoor potluck! If you want to transport the meat in the slow cooker, wrap the slow cooker in a towel or newspaper to keep it warm and place in a box that will stay flat in your car. Serve within an hour, or plug in the slow cooker at the new destination and set on Low to keep the food warm for hours.*

**1 Sandwich:** Calories 350; Total Fat 11g (Saturated Fat 3g, Trans Fat 0.5); Cholesterol 70mg; Sodium 900mg; Total Carbohydrate 34g (Dietary Fiber 1g) • **Exchanges:** 2 Starch, 1 Vegetable, 3 Lean Meat • **Carbohydrate Choices:** 2

# Onion and Bacon Cheese Sandwiches

4 slices bacon, cut into ½-inch pieces

1 medium onion, thinly sliced

8 slices (¾ oz each) Cheddar cheese

8 slices Vienna bread, ½ inch thick

1 In 12-inch nonstick skillet, cook bacon over medium heat about 4 minutes, stirring occasionally, until almost cooked.

2 Add onion to skillet. Cook 2 to 3 minutes, turning occasionally, until tender. Remove bacon and onion from skillet. Reserve 1 tablespoon drippings in skillet.

3 To make each sandwich, layer cheese, bacon and onion between 2 bread slices. Place 2 sandwiches in drippings in skillet. Cover; cook over medium-low heat 3 to 5 minutes, turning once, until bread is crisp and golden brown and cheese is melted. Repeat with remaining sandwiches.

**4 sandwiches**

## Make it a Meal

*Yum, don't these sandwiches sound good? Throw your favorite frozen French fry product into the oven to serve with the sandwiches, or how about kettle-cooked potato chips? For a great no-brainer French fry dip that's a notch up from ketchup and barbecue sauce, try Cheddar-flavored sour cream or onion- and chive-flavored sour cream.*

**1 Sandwich:** Calories 350; Total Fat 19g (Saturated Fat 10g; Trans Fat 0.5g); Cholesterol 55mg; Sodium 730mg; Total Carbohydrate 27g (Dietary Fiber 2g) • **Exchanges:** 2 Starch, 1½ High-Fat Meat, 1 Fat • **Carbohydrate Choices:** 2.

Prep Time **20 Minutes**

Start to Finish **20 Minutes**

# Veggie Focaccia Sandwiches

½ medium yellow bell pepper, cut into ½-inch strips

½ medium green bell pepper, cut into ½-inch strips

1 small onion, cut into ¼-inch slices

2 tablespoons balsamic vinaigrette or Italian dressing

1 round focaccia bread (8 inch), cut into 4 wedges

2 tablespoons chopped fresh basil leaves

½ cup shredded mozzarella cheese (2 oz)

2 plum (Roma) tomatoes

1 Spray 8- or 10-inch skillet with cooking spray; heat over medium-high heat. Add bell peppers, onion and vinaigrette to the skillet. Cook 4 to 5 minutes, stirring occasionally, until peppers are crisp-tender; remove from heat.

2 Split each focaccia wedge horizontally. Spoon ¼ of vegetable mixture onto each bottom half of focaccia wedge; sprinkle with basil and cheese. Top with tomatoes and tops of focaccia wedges.

**4 sandwiches**

**Lighten Up Veggie Focaccia Sandwiches:** *Use fat-free balsamic vinaigrette to reduce the fat to 9 grams and the calories to 250 per serving.*

## Budget
### Saver

*Try making these Italian-style sandwiches in summertime, when many of the ingredients will be at their peak of flavor—and probably cheaper as well. To save even more money, substitute 1 whole green bell pepper for the ½ green and ½ yellow bell peppers.*

**1 Sandwich:** Calories 280; Total Fat 12g (Saturated Fat 3g, Trans Fat 0g); Cholesterol 10mg; Sodium 660mg; Total Carbohydrate 35g (Dietary Fiber 2g) • **Exchanges:** 2 Starch, 1 Vegetable, 2 Fat • **Carbohydrate Choices:** 2

# Italian Steak Sandwiches

1 tablespoon butter or margarine

1 medium onion, thinly sliced

4 beef cube steaks (about 1½ lb)

½ teaspoon salt

¼ teaspoon pepper

¼ cup basil pesto

4 kaiser buns, split (toasted in oven if desired)

4 slices (about ¾ oz each) mozzarella cheese

1 medium tomato, thinly sliced

1 In 12-inch nonstick skillet, melt butter over medium-high heat. Cook onion in butter 3 to 4 minutes, stirring frequently, until tender; push to side of skillet.

2 Add beef steaks to skillet; sprinkle with salt and pepper. Cook 5 to 8 minutes, turning once, for medium doneness (160°F).

3 Spread pesto on cut sides of buns. Layer steaks, cheese, onion and tomato in buns.

**4 sandwiches**

## Instant
## Success!

*Have you ever thought of putting that killer spinach dip you can buy from the deli or refrigerated case on a sandwich? Try it if you don't have the pesto on hand. Pick up a tub of potato salad or some other wonderful concoction from the deli to go with these sandwiches.*

**1 Sandwich:** Calories 600; Total Fat 29g (Saturated Fat 11g; Trans Fat 1.5g); Cholesterol 95mg; Sodium 880mg; Total Carbohydrate 32g (Dietary Fiber 2g) • **Exchanges:** 2 Starch, 6½ Very Lean Meat, 5 Fat • **Carbohydrate Choices:** 2

# Grilled Portabella and Bell Pepper Sandwiches

6 fresh medium portabella mushroom caps

1 large bell pepper, cut into ¼-inch slices

1 large red onion, sliced

1 tablespoon olive or vegetable oil

½ teaspoon seasoned salt

1 round focaccia bread (8 or 9 inch)

¼ cup mayonnaise or salad dressing

¼ cup basil pesto

4 leaf lettuce leaves

1 Heat gas or charcoal grill. Brush mushrooms, bell pepper and onion with oil. Sprinkle with seasoned salt. Place vegetables in grill basket (grill "wok").

2 Place grill basket on grill. Cover grill; cook over medium heat 10 to 12 minutes, shaking grill basket occasionally to turn vegetables, until bell pepper and onion are crisp-tender and mushrooms are just tender.

3 Cut bread horizontally in half. In small bowl, mix mayonnaise and pesto; spread over cut sides of bread. Layer lettuce and grilled vegetables on bottom half of bread. Add top of bread. Cut into 6 wedges.

**6 sandwiches**

## Instant
## Success!

*It's easy to clean mushrooms just before using by wiping them off with a damp paper towel. If you find that the mushrooms are very watery after cooking, pat them dry before making the sandwiches.*

**1 Sandwich:** Calories 350; Total Fat 22g (Saturated Fat 4.5g; Trans Fat 0g); Cholesterol 10mg; Sodium 470mg; Total Carbohydrate 28g (Dietary Fiber 2g)• **Exchanges:** 1½ Starch, 1 Vegetable, ½ High-Fat Meat, 3½ Fat • **Carbohydrate Choices:** 2

# Peppered Pork Pitas with Garlic Spread

Prep Time **20 Minutes**
Start to Finish **20 Minutes**

⅓ cup mayonnaise or salad dressing

2 tablespoons milk

2 cloves garlic, finely chopped

1 lb boneless pork loin chops, cut into thin bite-size strips

1 tablespoon olive or vegetable oil

1 teaspoon coarsely ground pepper

1 jar (7 oz) roasted red bell peppers, drained, sliced

4 pita fold breads (7 inch)

1  In small bowl, mix mayonnaise, milk and garlic; set aside.

2  In medium bowl, mix pork, oil and pepper. Heat 12-inch skillet over medium-high heat. Cook pork in skillet 5 to 6 minutes, stirring occasionally, until pork is lightly browned on outside and no longer pink in center. Stir in bell peppers; heat until warm.

3  Heat pita folds as directed on package. Lightly spread one side of each pita fold with garlic mixture. Spoon pork mixture over each; fold up.

**4 sandwiches**

## Speed it Up

*Speed it up by using jarred chopped garlic and pork chow mein meat instead of fresh garlic and the pork chops.*

**1 Sandwich:** Calories 550; Total Fat 27g (Saturated Fat 6g; Trans Fat 0g); Cholesterol 75mg; Sodium 520mg; Total Carbohydrate 44g (Dietary Fiber 2g) • **Exchanges:** 3 Starch, 3 Lean Meat, 3 Fat • **Carbohydrate Choices:** 3

Prep Time **15 Minutes**
Start to Finish **15 Minutes**

## Budget
### Smart

*A week of "brown-bagging" sandwiches like these will really make a dent in your food budget if you've been hitting the sandwich counter a lot recently at lunch time. All the versions are easy and quick. Make sure to store the sandwiches in the fridge.*

# Tuna Salad Sandwiches

2 cans (6 oz each) tuna in water, drained

1 medium stalk celery, chopped (½ cup)

1 small onion, chopped (¼ cup)

½ cup mayonnaise or salad dressing

1 teaspoon lemon juice

¼ teaspoon salt

¼ teaspoon pepper

8 slices bread

**1** In medium bowl, mix all ingredients except bread.

**2** Spread tuna mixture on 4 bread slices. Top with remaining bread slices.

**Lighten Up Tuna Salad Sandwiches:** *Use fat-free mayonnaise for a tuna salad sandwich with 3 grams of fat and 240 calories.*

**Chicken Salad Sandwiches:** *Substitute 1½ cups chopped cooked chicken or turkey for the tuna. Omit the lemon juice.*

**Egg Salad Sandwiches:** *Substitute 6 Hard-Cooked Eggs (page 261), chopped, for the tuna. Omit the lemon juice.*

**Ham Salad Sandwiches:** *Substitute 1½ cups chopped cooked ham for the tuna. Omit the salt and pepper. Substitute 1 teaspoon yellow mustard for the lemon juice.*

**4 sandwiches**

**1 Sandwich:** Calories 410; Total Fat 24g (Saturated Fat 4g, Trans Fat 0g); Cholesterol 30mg; Sodium 870mg; Total Carbohydrate 29g (Dietary Fiber 1g) • **Exchanges:** 2 Starch, 2 Very Lean Meat, 4 Fat • **Carbohydrate Choices:** 2

# Lemon-Pepper Fish Fillet Sandwiches

Prep Time **15 Minutes**
Start to Finish **15 Minutes**

2 tablespoons whole-grain yellow cornmeal

2 tablespoons all-purpose flour

1 teaspoon seasoned salt

½ teaspoon lemon-pepper seasoning

1 tablespoon canola oil

2 walleye fillets (about 6 oz each), each cut crosswise in half

¼ cup tartar sauce

4 100% whole wheat or rye sandwich buns, toasted

1 cup shredded lettuce

1 In shallow bowl, mix cornmeal, flour, seasoned salt and lemon-pepper seasoning.

2 In 12-inch nonstick skillet, heat oil over medium-high heat. Coat fish fillets with flour mixture. Cook in oil 4 to 6 minutes, turning once, until fish flakes easily with fork.

3 Spread tartar sauce on cut sides of toasted buns. Layer lettuce and fish fillets in buns.

**4 sandwiches**

## Instant
## Success!

*If you can't find walleye, you can substitute other medium-textured white fish fillets like hake, flounder or catfish. It's fine to buy what's on sale, but make sure the fish is fresh (the flesh should be shiny, firm and elastic and spring back when touched). Frozen fillets should be tightly wrapped and frozen solid with little or no ice crystals, or dark or dry spots that may indicate freezer burn.*

**1 Sandwich:** Calories 330; Total Fat 14g (Saturated Fat 2g, Trans Fat 0g); Cholesterol 50mg; Sodium 930mg; Total Carbohydrate 29g (Dietary Fiber 2g) • **Exchanges:** 1½ Starch, ½ Other Carbohydrate, 2 Very Lean Meat, 2½ Fat • **Carbohydrate Choices:** 2

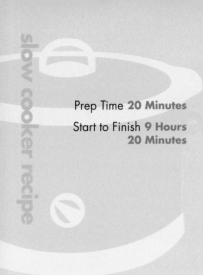
Prep Time **20 Minutes**

Start to Finish **9 Hours
20 Minutes**

# Jerk Pork Sandwiches

1 boneless pork shoulder roast (2½- to 3-lb)

1 medium onion, chopped (½ cup)

3 tablespoons Caribbean jerk seasoning

½ cup chili sauce

½ cup purchased corn relish

2 tablespoons chopped fresh cilantro

1 cup shredded lettuce

8 pita fold breads or split potato rolls

1 Spray 3- to 4-quart slow cooker with cooking spray. Remove netting or strings from pork roast; cut pork into 2-inch pieces. Place pork and onion in cooker. Sprinkle with jerk seasoning; toss to coat. Pour chili sauce over top of the roast.

2 Cover and cook on Low heat setting 9 to 11 hours.

3 Place pork on cutting board; use 2 forks to pull pork into shreds. Return pork to cooker. In small bowl, mix corn relish and cilantro. To serve, layer lettuce, pork mixture and corn relish in pita fold breads.

**8 sandwiches**

## Instant
## **Success!**

*Look for Caribbean jerk seasoning in the spice section of the supermarket. Pork shoulder is one of the least expensive cuts of pork, and one of the most flavorful.*

**1 Sandwich:** Calories 450; Total Fat 18g (Saturated Fat 6g, Trans Fat 0g); Cholesterol 90mg; Sodium 760mg; Total Carbohydrate 36g (Dietary Fiber 3g) • **Exchanges:** 2½ Starch, 4 Lean Meat, ½ Fat • **Carbohydrate Choices:** 2½

# Grilled Italian Turkey Burgers

Prep Time **30 Minutes**
Start to Finish **30 Minutes**

½ lb ground turkey breast

3 tablespoons tomato pasta sauce

1 tablespoon finely chopped red onion

2 slices (1 oz each) mozzarella cheese, cut in half

½ baguette (8 inches), cut into two 4-inch pieces

2 lettuce leaves

2 slices red onion

Additional tomato pasta sauce, if desired

## Budget
### Smart

*Ground turkey is naturally lighter than beef, and often cheaper to boot. Avoid overmixing the ground turkey with other ingredients for a lighter textured burger.*

1 Heat gas or charcoal grill. In medium bowl, mix turkey, 3 tablespoons pasta sauce and chopped onion. Shape mixture into 2 patties, each about ¾ inch thick and the approximate shape of the baguette pieces.

2 Carefully brush grill rack with canola oil. Place patties on grill. Cover grill; cook over medium heat 12 to 15 minutes, turning once, until thermometer inserted in center of patties reads 165°F. Top patties with cheese. Cover grill; cook about 1 minute longer or until cheese is melted.

3 Cut baguette pieces in half horizontally. Place lettuce leaves on bottom halves; top with burgers and onion slices. Top with remaining baguette halves. Serve with additional pasta sauce.

**2 sandwiches**

**1 Sandwich:** Calories 450; Total Fat 15g (Saturated Fat 6g, Trans Fat 1g); Cholesterol 90mg; Sodium 710mg; Total Carbohydrate 40g (Dietary Fiber 3g) • **Exchanges:** 2 Starch, ½ Other Carbohydrate, 4½ Very Lean Meat, 2½ Fat • **Carbohydrate Choices:** 2½

# Broiled Dijon Burgers

Prep Time **20 Minutes**
Start to Finish **20 Minutes**

1 egg

2 tablespoons milk

2 teaspoons Dijon mustard

¼ teaspoon salt

⅛ teaspoon pepper

1 cup soft bread crumbs (about 2 slices bread)

1 small onion, finely chopped (¼ cup)

1 lb extra-lean (at least 90%) ground beef

6 whole wheat burger buns, split, toasted

1 Set oven control to broil. Spray broiler pan rack with cooking spray.

2 In medium bowl, mix egg, milk, mustard, salt and pepper. Stir in bread crumbs and onion. Stir in beef. Shape mixture into 6 patties, each about ½ inch thick.

3 Place patties on rack in broiler pan. Broil with tops about 5 inches from heat for about 10 minutes for medium, turning once, until meat thermometer inserted in center reads 160°F. Serve burgers on buns.

**6 sandwiches**

## Instant
## Success!

*Use whatever mustard you have on hand—even honey mustard would be good in these healthful, whole-grain burgers. The soft bread crumbs and onion stretch the meat without detracting from the beefy flavor. Avoid overmixing the beef mixture for a tender, juicier burger.*

**1 Sandwich:** Calories 270; Total Fat 9g (Saturated Fat 3g, Trans Fat 1g); Cholesterol 85mg; Sodium 470mg; Total Carbohydrate 25g (Dietary Fiber 3g) • **Exchanges:** 1½ Starch, 2½ Lean Meat • **Carbohydrate Choices:** 1½

# Italian Sausage Burgers

1 lb lean (at least 80%) ground beef

½ lb bulk mild or hot Italian sausage

2 tablespoons Italian-style dry bread crumbs

6 slices (¾ oz each) mozzarella cheese

12 slices Italian bread, ½ inch thick

½ cup sun-dried tomato mayonnaise

1 cup shredded lettuce

1 medium tomato, thinly sliced

1 Heat coals or gas grill for direct heat. In large bowl, mix beef, sausage and bread crumbs. Shape mixture into 6 patties, about ½ inch thick and 3½ inches in diameter.

2 Cover and grill patties 4 to 6 inches from medium heat 12 to 15 minutes, turning once, until meat thermometer inserted in center reads 160°F. Top patties with cheese. Cover and grill about 1 minute longer or until cheese is melted. Add bread slices to side of grill for last 2 to 3 minutes of grilling, turning once, until lightly toasted.

3 Spread toasted bread with mayonnaise; top 6 bread slices with lettuce, tomato and patties. Top with remaining bread slices.

**6 sandwiches**

## Instant
## Success!

*If you don't have sun-dried tomato mayonnaise, you can make your own: Combine ⅓ cup mayonnaise with about 2 tablespoons chopped sun-dried tomatoes. Regular mayonnaise works just fine as well. Be sure to use lean ground beef here, since the bulk sausage already contributes the fat needed to make the burgers juicy.*

**1 Sandwich:** Calories 490; Total Fat 31g (Saturated Fat 10g, Trans Fat 1g); Cholesterol 85mg; Sodium 750mg; Total Carbohydrate 25g (Dietary Fiber 2g) • **Exchanges:** 1½ Starch, 3½ High-Fat Meat, 1 Fat • **Carbohydrate Choices:** 1½

# Veggie and Bean Burgers

¼ cup uncooked instant rice

¼ cup boiling water

½ cup broccoli florets

2 oz fresh mushrooms (about 4 medium)

½ small red bell pepper, cut up

1 can (15 to 16 oz) garbanzo beans, rinsed, drained

1 egg

1 clove garlic

½ teaspoon seasoned salt

1 teaspoon instant chopped onion

⅓ cup Italian-style dry bread crumbs

3 tablespoons vegetable oil

4 whole wheat hamburger buns, split

Toppings (Cheddar cheese slices, lettuce, sliced tomato, sliced onion and mayonnaise), if desired

1 In medium bowl, stir rice and boiling water. Cover and let stand 5 minutes. Drain if necessary.

2 Meanwhile, in food processor, place broccoli, mushrooms and bell pepper. Cover and process, using quick on-and-off motions, to finely chop vegetables (do not puree). Stir vegetables into rice.

3 Add beans, egg, garlic and seasoned salt to food processor. Cover and process until smooth. Stir bean mixture, onion and bread crumbs into vegetable mixture.

4 Using about ½ cup vegetable mixture for each patty, shape into four ½-inch-thick patties.

5 In 10-inch nonstick skillet, heat oil over medium-high heat. Cook patties in oil 8 to 10 minutes, turning once, until brown and crisp. Serve on buns with toppings.

**4 sandwiches**

**Veggie and Bean "Meatballs":** *Heat oven to 400°F. Generously spray 15 × 10 × 1-inch pan with cooking spray. Shape vegetable mixture into 16 balls; place in pan. Generously spray tops of balls with cooking spray. Bake about 20 minutes or until crisp. Serve with pasta sauce (any flavor) or cheese sauce.*

1 Sandwich: Calories 460; Total Fat 16g (Saturated Fat 2.5g, Trans Fat 0g); Cholesterol 55mg; Sodium 540mg; Total Carbohydrate 61g (Dietary Fiber 9g) • **Exchanges:** 3½ Starch, 2 Vegetable, 2 Fat • **Carbohydrate Choices:** 4

## Budget
### Smart

*It's easier to make your own veggie burgers than you think and a lot cheaper than store-bought! These take only 25 minutes from start to finish.*

# Grilled Veggie Burger and Roasted Pepper Sandwiches

Prep Time **10 Minutes**
Start to Finish **25 Minutes**

1 package (10-oz) frozen meatless soy-protein burgers (4 burgers)

½ teaspoon salt

4 slices (¾ oz each) mozzarella cheese

4 whole-grain sandwich buns, split

¼ cup roasted-garlic mayonnaise

1 cup roasted bell peppers

1 medium tomato, sliced

1 Heat coals or gas grill for direct heat. Sprinkle burgers with salt.

2 Cover and grill burgers 4 to 6 inches from medium heat 8 to 10 minutes, turning once or twice, until thoroughly heated. Top each burger with cheese. Cover and grill about 1 minute or just until cheese is melted.

3 Spread cut sides of buns with garlic mayonnaise. Thinly slice roasted bell peppers. Layer tomato, burger and bell peppers in each bun.

**4 sandwiches**

## Instant Success!

*If you have the odds and ends of partially used bell peppers in your fridge, use them in this veggie burger sandwich. You don't even have to roast them! Just chop roughly and scatter on top of each burger.*

**Simple Swap:** *If you can't find roasted-garlic mayonnaise, just add a teaspoon of garlic powder or minced garlic to ¼ cup regular mayonnaise.*

**1 Sandwich:** Calories 450; Total Fat 24g (Saturated Fat 6g, Trans Fat 0g); Cholesterol 20mg; Sodium 1190mg; Total Carbohydrate 38g (Dietary Fiber 4g) • **Exchanges:** 2 Starch, 1 Vegetable, 2 Medium-Fat Meat, 2½ Fat • **Carbohydrate Choices:** 2½

# Grilled Fish Tacos

1 lb sea bass, red snapper, halibut or other firm white fish fillets

1 tablespoon olive or vegetable oil

1 teaspoon ground cumin or chili powder

½ teaspoon salt

¼ teaspoon pepper

8 corn tortillas (6 inch)

¼ cup sour cream

Toppers (shredded lettuce, chopped avocado, chopped tomatoes, chopped onion and chopped fresh cilantro), if desired

½ cup salsa

1  Brush grill rack with vegetable oil. Heat gas or charcoal grill.

2  Brush fish with oil; sprinkle with cumin, salt and pepper. Place fish on grill. Cover grill; cook over medium heat 5 to 7 minutes, turning once, until fish flakes easily with fork. Cut fish into 8 serving pieces.

3  Heat tortillas as directed on package. Spread sour cream on tortillas. Add fish, toppers and salsa.

**8 tacos**

## Speed it Up

*Put away the knife for those topper suggestions. Instead, pick up a layered Mexican dip from the deli case—a generous dollop of that would taste great! Or buy preshredded lettuce, guacamole and frozen chopped onions— so you just have to chop the tomatoes.*

**1 Taco:** Calories 160; Total Fat 6g (Saturated Fat 2g; Trans Fat 0g); Cholesterol 35mg; Sodium 290mg; Total Carbohydrate 13g (Dietary Fiber 2g) • **Exchanges:** 1 Starch, 1½ Very Lean Meat, 1 Fat • **Carbohydrate Choices:** 1

Betty Crocker Supper in a Snap

# Salsa-Rice Burritos

1½ cups salsa

1½ teaspoons chili powder

1 cup uncooked instant rice

1 can (15 oz) black beans, drained, rinsed

1 can (11 oz) whole kernel corn with red and green peppers, undrained

1½ cups shredded Cheddar cheese (6 oz)

8 flour tortillas (8 inch)

Additional salsa, if desired

1 In 10-inch skillet, heat 1½ cups salsa and the chili powder to boiling. Stir in rice; remove from heat. Cover; let stand 5 minutes.

2 Stir beans, corn and cheese into rice mixture.

3 Onto center of each tortilla, spoon about ½ cup rice mixture. Roll tortillas around filling; tuck ends under. Serve with additional salsa.

**8 burritos**

## Instant
## Success!

*If you're a meat lover and have a few extra minutes, cook up some chorizo or ground beef and stir it into the rice mixture in step 2. Some brands of chorizo come in heat-and-serve links—even easier!*

**1 Burrito:** Calories 390; Total Fat 11g (Saturated Fat 5g; Trans Fat 0.5g); Cholesterol 20mg; Sodium 680mg; Total Carbohydrate 58g (Dietary Fiber 6g) • **Exchanges:** 4 Starch, ½ Very Lean Meat, 1½ Fat • **Carbohydrate Choices:** 4

# Cheese Enchiladas

⅓ cup chopped green bell pepper

1 clove garlic, finely chopped, or
⅛ teaspoon garlic powder

1 tablespoon chili powder

1½ teaspoons chopped fresh or
½ teaspoon dried oregano leaves

¼ teaspoon ground cumin

1 can (15 oz) tomato sauce

1 medium onion, chopped (½ cup)

2 cups shredded Monterey Jack cheese
(8 oz)

1 cup shredded Cheddar cheese (4 oz)

½ cup sour cream

2 tablespoons chopped fresh parsley,
if desired

¼ teaspoon pepper

8 corn tortillas (5 or 6 inch)

Additional sour cream and chopped
green onions, if desired

1 Heat oven to 350°F.

2 In medium bowl, mix bell pepper, garlic, chili powder, oregano, cumin
and tomato sauce; set aside. In large bowl, mix onion, Monterey Jack cheese,
Cheddar cheese, ½ cup sour cream, the parsley and pepper.

3 Place 2 tortillas between dampened microwavable paper towels or
microwavable plastic wrap; microwave on High 15 to 20 seconds to soften.
Immediately spoon about ⅓ cup of the cheese mixture down one side of
each softened tortilla to within 1 inch of edge. Roll tortilla around filling;
place seam side down in ungreased 11 × 7-inch glass (2-quart) baking dish.
Repeat with remaining tortillas and cheese mixture.

4 Pour tomato sauce mixture over tortillas. Bake uncovered about
25 minutes or until hot and bubbly. Garnish with additional sour cream
and chopped green onions.

**4 servings**

**Beef Enchiladas:** *Add 1½ cups shredded or chopped cooked beef. In step
3, spoon about 2 tablespoons beef over the cheese mixture on each tortilla.*

**Chicken Enchiladas:** *Add 1½ cups shredded or chopped cooked chicken
or turkey. In step 3, spoon about 2 tablespoons chicken over the cheese
mixture on each tortilla.*

**1 Serving:** Calories 560; Total Fat 34g (Saturated Fat 21g, Trans Fat 1g); Cholesterol 100mg; Sodium 1090mg; Total Carbohydrate
36g (Dietary Fiber 6g) • **Exchanges:** 2 Starch, ½ Other Carbohydrate, 3 High-Fat Meat, 1½ Fat • **Carbohydrate Choices:** 2½

## Budget
Smart

*If your family loves
Mexican food, add these
cheese enchiladas to your
repertoire of budget-
friendly meals. The
uncooked enchiladas
can be prepared up to
24 hours ahead of time
and refrigerated, covered,
until you're ready to
bake them. You can
spice up the flavor by
adding a finely chopped
stemmed and seeded
jalapeño chile or two.*

Betty Crocker Supper in a Snap

# Chipotle and Black Bean Burritos

2 tablespoons vegetable oil

1 large onion, chopped (1 cup)

6 cloves garlic, finely chopped, or
¾ teaspoon garlic powder

1 can (15 oz) black beans, drained,
rinsed and mashed

2 to 3 chipotle chiles in adobo sauce
(from a 7-oz can), drained, finely
chopped (2 teaspoons)

4 flour tortillas (8 or 10 inch)

1 cup shredded mozzarella cheese
(4 oz)

1 large tomato, chopped (1 cup)

Chunky-style salsa, if desired

Sour cream, if desired

1 In 10-inch nonstick skillet, heat oil over medium–high heat. Add onion
and garlic; cook 6 to 8 minutes, stirring occasionally, until onion is tender.
Stir in mashed beans and chiles. Cook, stirring frequently, until hot.

2 Place ¼ of the bean mixture on center of each tortilla. Top with cheese
and tomato.

3 Fold one end of each tortilla up about 1 inch over filling; fold right
and left sides over folded end, overlapping. Fold remaining end down. Place
seam side down on serving platter or plate. Spoon on salsa and dollop of
sour cream.

**4 servings**

## Budget
Smart

*Many vegetarian
dishes are naturally
cost friendly, and these
20-minute burritos
are no exception!*

**1 Serving:** Calories 450; Total Fat 17g (Saturated Fat 6g, Trans Fat 0.5g); Cholesterol 15mg; Sodium 820mg; Total Carbohydrate 56g
(Dietary Fiber 12g) • **Exchanges:** 3 Starch, ½ Other Carbohydrate, 1½ Medium-Fat Meat, 1½ Fat • **Carbohydrate Choices:** 4

# Chicken Fajita Wraps

1 tablespoon chili powder

1 teaspoon salt

1¼ lb boneless skinless chicken breasts, cut into thin strips

1 tablespoon vegetable oil

1 bag (1 lb) frozen broccoli, red peppers, onions and mushrooms (or other combination)

8 flour tortillas (8 inch)

Salsa, if desired

1  In large bowl, sprinkle chili powder and salt over chicken; toss.

2  In 12-inch skillet, heat oil over high heat. Cook chicken in oil 3 to 4 minutes, stirring frequently, until no longer pink in center. Stir in vegetables. Cook about 4 minutes, stirring frequently, until vegetables are crisp-tender.

3  Onto center of each tortilla, spoon about ½ cup of the chicken mixture. Fold top and bottom ends of each tortilla about 1 inch over filling; fold right and left sides over folded ends, overlapping. Serve with salsa.

**4 sandwiches**

## Instant
## Success!

*It's all about options. If you can't find the frozen veggie combo suggested, try a 1-pound bag of frozen corn, broccoli and sweet red peppers or any of your favorites.*

**1 Sandwich:** Calories 520; Total Fat 15g (Saturated Fat 3.5g; Trans Fat 1g); Cholesterol 85mg; Sodium 1370mg; Total Carbohydrate 56g (Dietary Fiber 5g) • **Exchanges:** 3½ Starch, 1 Vegetable, 4 Very Lean Meat, 2 Fat • **Carbohydrate Choices:** 4

# Mexican Chicken Pizza with Cornmeal Crust

Prep Time **20 Minutes**
Start to Finish **40 Minutes**

1½ cups all-purpose flour

1 tablespoon sugar

1¼ teaspoons regular active dry yeast

¼ teaspoon coarse (kosher or sea) salt

¾ cup warm water

1 tablespoon olive oil

⅓ cup yellow cornmeal

Additional cornmeal

1½ cups Mexican cheese blend (6 oz)

1½ cups shredded cooked chicken breast

1 can (14.5 oz) organic fire roasted or plain diced tomatoes, drained

½ medium yellow bell pepper, chopped (½ cup)

¼ cup sliced green onions (4 medium)

¼ cup chopped fresh cilantro

1 Heat oven to 450°F. In medium bowl, stir together ¾ cup of the flour, the sugar, yeast and salt. Stir in warm water and oil. Beat with electric mixer on high speed 1 minute. Stir in ⅓ cup cornmeal and remaining ¾ cup flour to make a soft dough.

2 On lightly floured surface, knead dough until smooth and elastic, about 5 minutes. Cover and let rest 10 minutes.

3 Spray large cookie sheet with cooking spray; sprinkle with additional cornmeal. On cookie sheet, press dough into 4 × 10-inch rectangle; prick with fork. Bake 8 to 10 minutes or until edges just begin to turn brown.

4 Sprinkle with ½ cup of the cheese blend. Top with chicken, tomatoes and bell pepper. Sprinkle with remaining 1 cup cheese. Bake 6 to 8 minutes longer or until cheese is melted and edges are golden brown. Sprinkle with green onions and cilantro.

**6 servings**

## Speed it Up

*This hurry-up homemade technique makes it easy to save by making your pizza instead of ordering delivery—it's ready in 40 minutes!*

**1 Serving:** Calories 340; Total Fat 13g (Saturated Fat 6g, Trans Fat 0g); Cholesterol 55mg; Sodium 360mg; Total Carbohydrate 35g (Dietary Fiber 2g) • **Exchanges:** 2 Starch, 1 Vegetable, 2 Lean Meat, 1 Fat • **Carbohydrate Choices:** 2

# Barbecue Chicken Pizza

2 cups shredded rotisserie or other cooked chicken breast

⅓ cup barbecue sauce

1 package (10 oz) prebaked thin Italian pizza crust (12 inch)

3 plum (Roma) tomatoes, sliced

1 cup shredded Monterey Jack cheese (4 oz)

2 tablespoons chopped fresh cilantro leaves

1 Heat oven to 450°F. In small bowl, mix chicken and barbecue sauce. Place pizza crust on ungreased cookie sheet; spread chicken mixture over crust. Arrange tomatoes over chicken; sprinkle with cheese.

2 Bake 8 to 10 minutes or until cheese is melted and crust is browned. Sprinkle with cilantro.

**6 servings**

## Speed it Up

*On the move? Make barbecued chicken wraps! No baking needed! Instead of pizza crust, substitute 6 flour tortillas (6 to 8 inch). Spread chicken mixture evenly over wraps to within 1 inch of edge. Top with tomatoes, cheese and cilantro. Roll up tortillas tightly.*

**1 Serving:** Calories 300); Total Fat 11g (Saturated Fat 6g; Trans Fat 0g); Cholesterol 60mg; Sodium 710mg; Total Carbohydrate 27g (Dietary Fiber 1g) • **Exchanges:** 1½ Starch, ½ Other Carbohydrate, 3 Lean Meat • **Carbohydrate Choices:** 2

# Double-Cheese, Spinach and Chicken Pizza

1 package (14 oz) prebaked original Italian pizza crust (12 inch)

1 cup shredded Havarti cheese (4 oz)

2 cups washed fresh baby spinach leaves (from 10-oz bag)

1 cup diced rotisserie or other cooked chicken

¼ cup chopped drained roasted red bell peppers (from 7-oz jar)

½ teaspoon garlic salt

1 cup shredded Cheddar cheese (4 oz)

1 Heat oven to 425°F. Place pizza crust on ungreased cookie sheet.

2 Top with Havarti cheese, spinach, chicken, bell peppers, garlic salt and Cheddar cheese.

3 Bake 8 to 10 minutes or until crust is golden brown.

**6 servings**

## Speed it Up

*Why not buy bags of fresh spinach and shredded cheese? All the hard work is already done. By the way, you can use most any type of cheese in place of Havarti.*

**1 Serving:** Calories 380; Total Fat 19g (Saturated Fat 11g; Trans Fat 0.5g); Cholesterol 70mg; Sodium 800mg; Total Carbohydrate 30g (Dietary Fiber 2g) • **Exchanges:** 2 Starch, 2½ Lean Meat, 2 Fat • **Carbohydrate Choices:** 2

# Easy Philly Cheesesteak Pizza

1 can (13.8 oz) refrigerated pizza crust

2 cups frozen bell pepper and onion stir-fry (from 1-lb bag)

2 tablespoons creamy Dijon mustard-mayonnaise spread

8 oz thinly sliced cooked roast beef (from deli)

2 cups shredded American cheese (8 oz)

1 Heat oven to 425°F. Spray 12-inch pizza pan with cooking spray. Press pizza crust dough in pan. Bake 8 minutes.

2 Meanwhile, spray 10-inch skillet with cooking spray; heat over medium-high heat. Cook bell pepper mixture in skillet 4 to 5 minutes, stirring frequently, until crisp-tender; drain if necessary.

3 Spread mustard-mayonnaise spread over partially baked crust. Top with roast beef, bell pepper mixture and cheese. Bake 8 to 10 minutes or until crust is golden brown.

**6 servings**

Instant
## Success!

*Here's a quick take on the cheesesteak sandwich made famous in Philadelphia in the 1930s. Turning it into a hearty pizza means it can serve the whole family super-fast.*

**1 Serving:** Calories 420; Total Fat 20g (Saturated Fat 10g; Trans Fat 0.5g); Cholesterol 65mg; Sodium 1130mg; Total Carbohydrate 37g (Dietary Fiber 0g) • **Exchanges:** 1½ Starch, ½ Other Carbohydrate, 1 Vegetable, 2½ High-Fat Meat • **Carbohydrate Choices:** 2½

# Shrimp and Feta Pizza

Prep Time **10 Minutes**
Start to Finish **25 Minutes**

1 package (14 oz) prebaked original
   Italian pizza crust (12 inch)

1 tablespoon olive or vegetable oil

½ lb uncooked deveined peeled medium
   shrimp, thawed if frozen, tail shells
   removed

1 clove garlic, finely chopped

2 cups shredded mozzarella cheese
   (8 oz)

1 can (2¼ oz) sliced ripe olives, drained

1 cup crumbled feta cheese (4 oz)

1 tablespoon chopped fresh or
   1 teaspoon dried rosemary leaves

1 Heat oven to 400°F. Place pizza crust on ungreased cookie sheet.

2 In 10-inch nonstick skillet, heat oil over medium heat. Cook shrimp
and garlic in oil about 3 minutes, stirring frequently, until shrimp are pink.

3 Sprinkle 1 cup of the mozzarella cheese over pizza crust. Top with shrimp,
olives, remaining 1 cup mozzarella cheese and the feta cheese. Sprinkle with
rosemary. Bake 12 to 15 minutes or until cheese is melted.

**6 servings**

## Instant
## Success!

*Who says you need
tomato sauces on
pizza? This classy
version features two
kinds of cheese and
succulent shrimp, and
it's a mouthful!*

**1 Serving:** Calories 400; Total Fat 19g (Saturated Fat 10g; Trans Fat 0.5g); Cholesterol 100mg; Sodium 890mg; Total
Carbohydrate 32g (Dietary Fiber 2g) • **Exchanges:** 2 Starch, 3 Very Lean Meat, 3 Fat • **Carbohydrate Choices:** 2

# Antipasto French Bread Pizzas

1 loaf (12 inch) French bread, cut in half horizontally

¼ cup basil pesto

10 slices salami (3½ inches in diameter)

2 or 3 plum (Roma) tomatoes, thinly sliced

1 small green bell pepper, cut into thin rings

2 medium green onions, chopped (2 tablespoons)

¼ cup sliced ripe olives

6 slices (1½ oz each) provolone cheese

1 Heat oven to 425°F. Place bread halves, cut sides up, on ungreased cookie sheet. Spread with pesto. Top with salami, tomatoes, bell pepper, onions, olives and cheese.

2 Bake 8 to 10 minutes or until cheese is melted.

**6 servings**

## Instant
## Success!

*You know what they say: variety is the spice of life! For some quick substitutions, use pepperoni slices instead of salami and sliced or shredded mozzarella cheese for the provolone. No plum tomatoes today? Thinly slice regular tomatoes.*

**1 Serving:** Calories 380; Total Fat 24g (Saturated Fat 11g; Trans Fat 0.5g); Cholesterol 45mg; Sodium 1030mg; Total Carbohydrate 22g (Dietary Fiber 2g) • **Exchanges:** 1½ Starch, 2 High-Fat Meat, 1½ Fat • **Carbohydrate Choices:** 1½

# White Bean and Spinach Pizza

2 cups water

½ cup sun-dried tomato halves (not oil-packed)

1 can (15 to 16 oz) great northern or navy beans, drained, rinsed

2 medium cloves garlic, finely chopped

1 package (14 oz) prebaked original Italian pizza crust (12 inch)

¼ teaspoon dried oregano leaves

1 cup firmly packed spinach leaves, shredded

½ cup shredded Colby–Monterey Jack cheese blend (2 oz)

1 Heat oven to 425°F. Heat water to boiling. In small bowl, pour enough boiling water over dried tomatoes to cover. Let stand 10 minutes; drain. Cut into thin strips; set aside.

2 In food processor, place beans and garlic. Cover; process until smooth.

3 Place pizza crust on ungreased cookie sheet. Spread beans over pizza crust. Sprinkle with oregano, tomatoes, spinach and cheese. Bake 8 to 10 minutes or until cheese is melted.

**8 servings**

**1 Serving:** Calories 240; Total Fat 6g (Saturated Fat 3g, Trans Fat 0g); Cholesterol 10mg; Sodium 370mg; Total Carbohydrate 36g (Dietary Fiber 4g) • **Exchanges:** 2½ Starch, ½ Lean Meat, ½ Fat • **Carbohydrate Choices:** 2½

# Fresh Mozzarella and Tomato Pizza

Prep Time **35 Minutes**

Start to Finish **3 Hours 15 Minutes**

Italian-Style Pizza Dough (see recipe below)

4 oz fresh mozzarella cheese, well drained

2 plum (Roma) tomatoes, thinly sliced

¼ teaspoon salt

Fresh cracked pepper to taste

¼ cup thin strips fresh basil leaves

1 tablespoon chopped fresh oregano leaves

1 tablespoon small capers, if desired

1 tablespoon extra-virgin or regular olive oil

1 Make Italian-Style Pizza Dough.

2 Move oven rack to lowest position. Heat oven to 425°F. Grease cookie sheet or 12-inch pizza pan with oil. Press dough into 12-inch circle on cookie sheet or pat in pizza pan, using floured fingers. Press dough from center to edge so edge is slightly thicker than center.

3 Cut cheese into ¼-inch slices. Place cheese on dough to within ½ inch of edge. Arrange tomatoes on cheese. Sprinkle with salt, pepper, 2 tablespoons of the basil, the oregano and capers. Drizzle with oil.

4 Bake about 20 minutes or until crust is golden brown and cheese is melted. Sprinkle with remaining 2 tablespoons basil.

**8 servings**

**Italian-Style Pizza Dough:** *In large bowl, dissolve 1 packet regular or quick active dry yeast (2¼ teaspoons). Stir in ¾ cup all-purpose flour, 1 teaspoon extra-virgin or regular olive oil, ½ teaspoon salt and ½ teaspoon sugar. Stir in enough additional flour to make dough easy to handle. Place dough on lightly floured surface. Knead about 10 minutes or until smooth and springy. Grease large bowl with oil. Place dough in bowl, turning dough to grease all sides. Cover and let rise in warm place 20 minutes. Gently push fist into dough to deflate. Cover and refrigerate at least 2 hours but no longer than 48 hours. (If dough should double in size during refrigeration, gently push fist into dough to deflate.)*

## Budget Smart

*Making your own pizza dough is fun and inexpensive! You can also make this pizza with shredded mozzarella cheese. Just substitute 2 cups shredded mozzarella cheese (8 oz) for the fresh. Sprinkle 1 cup of the cheese over the dough. Add the remaining ingredients as directed—except sprinkle with the remaining 1 cup cheese before drizzling with the oil.*

**1 Serving:** Calories 140; Total Fat 5g (Saturated Fat 2g, Trans Fat 0g); Cholesterol 10mg; Sodium 300mg; Total Carbohydrate 17g (Dietary Fiber 1g) • **Exchanges:** 1 Starch, 1 Fat • **Carbohydrate Choices:** 1

# Canadian Bacon–Whole Wheat Pizza

Prep Time **15 Minutes**
Start to Finish **55 Minutes**

1 package regular active or fast-acting dry yeast

1 cup warm water (105°F to 115°F)

2½ cups whole wheat flour

3 tablespoons olive oil

½ teaspoon salt

1 tablespoon whole-grain cornmeal

1 can (8 oz) pizza sauce

2 cups finely shredded Italian mozzarella and Parmesan cheese blend (8 oz)

1 package (6 oz) sliced Canadian bacon, cut into fourths

1 small green bell pepper, chopped (½ cup)

1 In medium bowl, dissolve yeast in warm water. Stir in flour, 2 tablespoons of the oil and the salt. Beat vigorously with spoon 20 strokes. Let dough rest 20 minutes.

2 Move oven rack to lowest position. Heat oven to 425°F. Grease cookie sheet with remaining 1 tablespoon oil; sprinkle with cornmeal. Pat dough into 12×10-inch rectangle on cookie sheet, using floured fingers; pinch edges to form ½-inch rim.

3 Spread pizza sauce over crust. Top with cheese, bacon and bell pepper. Bake 15 to 20 minutes or until edge of crust is golden brown.

**8 servings**

## Instant
## Success!

*What a treat! You don't often find Canadian bacon on pizza, but it's delicious, and a 6-oz package won't stretch your wallet too far. You can also use sliced ham in place of the Canadian bacon.*

**1 Serving:** Calories 320; Total Fat 14g (Saturated Fat 6g, Trans Fat 0g); Cholesterol 35mg; Sodium 750mg; Total Carbohydrate 32g (Dietary Fiber 5g) • **Exchanges:** 1 Starch, 1 Other Carbohydrate, 2 Medium-Fat Meat, ½ Fat • **Carbohydrate Choices:** 2

# Very Veggie Pizza Pie

1 package (8 oz) sliced mushrooms (3 cups)

1 small zucchini, sliced (1 cup)

1 medium bell pepper, sliced

1 clove garlic, finely chopped

2 cups Bisquick Heart Smart® mix

¼ cup process cheese sauce or spread (room temperature)

¼ cup very hot water

½ cup pizza sauce

¾ cup shredded reduced-fat mozzarella cheese (3 oz)

1 Heat oven to 375°F. Spray cookie sheet with cooking spray. Spray 10-inch skillet with cooking spray; heat over medium-high heat. In skillet, cook mushrooms, zucchini, bell pepper and garlic about 5 minutes, stirring occasionally, until vegetables are crisp-tender.

2 In medium bowl, stir Bisquick mix, cheese sauce and hot water until soft dough forms. Place dough on surface sprinkled with Bisquick mix; roll in Bisquick mix to coat. Shape into a ball; knead about 5 times or until smooth. Roll or pat dough into 14-inch circle on cookie sheet. Spread pizza sauce over dough to within 3 inches of edge. Top with vegetable mixture. Sprinkle with cheese. Fold edge of dough over mixture.

3 Bake 23 to 25 minutes or until crust is golden brown and cheese is bubbly.

**8 servings**

## Budget
### Smart

*If you're having a party, this recipe is very easy to double, and it costs a lot less than sending out for pizza! It's almost as fast, too, thanks to dough that comes together in just a few minutes. This veggie version also helps keeps the cost down, but feel free to throw on some pepperoni or leftover cooked meat if you like.*

**1 Serving:** Calories 180; Total Fat 6g (Saturated Fat 2.5g, Trans Fat 0); Cholesterol 10mg; Sodium 470mg; Total Carbohydrate 25g (Dietary Fiber 1g) • **Exchanges:** 1 ½ Starch, 1 Vegetable, 1 Fat • **Carbohydrate Choices:** 1 ½

# 7 breakfast for dinner

## Instant "Evening" Breakfast

*"Breakfasts for dinner" can be both simple and hearty at the same time. Check out these easy and fun ideas!*

1 **Egg- and Sausage-Stuffed Muffins:** Top the bottom half of a toasted English muffin with a hot cooked brown-and-serve sausage patty and a fried egg or scrambled eggs. Add a slice of American cheese if you want, too! Top with remaining muffin half.

2 **Egg Tacos:** Fill taco shells with scrambled eggs. Sprinkle with shredded cheese, purchased guacamole, salsa, sour cream and sliced ripe olives.

3 **Ham and Scrambled Egg Pockets:** Fill pita breads halves with scrambled eggs that have been cooked with chopped deli ham; sprinkle with shredded cheese.

**4** Peanut Butter–Banana Pancakes: Heat maple-flavored syrup and peanut butter until mixture is hot and smooth (if too thick, add additional syrup). Top pancakes with sliced bananas, and serve with peanut butter–syrup mixture.

**5** Merry Cherry-Chip Pancakes: Stir cherry-flavored dried cranberries and miniature semisweet chocolate chips into pancake batter. Serve with your favorite syrup and whipped topping.

**6** Mexican Pancake Roll-Ups: Roll a pancake around a cooked sausage link; serve with warmed salsa or cheese dip.

**7** Bacon and Swiss Waffles: Stir crumbled cooked bacon and shredded Swiss cheese into waffle batter; serve cooked waffles with melted process cheese.

**8** Waffle and Fruit Bar: Serve waffles with several flavors of canned fruit pie filling and whipped topping.

**9** Easy Cream Cheese–Stuffed French Toast: Before making your favorite recipe, cut a small pocket in the side of 1- to 1½-inch-thick slices of French bread. Fill each slice with 1 tablespoon of your favorite fruit-flavored tub cream cheese, and cook as usual. Serve with strawberry, blueberry or maple syrup.

**10** Sausage Gravy and Biscuits: Heat frozen or ready-to-eat biscuits from the bakery section of the supermarket until hot; serve with sausage gravy made from a packet mix.

**This icon means:** 20 minutes or less

Prep Time **20 Minutes**
Start to Finish **20 Minutes**

# Monte Cristo Stuffed French Toast with Strawberry Syrup

12 slices French bread, ½ inch thick

¼ lb shaved or very thinly sliced cooked ham

3 slices (¾ oz each) Gruyère or Swiss cheese, cut in half

3 eggs

½ cup milk

2 tablespoons granulated sugar

1 tablespoon butter or margarine

Powdered sugar, if desired

¾ cup strawberry syrup

1 Top 6 slices of the bread evenly with ham and cheese, folding to fit. Top with remaining bread slices.

2 In small bowl, beat eggs, milk and granulated sugar with fork or wire whisk until well mixed; pour into shallow bowl.

3 In 12-inch nonstick skillet, heat butter over medium-low heat. Dip each side of each sandwich in egg mixture, allowing time for bread to soak up mixture. Add sandwiches to skillet. Cover; cook 2 to 3 minutes on each side or until golden brown. Sprinkle with powdered sugar. Serve with syrup.

**3 servings (2 sandwiches and ¼ cup syrup each)**

## Instant
## Success!

*Croque monsieur, or Monte Cristo sandwiches, are making a comeback! Traditionally a French-style grilled ham and cheese sandwich that has been dipped into a beaten egg mixture and fried in butter, this version becomes a rich and sensational French toast. Mix equal amounts of strawberry syrup and sour cream for a different topping flavor.*

**1 Serving:** Calories 850; Total Fat 22g (Saturated Fat 10g; Trans Fat 1g); Cholesterol 265mg; Sodium 1360mg; Total Carbohydrate 132g (Dietary Fiber 3g) • **Exchanges:** 6 Starch, 3 Other Carbohydrate, 2 Medium-Fat Meat, 1 Fat • **Carbohydrate Choices:** 9

# Cream Cheese and Jam Stuffed French Toast

12 slices French bread, ½ inch thick

6 tablespoons cream cheese, softened

¼ cup jam or preserves (any flavor)

3 eggs

½ cup milk

2 tablespoons granulated sugar

Powdered sugar, if desired

Fruit-flavored or maple-flavored syrup, if desired

1 Spread one side of 6 bread slices each with 1 tablespoon of the cream cheese. Spread one side of remaining bread slices with 2 teaspoons of the jam. Place 1 slice of each together to make 6 sandwiches.

2 In small bowl, beat eggs, milk and granulated sugar with fork or wire whisk until well mixed; pour into shallow bowl.

3 Spray griddle or skillet with cooking spray; heat griddle to 325°F or heat skillet over medium-low heat. Dip each side of sandwich into egg mixture. Cook sandwiches 2 to 3 minutes on each side or until golden brown. Transfer to plate; sprinkle lightly with powdered sugar. Serve with syrup.

**6 servings**

**1 Serving:** Calories 320; Total Fat 10g (Saturated Fat 5g; Trans Fat 0.5g); Cholesterol 125mg; Sodium 460mg; Total Carbohydrate 47g (Dietary Fiber 2g) • **Exchanges:** 2 Starch, 1 Other Carbohydrate, ½ Medium-Fat Meat, 1½ Fat • **Carbohydrate Choices:** 3

# Ham and Apple Pancakes

Prep Time **30 Minutes**
Start to Finish **30 Minutes**

1 can (21 oz) apple pie filling

2 cups Original Bisquick® mix

1 cup milk

2 eggs

¾ cup diced cooked ham

½ cup shredded Cheddar cheese
  (2 oz)

2 medium green onions, sliced
  (2 tablespoons), if desired

Ground cinnamon, if desired

1 In 1-quart saucepan, heat pie filling over low heat, stirring occasionally, until hot; keep warm.

2 Meanwhile, spray griddle or skillet with cooking spray. Heat griddle to 375°F or heat skillet over medium-low heat. In large bowl, beat Bisquick mix, milk and eggs with wire whisk or egg beater until smooth. Fold in ham, cheese and onions.

3 Pour batter by ¼ cupfuls onto hot griddle. Cook until edges are dry. Turn; cook other sides until golden brown. Serve with warm pie filling; sprinkle with cinnamon.

**4 servings (3 pancakes and ½ cup filling each)**

## Instant Success!

*If you're feeling just a tad adventurous, consider livening up the pancakes by adding 1 tablespoon Dijon mustard to the batter in step 2.*

**1 Serving:** Calories 550; Total Fat 19g (Saturated Fat 7g; Trans Fat 1.5g); Cholesterol 140mg; Sodium 1380mg; Total Carbohydrate 75g (Dietary Fiber 3g) • **Exchanges:** 2½ Starch, 2½ Other Carbohydrate, 1½ Medium-Fat Meat, 2 Fat • **Carbohydrate Choices:** 5

# Pancake and Sausage Stacks

1 package (7 oz) frozen brown-and-serve pork sausage patties (8 patties)

2 medium apples, chopped (2 cups)

1 cup maple-flavored syrup

½ teaspoon ground cinnamon

8 packaged frozen pancakes

1 In 12-inch nonstick skillet, mix all ingredients except pancakes. Heat to boiling; reduce heat to medium. Cook about 5 minutes, stirring occasionally, until apples are tender.

2 Meanwhile, prepare pancakes as directed on package.

3 For each serving, place 2 sausage patties on 1 pancake; spoon apple mixture over sausage. Top with additional pancake and apple mixture.

**4 servings**

## Make it a Meal

*Want to go vegetarian? Substitute heated frozen soy-protein breakfast sausage patties for the real deal. Fry up some refrigerated potato slices with chopped green onions for a side dish.*

**1 Serving:** Calories 660; Total Fat 20g (Saturated Fat 6g; Trans Fat 0.5g); Cholesterol 45mg; Sodium 890mg; Total Carbohydrate 107g (Dietary Fiber 3g) • **Exchanges:** 2 Starch, ½ Fruit, 4 ½ Other Carbohydrate, 1 High-Fat Meat, 2 Fat • **Carbohydrate Choices:** 7

# Ham and Swiss Pizza

6 eggs, beaten

1 package (10 oz) prebaked thin Italian pizza crust (12 inch)

¼ cup mayonnaise or salad dressing

2 tablespoons Dijon mustard

½ cup diced cooked ham

4 medium green onions, sliced (¼ cup)

¼ cup chopped red bell pepper

1 cup shredded Swiss cheese (4 oz)

1 Heat oven to 400°F. Spray 10-inch skillet with cooking spray; heat over medium heat.

2 Pour eggs into skillet. As eggs begin to set at bottom and side, gently lift cooked portions with metal spatula so that thin, uncooked portion can flow to bottom. Avoid constant stirring. Cook 3 to 4 minutes or until eggs are thickened throughout but still moist.

3 Place pizza crust on ungreased cookie sheet. In small bowl, mix mayonnaise and mustard; spread evenly over crust. Top with eggs, ham, onions, bell pepper and cheese. Bake about 10 minutes or until cheese is melted.

**6 servings**

## Instant
## Success!

*Go urban chic with this Italian version—use prosciutto instead of ham and half mozzarella, half Parmesan or Asiago for the Swiss cheese.*

**1 Serving:** Calories 370; Total Fat 22g (Saturated Fat 8g; Trans Fat 0g); Cholesterol 245mg; Sodium 690mg; Total Carbohydrate 24g (Dietary Fiber 1g) • **Exchanges:** 1½ Starch, 2 Medium-Fat Meat, 2½ Fat • **Carbohydrate Choices:** 1½

# Breakfast Burritos

8 eggs

¼ cup water

1 tablespoon butter or margarine

1 cup refried beans

½ cup chunky-style salsa

4 flour tortillas (10 inch)

1 cup shredded Cheddar cheese (4 oz)

Sour cream, if desired

Chopped fresh cilantro, if desired

1 In medium bowl, beat eggs and water with fork or wire whisk until well mixed.

2 In 12-inch nonstick skillet, melt butter over medium heat. Pour egg mixture into skillet. As mixture begins to set at bottom and side, gently lift cooked portions with metal spatula so that uncooked portion can flow to bottom. Cook 4 to 5 minutes or until eggs are thickened throughout but still moist; remove from heat and keep warm.

3 Spread refried beans and salsa on tortillas to within ½ inch of edge. Sprinkle with cheese. Place on microwavable plate; microwave each burrito uncovered on High 45 to 60 seconds or until tortilla and beans are very warm and cheese is starting to melt.

4 Cut eggs into strips, using plastic pancake turner. Divide strips evenly on centers of tortillas. Fold top and bottom ends of each tortilla about 1 inch over filling; fold right and left sides over folded ends, overlapping. Serve with sour cream and cilantro.

**4 servings**

## Instant
## Success!

*Despite their name, refried beans don't have to be fried in oil or loaded with fat to be high in flavor. Canned refried beans come in regular and fat-free versions.*

**1 Serving:** Calories 580; Total Fat 28g (Saturated Fat 13g; Trans Fat 1g); Cholesterol 465mg; Sodium 970mg; Total Carbohydrate 50g (Dietary Fiber 5g) • **Exchanges:** 3 Starch, ½ Other Carbohydrate, 3 Medium-Fat Meat, 2 Fat • **Carbohydrate Choices:** 3

# Bacon and Tomato Frittata

8 eggs

¼ teaspoon salt-free garlic-and-herb seasoning

¼ teaspoon salt

2 teaspoons vegetable oil

4 medium green onions, sliced (¼ cup)

2 large plum (Roma) tomatoes, sliced

½ cup shredded sharp Cheddar cheese (2 oz)

2 tablespoons real bacon pieces (from 2.8-oz package)

2 tablespoons sour cream

1 In medium bowl, beat eggs, garlic-and-herb seasoning and salt with fork or wire whisk until well blended; set aside.

2 In 10-inch nonstick ovenproof skillet, heat oil over medium heat. Add onions; cook and stir 1 minute. Reduce heat to medium-low. Pour in egg mixture. Cook 6 to 9 minutes, gently lifting edges of cooked portions with metal spatula so that uncooked egg mixture can flow to bottom of skillet, until set.

3 Set oven control to broil. Top frittata with tomatoes, cheese and bacon. Broil with top 4 inches from heat 1 to 2 minutes or until cheese is melted. Top each serving with sour cream.

**4 servings**

## Instant
## Success!

*If you don't have an ovenproof skillet, just wrap the skillet handle in a double layer of heavy-duty foil. Look for ready-to-use bacon pieces near the salad dressings in the store. They're shelf stable until opened, then they need to go in the fridge.*

**1 Serving:** Calories 260; Total Fat 20g (Saturated Fat 8g; Trans Fat 0g); Cholesterol 450mg; Sodium 470mg; Total Carbohydrate 3g (Dietary Fiber 0g) • **Exchanges:** 2½ Medium-Fat Meat, 1½ Fat • **Carbohydrate Choices:** 0

# Eggs and Sausage Skillet

1 package (12 oz) bulk reduced-fat
  pork sausage

4 oz fresh mushrooms, sliced
  (1½ cups)

3 cups frozen potatoes O'Brien (from
  28-oz bag), thawed

½ teaspoon salt

⅛ teaspoon pepper

6 eggs

1 cup shredded Swiss cheese (4 oz)

1 large tomato, chopped (1 cup)

1   In 12-inch nonstick skillet, cook sausage over medium-high heat 5 to
7 minutes, stirring frequently, until no longer pink.

2   Stir mushrooms, potatoes, salt and pepper into sausage. Cook over
medium heat about 8 minutes, stirring frequently, until potatoes begin to
brown. Reduce heat to low.

3   Using back of spoon, make 6 indentations in potato mixture. Break
1 egg into each indentation. Cover and cook 8 to 10 minutes or until egg
whites are set and yolks are beginning to thicken.

4   Sprinkle with cheese and tomato. Cover and cook 3 to 4 minutes or
until cheese is melted.

**6 servings (1 cup each)**

## Budget
### Smart

*Breakfast for dinner's a
tried-and-true solution
to the daily dinner
dilemma. Look for bulk
pork sausage on sale,
and freeze any extra in
6-oz portions so you
can defrost and use only
the amount you need.*

**1 Serving:** Calories 310; Total Fat 16g (Saturated Fat 5g, Trans Fat 0g); Cholesterol 240mg; Sodium 670mg; Total Carbohydrate
21g (Dietary Fiber 3g) • **Exchanges:** 1 Starch, 1 Vegetable, 2 High-Fat Meat, ½ Fat • **Carbohydrate Choices:** 1½

# Scrambled Eggs with Havarti and Wine

Prep Time **20 Minutes**
Start to Finish **20 Minutes**

8 eggs

¼ cup dry white wine or nonalcoholic wine

¼ teaspoon salt

¼ teaspoon pepper

2 tablespoons chopped fresh parsley

2 medium green onions, sliced (2 tablespoons)

2 tablespoons butter or margarine

4 oz Havarti cheese with dill weed, cut into ½-inch cubes

Additional chopped fresh parsley or dill weed, if desired

1 In medium bowl, beat eggs, wine, salt, pepper, 2 tablespoons parsley and the onions thoroughly with fork or wire whisk until well mixed.

2 In 10-inch nonstick skillet, heat butter over medium heat just until butter begins to sizzle. Pour egg mixture into skillet. Sprinkle cheese evenly over eggs.

3 As mixture begins to set at bottom and side, gently lift cooked portions with spatula so that thin, uncooked portion can flow to bottom. Avoid constant stirring. Cook 3 to 4 minutes or until eggs are thickened throughout but still moist. Garnish with additional parsley.

**4 servings**

## Make it a Meal

*When this recipe made a showing in our test kitchens, people raved. It's luscious, creamy and sophisticated—perfect for a special brunch as well as a light, elegant dinner. Serve the eggs with hash browns and brown-and-serve sausage links or bacon and some warmed scones or muffins.*

**1 Serving:** Calories 320; Total Fat 27g (Saturated Fat 14g; Trans Fat 0.5g); Cholesterol 470mg; Sodium 530mg; Total Carbohydrate 2g (Dietary Fiber 0g) • **Carbohydrate Choices:** 0

# Country Eggs in Tortilla Cups

4 flour tortillas (6 inch)

Cooking spray

4 eggs

¼ cup milk

¼ teaspoon salt

1 tablespoon butter or margarine

3 cups frozen shredded hash brown potatoes (from 32-oz bag)

¼ cup chopped green bell pepper

¼ cup shredded Cheddar cheese (1 oz)

Salsa, if desired

Sour cream, if desired

1 Heat oven to 400°F. Turn 4 (6-ounce) custard cups upside down onto cookie sheet. To make the tortillas more pliable, warm them as directed on the package. Spray both sides of each tortilla lightly with cooking spray. Place tortilla over each cup, gently pressing edges toward cup. Bake 8 to 10 minutes or until light golden brown. In small bowl, beat eggs, milk and salt with fork or wire whisk until well mixed; set aside.

2 Meanwhile, melt butter in 10-inch nonstick skillet over medium-high heat. Cook potatoes and bell pepper in skillet for 6 to 8 minutes, stirring occasionally, until potatoes are light golden brown; reduce heat to medium. Push potatoes to one side of skillet; carefully pour eggs into open side of skillet. Cook about 3 minutes, stirring occasionally, until eggs are almost set; sprinkle with cheese and cover 1 minute or until cheese melts.

3 Remove tortillas from cups; place upright on serving plates. Spoon ¼ each of the potatoes and eggs into each tortilla cup. Serve with salsa and sour cream.

**4 servings**

## Speed it Up

*Look for ready-to-eat fried tortilla "bowls" in your supermarket. Or copy the new restaurant style of tortilla bowls, which is simply to fit fresh tortillas into bowls—no frying or baking! Serve with fresh fruit or a green salad.*

**1 Serving:** Calories 350; Total Fat 16g (Saturated Fat 8g, Trans Fat 0.5g); Cholesterol 190mg; Sodium 480mg; Total Carbohydrate 36g (Dietary Fiber 3g) • **Exchanges:** 2½ Starch, 1 Medium-Fat Meat, 2 Fat • **Carbohydrate Choices:** 2½

# Potato, Bacon and Egg Scramble

5 slices bacon

1 lb small red potatoes (6 or 7), cubed

6 eggs

⅓ cup milk

¼ teaspoon salt

⅛ teaspoon pepper

2 tablespoons butter or margarine

4 medium green onions, sliced (¼ cup)

1 In 10-inch skillet, cook bacon over medium heat 8 to 10 minutes, turning occasionally, until crisp and brown. Remove from skillet; drain on paper towels. Crumble bacon.

2 Meanwhile, in 2-quart saucepan, heat 1 inch water to boiling. Add potatoes. Cover; heat to boiling. Reduce heat to medium-low. Cook covered 6 to 8 minutes or until potatoes are tender; drain. In medium bowl, beat eggs, milk, salt and pepper with fork or wire whisk until well mixed; set aside.

3 In 10-inch skillet, melt butter over medium-high heat. Cook potatoes in butter 3 to 5 minutes, turning potatoes occasionally, until light brown. Stir in onions. Cook 1 minute, stirring constantly.

4 Pour egg mixture into skillet. As mixture begins to set at bottom and side, gently lift cooked portions with metal spatula so that thin, uncooked portion can flow to bottom. Avoid constant stirring. Cook 3 to 4 minutes or until eggs are thickened throughout but still moist. Sprinkle with crumbled bacon.

**5 servings**

## Speed it Up

*We're lucky to have so many really high-quality, great-tasting convenience foods available. If you don't have time to cube potatoes, use purchased refrigerated cubed potatoes instead.*

**1 Serving:** Calories 260; Total Fat 15g (Saturated Fat 6g; Trans Fat 0g); Cholesterol 275mg; Sodium 420mg; Total Carbohydrate 18g (Dietary Fiber 2g) • **Exchanges:** 1 Starch, 1½ Medium-Fat Meat, 1½ Fat • **Carbohydrate Choices:** 1

# Veggie Cream Cheese Omelets

Prep Time **20 Minutes**
Start to Finish **20 Minutes**

8 eggs

¼ teaspoon salt

⅛ teaspoon pepper

2 tablespoons butter or margarine

1 cup 1-inch pieces fresh asparagus

½ red bell pepper, cut into thin slivers

½ cup garden vegetable cream cheese spread (from 8-oz container)

2 tablespoons chopped fresh chives

1 In medium bowl, beat eggs, salt and pepper with fork or wire whisk until well blended; set aside. In 8-inch nonstick omelet pan or skillet, heat 2 teaspoons of the butter over medium heat. Cook asparagus and bell pepper in butter 3 to 4 minutes, stirring frequently, until crisp-tender; remove from pan.

2 Add 2 teaspoons of the butter to pan. Increase heat to medium-high. Pour half of the egg mixture (scant 1 cup) into pan. As mixture begins to set at bottom and side, gently lift cooked portions with spatula so that thin, uncooked portion can flow to bottom. Avoid constant stirring. Cook 3 to 4 minutes or until eggs are thickened throughout but still moist.

3 Spoon ¼ cup of the cream cheese in dollops evenly over omelet; top with half of the asparagus and bell pepper. Tilt skillet and slip pancake turner under omelet to loosen. Remove from heat. Fold omelet in half; remove omelet from skillet. Repeat with remaining ingredients. To serve, cut each omelet crosswise in half; sprinkle with chives.

**4 servings**

## Make it a Meal

*Toast some English muffins or crumpets, butter them and offer some jelly and preserves, and you're good to go!*

1 **Serving:** Calories 300; Total Fat 25g (Saturated Fat 12g; Trans Fat 0.5g); Cholesterol 465mg; Sodium 520mg; Total Carbohydrate 4g (Dietary Fiber 0g) • **Exchanges:** 2½ Medium-Fat Meat, 2½ Fat • **Carbohydrate Choices:** 0

# Green Chile, Egg and Potato Bake

Prep Time **20 Minutes**

Start to Finish **1 Hour 30 Minutes**

3 cups frozen diced hash brown potatoes (from 2-lb bag), thawed

½ cup frozen whole kernel corn, thawed

¼ cup chopped roasted red bell peppers (from 7-oz jar)

1 can (4.5 oz) chopped green chiles, undrained

1½ cups shredded Colby–Monterey Jack cheese (6 oz)

10 eggs

½ cup small curd cottage cheese

½ teaspoon dried oregano leaves

¼ teaspoon garlic powder

4 medium green onions, chopped (¼ cup)

1 Heat oven to 350°F. Spray 11 × 7-inch (2-quart) glass baking dish with cooking spray. In baking dish, layer potatoes, corn, bell peppers, chiles and 1 cup of the shredded cheese.

2 In medium bowl, beat eggs, cottage cheese, oregano and garlic powder with wire whisk until well blended. Slowly pour over potato mixture. Sprinkle with onions and remaining ½ cup cheese.

3 Cover and bake 30 minutes. Uncover and bake about 30 minutes longer or until knife inserted in center comes out clean. Let stand 5 to 10 minutes before cutting.

**8 servings**

## Easy
### Add-On

*This "egg"-cellent Mexican-style bake will be the hit of your next brunch! If you're looking for other ways to use the rest of the jarred roasted red bell peppers, try Chicken Alfredo (page 103), Florentine Tuna Tetrazzini (page 245) and Peppered Pork Pitas with Garlic Spread (page 345).*

**1 Serving:** Calories 270; Total Fat 14g (Saturated Fat 7g, Trans Fat 0g); Cholesterol 285mg; Sodium 530mg; Total Carbohydrate 20g (Dietary Fiber 2g) • **Exchanges:** 1½ Starch, 1½ Medium-Fat Meat, 1 Fat • **Carbohydrate Choices:** 1

# Italian Frittata with Vinaigrette Tomatoes

| | |
|---|---|
| 1 can (14 oz) vegetable or chicken broth | 6 eggs |
| ¾ cup uncooked bulgur wheat | ⅓ cup fat-free (skim) milk |
| 1 medium zucchini, sliced, slices cut in half crosswise (1½ cups) | ¼ teaspoon salt |
| 1 cup sliced fresh mushrooms (3 oz) | ¼ teaspoon pepper |
| 1 small red bell pepper, chopped (½ cup) | ½ cup shredded mozzarella cheese (2 oz) |
| 1 small onion, chopped (¼ cup) | 3 medium plum (Roma) tomatoes, chopped, drained (1 cup) |
| ½ teaspoon dried oregano leaves | 2 tablespoons balsamic vinaigrette dressing |
| ½ teaspoon dried basil leaves | |

1 In 12-inch nonstick skillet, heat broth to boiling over high heat. Stir in bulgur; reduce heat to low. Top bulgur evenly with zucchini, mushrooms, bell pepper and onion. Sprinkle with oregano and basil. Cover; cook 12 minutes. Fluff bulgur with spatula, mixing with vegetables.

2 Meanwhile, in medium bowl, beat eggs, milk, salt and pepper with wire whisk until well blended.

3 Pour egg mixture evenly over bulgur mixture. Increase heat to medium-low. Cover; cook 5 minutes. Remove cover; sprinkle with cheese. Cook uncovered 5 to 7 minutes or until sharp knife inserted in center of egg mixture comes out clean.

4 Meanwhile, in medium microwavable bowl, mix tomatoes and dressing. Microwave uncovered on High 30 seconds to blend flavors.

5 Cut frittata into wedges (bulgur will form a "crust" on the bottom; use spatula to lift wedge out of skillet). Top with tomato mixture.

**6 servings**

**1 Serving:** Calories 230; Total Fat 10g (Saturated Fat 3.5g, Trans Fat 0g); Cholesterol 215mg; Sodium 560mg; Total Carbohydrate 20g (Dietary Fiber 4g) • **Exchanges:** 1 Other Carbohydrate, 1 Vegetable, 1½ Very Lean Meat, 2 Fat • **Carbohydrate Choices:** 1

## Budget Smart

*Eggs for dinner! Eggs are a tasty, easy and inexpensive alternative to meat. Here they're used in a 30-minute veggie frittata with a delicious whole-grain "crust" made of bulgur. Bulgur is one of the fastest whole grains to prepare, and can be served instead of rice or couscous.*

# helpful nutrition and cooking information

## Nutrition Guidelines

We provide nutrition information for each recipe that includes calories, fat, cholesterol, sodium, carbohydrate, and fiber. Individual food choices can be based on this information.

Recommended intake for a daily diet of 2,000 calories as set by the Food and Drug Administration

| | |
|---|---|
| Total Fat | Less than 65g |
| Saturated Fat | Less than 20g |
| Cholesterol | Less than 300mg |
| Sodium | Less than 2,400mg |
| Total Carbohydrate | 300g |
| Dietary Fiber | 25g |

### Criteria Used for Calculating Nutrition Information

- The first ingredient was used wherever a choice is given (such as ⅓ cup sour cream or plain yogurt).

- The first ingredient amount was used wherever a range is given (such as 3- to 3½–pound cut-up broiler-fryer chicken).

- The first serving number was used wherever a range is given (such as 4 to 6 servings).

- "If desired" ingredients and recipe variations were not included (such as sprinkle with brown sugar, if desired).

- Only the amount of a marinade or frying oil that is estimated to be absorbed by the food during preparation or cooking was calculated.

### Ingredients Used in Recipe Testing and Nutrition Calculations

- Ingredients used for testing represent those that the majority of consumers use in their homes: large eggs, 2% milk, 80%–lean ground beef, canned ready-to-use chicken broth and vegetable oil spread containing not less than 65 percent fat.

- Fat-free, low-fat or low-sodium products were not used, unless otherwise indicated.

- Solid vegetable shortening (not butter, margarine, nonstick cooking sprays or vegetable oil spread as they can cause sticking problems) was used to grease pans, unless otherwise indicated.

### Equipment Used in Recipe Testing

We use equipment for testing that the majority of consumers use in their homes. If a specific piece of equipment (such as a wire whisk) is necessary for recipe success, it is listed in the recipe.

- Cookware and bakeware without nonstick coatings were used, unless otherwise indicated.

- No dark-colored, black or insulated bakeware was used.

- When a pan is specified in a recipe, a metal pan was used; a baking dish or pie plate means ovenproof glass was used.

- An electric hand mixer was used for mixing only when mixer speeds are specified in the recipe directions. When a mixer speed is not given, a spoon or fork was used.

## Cooking Terms Glossary

BEAT: Mix ingredients vigorously with spoon, fork, wire whisk, hand beater or electric mixer until smooth and uniform.

BOIL: Heat liquid until bubbles rise continuously and break on the surface and steam is given off. For rolling boil, the bubbles form rapidly.

CHOP: Cut into coarse or fine irregular pieces with a knife, food chopper, blender or food processor.

CUBE: Cut into squares ½ inch or larger.

DICE: Cut into squares smaller than ½ inch.

GRATE: Cut into tiny particles using small rough holes of grater (citrus peel or chocolate).

GREASE: Rub the inside surface of a pan with shortening, using pastry brush, piece of waxed paper or paper towel, to prevent food from sticking during baking (as for some casseroles).

JULIENNE: Cut into thin, matchlike strips, using knife or food processor (vegetables, fruits, meats).

MIX: Combine ingredients in any way that distributes them evenly.

SAUTÉ: Cook foods in hot oil or margarine over medium-high heat with frequent tossing and turning motion.

SHRED: Cut into long thin pieces by rubbing food across the holes of a shredder, as for cheese, or by using a knife to slice very thinly, as for cabbage.

SIMMER: Cook in liquid just below the boiling point on top of the stove; usually after reducing heat from a boil. Bubbles will rise slowly and break just below the surface.

STIR: Mix ingredients until uniform consistency. Stir once in a while for stirring occasionally, often for stirring frequently and continuously for stirring constantly.

TOSS: Tumble ingredients (such as green salad) lightly with a lifting motion, usually to coat evenly or mix with another food.

# metric conversion guide

## VOLUME

| U.S. Units | Canadian Metric | Australian Metric |
|---|---|---|
| ¼ teaspoon | 1 mL | 1 ml |
| ½ teaspoon | 2 mL | 2 ml |
| 1 teaspoon | 5 mL | 5 ml |
| 1 tablespoon | 15 mL | 20 ml |
| ¼ cup | 50 mL | 60 ml |
| ⅓ cup | 75 mL | 80 ml |
| ½ cup | 125 mL | 125 ml |
| ⅔ cup | 150 mL | 170 ml |
| ¾ cup | 175 mL | 190 ml |
| 1 cup | 250 mL | 250 ml |
| 1 quart | 1 liter | 1 liter |
| 1½ quarts | 1.5 liters | 1.5 liters |
| 2 quarts | 2 liters | 2 liters |
| 2½ quarts | 2.5 liters | 2.5 liters |
| 3 quarts | 3 liters | 3 liters |
| 4 quarts | 4 liters | 4 liters |

## WEIGHT

| U.S. Units | Canadian Metric | Australian Metric |
|---|---|---|
| 1 ounce | 30 grams | 30 grams |
| 2 ounces | 55 grams | 60 grams |
| 3 ounces | 85 grams | 90 grams |
| 4 ounces (¼ pound) | 115 grams | 125 grams |
| 8 ounces (½ pound) | 225 grams | 225 grams |
| 16 ounces (1 pound) | 455 grams | 500 grams |
| 1 pound | 455 grams | ½ kilogram |

## MEASUREMENTS

| Inches | Centimeters |
|---|---|
| 1 | 2.5 |
| 2 | 5.0 |
| 3 | 7.5 |
| 4 | 10.0 |
| 5 | 12.5 |
| 6 | 15.0 |
| 7 | 17.5 |
| 8 | 20.5 |
| 9 | 23.0 |
| 10 | 25.5 |
| 11 | 28.0 |
| 12 | 30.5 |
| 13 | 33.0 |

## TEMPERATURES

| Fahrenheit | Celsius |
|---|---|
| 32° | 0° |
| 212° | 100° |
| 250° | 120° |
| 275° | 140° |
| 300° | 150° |
| 325° | 160° |
| 350° | 180° |
| 375° | 190° |
| 400° | 200° |
| 425° | 220° |
| 450° | 230° |
| 475° | 240° |
| 500° | 260° |

**NOTE:** The recipes in this cookbook have not been developed or tested using metric measures. When converting recipes to metric, some variations in quality may be noted.

# index

Underscored page references indicate sidebar text. **Boldfaced** page references indicate photographs.